CELTIC
Women
IN MUSIC

QUARRY MUSIC BOOKS

Celtic Tides: Traditional Music in a New Age
by Martin Melhuish
(with CD and video companion from Putamayo World Music)

Celtic Quest: Loreena McKennitt
by Geoff Hancock

Country Women in Music: Man, I Feel Like a Woman
by Jim Brown

Righteous Babe: Ani DiFranco
by Raffaele Quirino

Building a Mystery: Sarah McLachlan and Lilith Fair
by Judith Fitzgerald

Ironic: Alanis Morissette
by Barry Grills

Falling Into You: Celine Dion
by Barry Grills

CELTIC

Women

IN MUSIC

A Celebration of Beauty and Sovereignty

MAIRÉID SULLIVAN

QUARRY
MUSIC
BOOKS

DEDICATION

*This book would not have been completed but for the
computer wizardry, huge amount of time and effort given to
interview transcription and general editing by
my fellow traveler, beloved companion and partner, Ben Kettlewell.
Thank you Ben for your dedication
and endless patience and encouragement.*

The publisher gratefully acknowledges the support of
The Canada Council for the Arts and the Department
of Canadian Heritage, Book Publishers Industry Development
Program, for writing and publishing in Canada.

ISBN 1-55082-246-2

Cover art portraying Siobhán Peoples and her parents by Kathryn Kingcome,
reproduced by permission of the artist. Unless otherwise credited here, all images in this
book were supplied by the artists themselves or their recording labels. We are pleased to
acknowledge the individuals so credited for their co-operation in supplying photographs.

Sheila Chandra, page 38: Sheila Rock; Mary Coughlan, page 47: Amelia Stein;
Eileen Ivers, page 68: John Kuczala; Alison Kinnaird, page 81: Mark Jackson;
Mary Jane Lamond, page 89: Derek Shapton; Loreena McKennitt, page 116:
Elisabeth Feryn; Susan McKeown, page 122: John-Francis Bourke; Siobhán Peoples,
page 178: Kathryn Kingcome; Bonnie Rideout, page 193: Chris Moscatiello;
June Tabor, page 220: Tom Howard.

Color Insert: Susan McKeown: John-Francis Bourke;
Bonnie Rideout: Chris Moscatiello; Sheila Chandra: Sheila Rock.

Design by Susan Hannah.

Copyediting and typesetting by Kate Archibald-Cross.

Printed and bound in Canada by
AGM Marquis, Cap-Saint-Ignace, Quebec.

Published by Quarry Press Inc., P.O. Box 1061, Kingston, Ontario
K7L 4Y5 Canada, www.quarrypress.com

THE CANADA COUNCIL | LE CONSEIL DES ARTS
FOR THE ARTS | DU CANADA
SINCE 1957 | DEPUIS 1957

Canada

CONTENTS

MAIRÉID SULLIVAN

BIOGRAPHY

Mairéid Sullivan was born on a farm at Lisheens, Kealkill, West Cork, Ireland, where she was encouraged by her parents to sing traditional Irish songs. In her twelfth year, she moved with her family to San Francisco, California. She later moved to Australia where the legendary Donal Lunny produced DANCER, her first recording, in 1994 (Lyrebird Music).

Mairéid returned to California and recorded FOR LOVE'S CARESS – A CELTIC JOURNEY (Lyrebird Music) in 1998. She performed with Derek Bell of The Chieftains which resulted in the recording of A CELTIC EVENING WITH DEREK BELL, FEATURING MAIRÉID SULLIVAN (Clarity Sound and Light). *Los Angeles Times* music critic Don Heckman has called her music a combination of "poetic originals and traditional gems," while declaring that her "ethereal voice" evokes the "serene presence of a Celtic priestess." Her songs appear on two compilations, CELTIC VOICES – WOMEN OF SONG (Narada Records, 1995) and CELTIC TWILIGHT 3 LULLABIES (Hearts O'Space Records, 1996).

Mairéid's articles and essays on various aspects of Celtic culture have been published in many journals and publications. Her insights have been cited as essential for understanding contemporary Celtic music in Martin Melhuish's book, *Celtic Tides: Traditional Music in a New Age*. Her own collection of prose poetry, *Ancient Self – Memoirs*, was published in 1997.

INTRODUCTION

Thirty women artists, musicians from all over the Celtic world – Ireland, Scotland, England, Canada, The United States, and Australia – fill these pages with their wonderful personalities, insights, and stories. Gathered here for the first time are the 'keepers' of traditional Celtic music with the composers of 'innovative' Celtic music, musicians reclaiming ancient techniques of playing the harp, for example, with others setting new lyrics to old melodies, all leading lights in contemporary music, world music, new age music, folk music, classical music, and jazz. There can be no doubt that these women have helped to inspire the current renaissance of Celtic music. Anyone who reads these interviews will understand immediately why the genre is flourishing. These women fill the air with the 'perfume of joy' as they call to us from the depths of their own passion and beauty, proud heirs of the musical and spiritual grace of their Celtic ancestors.

While conducting these interviews, I often felt as if I was visiting these women in their homes 'for tea'. We were able to talk informally about the things that truly matter, while the children were busy playing in the garden. They have opened the door to their world for us to come in and explore their life stories, their views, and the themes that inform their music. They share personal stories from their childhood and from their experiences as world travelers and performers. They tell about how they found themselves working as musicians, and how they managed their careers and their families at the same time. They tell us who their musical mentors are, and speak of their responsibility to the next generation of Celtic artists. They show us how they have led music lovers to a deeper appreciation of the Celtic muse. These women are steeped in Celtic culture in unique ways. Each is a bearer of a living tradition. Through their eyes we see the unique qualities of the musical style and cultural tradition that have captured the hearts and the imagination of music lovers everywhere.

What are the qualities of Celtic music and culture that draw so many people to the fire of this tradition? And why have women become the keepers of the flame?

Many have tried to answer this question in scholarly treatises on the history of the Celts and the role women have played in this society since these people first emerged as a 'race' from their Indo-European family and began to migrate across Western Europe, perhaps even into the Indian subcontinent, then across the oceans to the New World in North America and Australia and New Zealand. The name 'Celt' was first derived from the Greek word 'keltoi' or 'keltori' and means the hidden people or outsiders. The word Celtic is used by scholars to define the shared roots of the Gaelic languages and is now applied as a general reference to people of Irish, Scottish, Welsh, Cornish, Briton, Celt-Iberian, and Manx heritage. Archeological discoveries suggest that the early Celts developed a rich and sophisticated tribal culture which reached an apogee around 500 BC. They didn't have a centralized government but rather were united inter-tribally by their shared language and world-view or philosophy. The Druids were their intellectual class, incorporating all the professions.

Slowly, the Celts were pushed westward by the expansion of the Roman Empire. Iberia (Spain), Scotland, Cornwall, The Isle of Man, Wales, and Brittany were the last geographic frontiers of the Celts. Ireland was the "last stand" for ancient Celtic culture. By the 17th century the Irish intelligentsia was destroyed. Ireland's ancient Celtic (Druidic) Bardic Schools, the oldest established centers of learning in all of recorded European history, were closed by the English. Legend has it that these schools were as old as the first millennium BC. Celtic language, law, music, and religious practice were banned. Those who had the opportunity escaped to the New World, while others were transported to work as indentured slaves in English plantations, against their will. Thirty percent of North Americans can claim links with Celtic culture. There are forty million Americans with direct Celtic roots and thirty million more with indirect Celtic roots. Forty percent of Australians come from Celtic origins.

Throughout this history, the idea of personal sovereignty and gender equality has distinguished the Celts from other Indo-European races. A growing body of evidence shows that before the Roman conquest Celtic women had achieved political, economic, and philosophical equality with men. 'Anam Chara' is the old Celtic/Irish name for the true relationship between men and women, where we meet in freedom and unite to mirror each other, where our invisible souls become visible to one another. Indeed, ancient Celtic culture offers wonderful support for the promotion of harmony between the sexes, showing that men and women can enjoy a fruitful partnership, including companionship in the quest for enlightenment. Women of Celtic origin traditionally shared the archetypal roles of warrior and nurturer with men. They balanced their 'masculine' martial power and strength with 'feminine' humor and mastery of the healing arts and music – especially music, which became the repository for Celtic history, legend, and that ineffable force we call spirit.

The Celtic spirit was eventually suppressed by patriarchal forces like the Roman Catholic Church and the various conquering empires, Roman and British, though not destroyed, as the women artists interviewed in this book make clear. When we look back at European history in this light, we see the expansion of patriarchal society directly related to the destruction of ancient feminine/goddess focused cultures. Having been born and raised in Catholic Ireland, I have always been astonished by the contradiction between the history of the establishment of the Roman Catholic Church (and the later Protestant Churches) and the tenets of Christianity. True Christian spirituality has always been congruent with women's values, but Western European women who, from ancient Celtic times, enjoyed positions of leadership on every level in traditional cultures, were singled out by the Church's imperial laws. The Church stripped women of their free will and political power, laying at their feet responsibility for 'original sin'. The whole of the Western world has suffered trauma to the collective consciousness as a result of this setback to civilized society, especially Celtic culture, which had attained an unprecedented balance between men and women. Jungian psychologists talk about the deleterious psychic effects of this historical oppression of the feminine in our nature, both for men and women, where the growth of rational science and technology out of our dominant masculine energy has stifled our intuitive and poetic nature.

But this feminine sensibility now seems to be recovering from being the lost soul of Western society, rediscovered and celebrated by artists like the women profiled in this book. In their way of living and in their music, these women encourage us to recreate reverence for truly feminine sensitivity in both men and women. When women are fully empowered, they nurture. Nurtured and nurturing, we develop strength and confidence. This may be the antidote to the alienation we feel living in modern society. With compassion and intelligence, we can understand each other, forgive our adversarial ways, and bridge gaps created by the philosophy of dualism which sees everything in terms of "good versus evil" and which results in political strategies based on fear. Music has this power to touch the heart – to cut through claustrophobic dogmas, abstract ideologies, and social stratas of age and class – to restore the Celtic spirit of personal sovereignty and love of beauty.

Now, this self-image is offered to all people who claim Celtic ancestry. Celts as far-flung as Latin America, Australasia, and India are awakening to their ethnic heritage through the renaissance of Celtic music. Buoyant and mystical, Celtic music thrills us, entrancing the soul with jigs and reels and slow airs. The soul reveals itself through emotional gestures and experiences another means of expression and celebration – "the music of the spheres." Music is a truth our bodies know, rhythms and reflections of what we feel. Celtic music takes this truth into another dimension, merging traditional ways of playing and singing with something new and innovative. Celtic musicians must know the cultural ethos of their music. They find the mode that has survived in a traditional form, then while retaining its identity, they improvise a new idea in the moment of play. This liberates the tradition with a contemporary idea so subtle that it enhances the vitality of the music.

Celtic music is now front and center on the world stage. Throughout the Celtic diaspora as well as in Scotland and Ireland, Celtic music festivals have become important gathering places for thousands of music lovers. These events offer a heightened sense of community among organizers and audiences, local and visiting artists. Well-established festivals book over three hundred performers for their programs, and there is at least an equal number of artists who apply, unsuccessfully, to perform. Even the ever-popular Scottish Highland Games are broadening their music programs to include the new and old music of their Celtic cousins. The growing mainstream appeal of Celtic-influenced music and a growing fascination for unaccompanied singing in the sean-nos 'old style' of the Gaelic language as well as for music played on the old instruments has restored a love for traditional Celtic music and culture. Music has become the conduit to the ancient Celtic myths and philosophies, which are coming to life again to feed starved imaginations. The thirty women artists interviewed here are all very much aware of this tradition and accept gladly the responsibility to feed our hunger for beauty and quest for freedom.

inTeRView

The idea of compiling a series of interviews with Celtic women musicians arose when I was being interviewed myself by Australian writer Gary Lewis after the release of my second album, FOR LOVE'S CARESS – A CELTIC JOURNEY. As Gary and I explored the 'themes' of my life and music, I began to wonder if other women artists shared similar experiences, beliefs, and values. To my delight, they did, but even more important to me, they had much to teach me about my heritage, my culture, and myself as a Celtic woman artist. To create a further context for their insights and opinions, my conversation with Gary Lewis follows.

GARY Lewis In the liner notes accompanying your latest CD, FOR LOVE'S CARESS – A CELTIC JOURNEY, you tell us that "ancient travelers navigated by the stars." On the cover you are, in fact, with the stars, set in the Milky Way with the Southern Cross. Australia's Southern Cross constellation, along with memories of your Irish childhood, seem to inform your present reality. You state that your journey is one of personal unfolding "with my companion musicians and our audience," and that ancient Celtic culture is employed by you because "it is the only historic cultural precedent I have found in my hunt for philosophical treasure, thus far, that promotes the concept of 'personal sovereignty' as central to a successful life's journey." You say that this way of life has little to do with where one dwells, because in the sense of the inner life, we are travelers in the imagination as well as on the physical plane "and our thoughts and feelings are our landing places." You want to connect with people of like mind ... these companions are like stars which help you to navigate through your life. Do you see this as a metaphor for your own experience?

MAIRÉID SULLIVAN   I call it my sense of 'indigenous' memory.

G.L.   Is this 'indigenous' memory' one of the magnetic fields which attract you, or a reflection of the light that guides you?

M.S.   I love concepts like that. I love concepts that come out of the ancient wisdom archetypes as much as I love the concepts that come out of the most up-to-date research. For example, the ancient concepts of yearning, journeying, infinity, eternity, heaven, magic, angels, spirits, fairies, luminous beings, enchantment, vision, divine, sacred and then the modern concepts, quantum consciousness, a quark, the speed of light, tachyonic sound, morphic resonance, electromagnetic fields. I find contemplating the old and the new concepts equally challenging and very exciting. I love words that aim to define the thinking processes of the most serious and profound human minds from any time. I love the effort to capture subtle perceptions in words, be it by poets or saints, scientists or philosophers. So, I don't mind whether you say it's a guiding star or magnetic pull. Either way we are talking about experiencing the phenomenon of 'special attraction'.

G.L.   Can you tell us how this has shaped your sense of your own life's mission, your philosophy?

M.S.   I really enjoy exploring the concept of a personal 'mission'. If I ask myself, in my quietest moment, "what am I here for, what is my life purpose?" then I am articulating a 'mission statement'.

There are so many issues that call for us to make commitments at various times in life: concern for the environment, care of children, and many community responsibilities. It is very important to find interests that draw upon the source of joy and enthusiasm, to sustain us through struggles we will surely encounter along the way. Laughter and playfulness are very important to me, so anything I do must allow for plenty of spontaneity.

When I 'step back' far enough from the challenges of life, I visualize the vast universe before me. I call it 'infinite intelligence' ... or 'God'. As soon as I begin thinking about what 'God' means to me, I am transported into a familiar bliss and joy and I'm filled with love and delight. I am lifted into realms of feeling that are so healthy, so complete and satisfying … in that moment that I just want to sing! My true 'mission' is to bring this source of joy and delight into every aspect of my creativity – every moment. I want to meet people who can stand there with me and share their own appreciation of 'infinite intelligence', of 'God', their joy and, ultimately, their 'love'.

G.L. Why do you think you chose a musical career?

M.S. Almost everyone who is asked that question answers that the music chose them. I would say the same thing.

G.L. Can you describe the phenomenon of being chosen?

M.S. I have a sense of being chosen to sing, in that I feel I am in a meeting place halfway between the song and the listener.

G.L. Tell us about your first adventures in performance.

M.S. There really was no break in my singing from my early childhood in the community of my family. When my family moved to the United States, I sang in the school choir as well as solo, for various community events. My professional career 'happened' in Melbourne. I was twenty years old when I went there with my father on a month-long holiday. When we arrived in Melbourne, I met wonderful people right away and I put off leaving. I had to go to the Immigration Department to extend my tourist visa, and when I was walking back, I saw a sign over a door which said, "Outpost Inn – Folk and Jazz Music." I walked in through the big heavy oak door and peeped around the corner. There, at a table, sat three people who turned and invited me in.

The Outpost Inn was organized by several teachers, two ex-Catholic priests, university students, writers, musicians, and other 'artistic' idealists. It was a very 'heady' environment all around. It was great! There was a meditation room in the basement where anyone could go for silent contemplation. I still hold several of those people dear to my heart, though I am out of touch with most of them at the moment. A few of us started a household together. One of us called it the 'commune' as a joke, but that name stuck. It was a big Victorian terrace house in North Melbourne, with a huge shop space at the front. It became one of the major venues for music and dance performances. Melbourne was a great city then, as it is now. Theater was going through a major revival, and there were a few important music venues that featured extremely vibrant jazz, contemporary and folk music. The city was alive with great creativity and I thrived there.

I started singing a few songs, casually, at the Outpost Inn, because I felt so comfortable there. I soon began performing at all the surrounding 'appropriate' venues. It developed very naturally. I was the only person singing the old traditional songs, unaccompanied, at that time. I did have a good size repertoire of songs that people liked to hear. I also sang with other musicians.

The beauty of unaccompanied singing is that I can simply sing the songs as they come to mind. The songs surprise me by filtering to the fore of my memory, inspired by the audience, when I haven't planned a set. Then I sing them with more delight because I remember them suddenly. It's very similar to the surprise and delight one would experience on meeting an old friend unexpectedly. That makes for inspired singing.

G.L. What was informing you in decisions about your repertoire? What were you choosing and why? Were there any linkages, any unifying principles in the collection?

M.S. Before going to Melbourne, I collected traditional songs that I could sing by myself, most of the time. But in Melbourne I also sang songs written by contemporary musicians and friends. I look for the poetry and the melody, as well as the rhythm in the song. I prefer the slow airs and ballads. I like finding the 'groove' that the song sits best in, be it accompanied or unaccompanied. There is always a groove that makes me feel the listeners are 'in' the song. But I also love the variety of rhythms and feels that a group of musicians can create.

When I find a new song I want to learn, I get so excited about it that I sing it constantly, non-stop day and night, testing it out in different sound environments and shaping the way I want to sing it. That is good for both the voice and the spirit. I have seen my facial expression change within a half-hour of constant singing. Something happens to the body chemistry and there is a glow that occurs. Singing is a very healthy activity.

G.L. What sort of feedback were you getting from people? How were you being inspired by people?

M.S. The inspiration flows from the quality of the stillness and the silence experienced while singing. I love the suspended, vibrant concentration that happens when I sing, especially with the slow airs.

G.L. Could you tell a little more about the formation of your music preceding the Melbourne days?

M.S. I sang unaccompanied from my earliest childhood. It is so unfettered, so simple, and such a completely fulfilling experience.

G.L. Can you remember some of the circumstances in which you learned these songs?

M.S. Well, my mother taught me the songs when I was very young, from around five or six years old. I would sing them for the extended family and friends in our community, in West Cork. I started collecting for myself during my adolescence in San Francisco.

G.L. Was there a Christian upbringing and a renunciation?

M.S. Yes, in a way, there was. But it was not so cut and dry. My early upbringing had significant features which supported my spiritual journey. My mother was a very devout woman who came from a wonderfully devout and fine family. There is a community holy well, Lady's Well, at the foot of a hill on her family's farm. Many neighboring families had their own statues there, set over the water, with a kneeling rail surrounding the shrine. We'd go there with our mother and pick bluebells and daisies and such, on the way, for the altar.

My brother, John, was very proud of the altar he had made 'for God' in the house. We always tended to 'his' altar with flowers and candles. He was like our little 'priest', for awhile. My home life in Ireland holds very tender memories of deep devotion and kindness. My mother, her mother, and her aunt, who lived with us, were responsible for passing on those sensibilities to us. We all lived on my mother's family farm, which was set high on a hill with a 360-degree view. It is a beautiful place.

I learnt the spiritual life more by osmosis in my younger years. I had a full inner life when we first moved to the United States, to an infinitely more secular society. Even though I later made a serious effort to seek out religious community, structured religious life was not fulfilling for me. But I found a vast array of literature that helped me greatly – Kahlil Gibran, Alan Watts, Elizabeth Barrett-Browning and W.B. Yeats – when I first arrived in San Francisco. I learnt that we use a small part of our brains for processing information and that our unconscious brain power can be directed toward personal fulfillment and enlightenment.

G.L. To what extent was popular culture, in San Francisco, shaping your experience?

M.S. Looking back, I believe I was very 'precious' about popular culture. If it was popular and mainstream, I shunned it. The Beatles for example, and Bob Dylan, were among the biggest icons when we arrived in San Francisco, and I just didn't get excited about them. But then, that's not so surprising since I had just arrived from rural Ireland. I had never experienced urban life before, except for the occasional huge adventure of a trip to Cork City. By my mid-teens I got into the swing of the lifestyle. I went with friends to a lot of the big rock concerts – Jimi Hendrix, The Doors, Janet Joplin, Ravi Shankar, Leonard Cohen, Jefferson Airplane, the list goes on. San Francisco was the place to be in those days. The lifestyle was vibrant. I loved dancing and the whole spectacle of the performances, but something kept me from appreciating the 'poetry' or the 'meaning' in those artists social agendas. I'm sure that had something to do with the fact that I was very shy and preferred serious conversation with one friend at a time. I spent a lot of time sharing books and talking about the mysteries of life. I feel I lived a double life then.

G.L. In these complex adolescent years, how did San Francisco seem to you?

M.S. San Francisco had a very strong Irish community. I think it still does. We lived within the Irish community almost exclusively. My father was a very social person. From age thirteen, my parents took me to the Irish dances for a couple of years. My father was a great dancer and he liked to dance with me because I could 'fly' around the room with him. I loved that, too. There were Irish showbands playing songs that had a strong nostalgic twist to them. My father was also a wonderful tenor of the John McCormac style. He sang the slow, beautifully melodic old 'parlor songs'. Being such a social person, he always had men over to the house and they would engage in heated discussion about social and political issues of the day. My father was a passionate socialist and an 'devout' atheist. His favorite saying was "The Church is the next best business to the Post Office." He was very informed about both the union movement and corporate interests. He was a very engaging conversationalist. His men friends were also. They were all very passionate about issues of solidarity and egalitarianism.

He was a master horseman. In his prime, in Ireland and Canada, he trained horses for jumping. He was also a very highly skilled marksman. I have seen my father shoot a deer while riding his horse at a gallop.

G.L. There was a long journey ahead of you that would bring you up to the stage of your first recording on DANCER – a couple of decades almost – and the achievement of your current distinctive musical style. Could you speak to that for a few minutes?

M.S. Many years ago, I discovered a love for unusual poetry and melodies, mostly written by my friends or by well-known contemporary writers. There were several difficult factors to meld together in the collection I gathered. That convergence is continuing to grow with my own writing.

There was a space of several years break from regular performance before I came back to my singing full-time in 1992 and to my first recording in 1994. DANCER is the result of having survived one of my greatest personal 'dark nights of the soul' experiences. While living in Australia with my daughter, Brigette, I took on the 'job' of step-mother, for ten years, to three children who had special health problems. Since I couldn't travel anymore, I 'fell into' a career as a marketing consultant in the mainstream performing arts establishment. I worked for The Victoria State Opera, The Melbourne International Festival of the Arts, The Australian Ballet, and many other arts, educational and environmental organizations. But I was never comfortable with the 'professional' identity I began to develop in doing that work. I started that 'career' as a series of community initiatives focused around arts programming, and it grew out of proportion to my own expectations. But the work did build courage because I learned, over several years, that I could over-ride my own shyness when I focused on promoting someone else's strength to communicate concisely other people's artistic or educational endeavors. Understanding the strengths of the many artists I have represented has given me a very eclectic experience that has formed the basis of my confidence as an adult.

There were personal factors, culminating in a very unhappy divorce, and consequently, no longer needing to support a family, that helped me to bring that entire phase of my journey to an end. While going through the divorce and other dramas, my hair fell out in clumps. I had to apply everything I knew to survive unbelievable emotional pain. I prayed, meditated, constantly read positive affirmations to keep my thoughts and feelings focused. To cut a long story short, I will be eternally thankful for the support of my mother and several friends, and, uniquely, a wonderful Melbourne based musician and friend, Chris Stellar, who persuaded me that I had original songs in me and that I should begin to write songs. I didn't truly believe him, but he was so insistent that I sat down one evening with pen and paper before me and wrote my own first poem/song – melody and all. That was just before midnight on New Year's Eve 1991 and the song is *Dreaming the Dreaming*. "Recall what you knew when you were nursed in the sea of beginning … Dreaming the dreaming, wake to the dreaming of old." It was written intentionally with the Aboriginal concept of 'Dreaming'. I felt drawn to look through the prism of the ancient culture of aboriginal Australians.

From then on, my prayers became poems. I began to write prolifically to reach deeper roots of thought and feeling and to remember my inner source of freedom and joy … and it worked.

G.L.   So, you were beginning to delve into the unconscious. The aboriginal Dreaming was a link you needed in order to begin the process of searching for your own spiritual and indigenous roots?

M.S.   Absolutely! To me, the aboriginal people of Australia give living proof of the profound and sacred wisdom attained in ancient civilizations.

G.L.   The linkages are very much alive, whereas for many of us, whatever our origin, as you say in so many ways, that consciousness has gone into hiding. We may be able to retrieve it. We may be able to rediscover it.

M.S.   That is my view. There is a depth in the Australian aboriginal way of thinking that is hard, if not impossible, for us to comprehend but we know it is authentic. There are aboriginal people alive today who still carry a view of reality and human potential inherited from their most ancient ancestry, from forty-thousand years ago. Whenever I have experienced the faintest glimmer of insight into this, I have seen that their view is much more powerful than the hybrid definitions of infinity that we have inherited and enclosed ourselves in. Our theologies don't come near its scope of power.

G.L.   Where was the next landmark? Was it the incubation of DANCER?

M.S. I began the process of launching my music project. When DANCER was released, it received such wonderful reviews from everyone. In fact, one of the things that really amused and thrilled me is that it was reviewed by The *Melbourne Herald*'s classical reviewer the same day that the first Three Tenors' CD was reviewed. He gave them three stars and he gave DANCER three and a half stars!

I was at home at that time, with a visiting friend, and as I was standing with my back to the fire, I remember saying to her, "I feel like I am surrounded by laughing . . . angels." I had to search for the word 'angels' because it wasn't a word I used normally. The expanded feeling that came to me was similar to the pantheon of compassionate archetypes I felt surrounded by in my adolescence. Those feelings were a great source of encouragement. The success of that whole creative effort, culminating in the making of DANCER, restored me to my joy and delight.

G.L. You had developed a trust in fate and trust in chance to lead you on the right course.

M.S. Yes. I do believe I have a life purpose, a service that I can give to the world, but I don't want to fix it in any one definition. I want to keep building on my interpretation with new experiences. So, I act as if I have the highest imaginable purpose to serve and grow, in trust that I will bring it to fuller consciousness as I go along. I strive to keep it simple and to keep doubt at bay.

The Irish poet, John Montague's 'The Slow Dance' was the inspiration for my song *Rapture*. Montague describes a primordial human, a man, dancing on the quaking clay of the earth, surrounded by antlered trees, amidst the thundering and lightening elements of fire. The culmination of the poem is, "No one was meant to watch, least of all himself." When I read those words, I immediately knew that the culmination of evolution would be that everyone is meant to watch, most of all ourselves.

G.L. What happened when you arrived in California?

M.S. My 'trust in fate' unveiled great rewards for me as soon as I landed on these shores. There have been so many adventures that I could write a book about it all. I have crossed this vast country many times, performed in all kinds of venues, and met many wonderful people. While I have had to surmount difficulties, I have achieved important relationships on many levels of mutual respect, inspiration, support, and love, in both my musical and my personal life. I feel blessed. I basically follow the view that if I am happy in this moment then I shouldn't want to change anything at all in my past because every detail of my past led me to this moment.

G.L. Moving right along, what kinds of venues do you prefer and how do you prepare for performance?

M.S. I love the sense of occasion that a concert presents. The performer is central to it, so it's a big responsibility. A good sound system or a good natural acoustic really is very important. It is a wonderful thing to sing in a room where both you and the audience can hear perfectly. If I have the band playing with me, I want a good sound system with good fold-back monitors so that I can hear myself over the instruments. I adore the big sound of a festival stage, with the sound booming out over acres of space. That can be a very powerful experience. A good sound helps me hear the subtle nuances of my voice; I don't want to just fly across the notes. So much of it is a matter of perception. I like to prepare by giving thanks for the opportunity to be there.

G.L. Is there an instance when, try as you may, an audience has not warmed to what you are doing?

M.S. Never! The songs themselves don't allow that. Tenacity is the word, you know. If I am singing a song and I feel the listeners are not engaged, I don't give up. I make a bigger effort to go more deeply into the meaning of the song, because I know that the song itself will spring to life and draw the listeners to it. The groove is everything to me. Even a rubato song has a rhythm that helps the song come alive in a unique way.

G.L. Why don't we focus now on Celtic music and ask why it's become so popular. What is the genre all about in your view? Is Celtic music a reflection of a broader interest in Celtic culture and, if so, why should it be happening now?

M.S. There are many streams to it, and that is what I find so fascinating. Until the last ten or twenty years, formal study had become very narrowly focused but now inter-disciplinary training at university level encourages people to become eclectic in their interests, for the love of learning. Now many streams of interest are being studied by a wider, more educated public.

In Celtic studies there are the historical, archeological and anthropological streams, the political and economic streams, the philosophical, theological and occult streams, and then the artistic streams – music, dance, theater, literature, the visual arts and crafts. These are all very active. Right now, each of these 'streams' is peaking, in terms of drawing popular interest.

There is lively discussion going on in archeological circles about the various interpretations that can be applied to old and new discoveries, alike. There is a circle of linguistic scholars who have a very strong case to present in defining the roots of Celtic heritage through the Celtic languages. Then the philosophical, theological and occult schools of thought are also finding a tremendous amount of rejuvenation where the popular goddess movements, the Wiccan and Druidic circles, and proponents of Celtic Christianity are taking a new approach to the old melding of Christian and pre-Christian philosophy. Psychologists and psychoanalysts are also offering amazing interpretations from the rich source of archetypes in ancient Celtic mythology and lore.

We shouldn't forget the independent adventurers, scholars and researchers, historians, philosophers, scientists and spiritual seekers, who may have explored and correlated Occidental and Oriental thinking, and who have discovered a whole new source of inspiration and information in the roots of Celtic culture.

Of course, as the saying goes, we must "sort the wheat from the chaff." On the negative side, it should be no surprise that the Celtic genre is being used as a marketing ploy by many business interests whose unprecedented exploitations have both contributed to the promotion and to the distortion of the genre on many levels. There are some very fanciful interpretations being applied to the genre. But we need to remember that this is alongside brilliant analysis and creativity coming from the highest level of scholarship and art. We see all of this reflected in the explosion of books and recordings available now.

Needless to say, there is much re-writing of history going on from all points of view. We are all editing reality – as we should be! People in all of these legitimate streams of interest are editing their own histories, too. There is so much information to assimilate now that it is almost a game, but a game with serious implications – the best kind.

G.L.   What is the genre all about in your view?

M.S.   Celtic culture has always been about the flourishing of individual freedom. It has been a hidden and suppressed culture for so long because, for complex historical reasons, the ideals of individual freedom, free speech, and access to learning, etc., have not been available to the general public until relatively recent times. The genre offers so many exciting and imaginative 'ways' that are equally engaging and stimulating and promoting of individual expression.

G.L.   What is your own way?

M.S.   I like to think, "I am protecting my joy." I've always looked for ways to sustain and maintain high energy, joy and bliss in my life, and I have found valuable precedents in ancient Celtic philosophy, all the more delighting because it is my own heritage, my ancestry. Music, dance, and writing are my 'ways' for expression of my inspiration.

G.L.   How and why does it illicit bliss in you?

M.S.   I have a very high degree of enthusiasm and respect for people who are seriously involved in researching, practicing, and promoting many cultures. A sense of continual learning creates stepping stones to my personal 'comfort zone'. When I feel that my life's work and my relationships are fulfilling, I become very thankful and that leads me straight into great joy and bliss.

G.L.   You have described, in your writings, the essence of the Celtic genre as discovery, passion, and poetry. All of those aspects are exemplified in great abundance in your work. Is that a fair summation of how you see the tradition of Celtic culture as you give expression to it?

M.S. Discovery, passion, and poetry – what else is there, really? Good company, good music, poetry and conversation and a good 'drop' of whatever you like to go with it – it's 'the craic', as the Irish say. The discovery inspires the passion and its expression in words and music. It's all about the creativity of the individual in any given moment, and the capacity to consciously create and share an experience of 'the good life'.

G.L. Could you explain the origin of the notion of 'personal sovereignty'?

M.S. I was living in Australia when I set out to seriously study ancient Celtic heritage, back in 1991. Before that time I had spent years studying the development of Chinese history and philosophy. I was hugely surprised to discover that there was so much that I didn't know about the ancient Celts. I knew some Celtic history but I certainly hadn't accessed the depth of information that I have since gleaned deeper understanding from.

'Personal sovereignty' is a concept that can be traced way back in very ancient Celtic history. It has similarities to ancient Yogic theories. Consciousness 'in the body' is a vast field of exploration with an amazing pedigree. In ancient Europe, as in India, knowledge through 'body consciousness' had realized a great height of wisdom. Today's science tells us that ninety-nine-point-nine percent of every cell in the body is empty space and that every thought effects the chemistry of the whole body. Every thought has a chemical attached to it.

Rupert Sheldrake's theory is that memory and other information is stored within the microtubules of every cell. These are alive, self-organizing and causal information systems called holodynes. We can learn to access them and transform them. Holodynes exist within a quantum field dynamic that creates a 'morphogenic' effect which resists change. To transform these fields, we need to understand 'field shifting'. The ancient Celts called it 'shapeshifting'.

I use traditional Irish dancing as my metaphor to show how we can comprehend this greater dimension of insight. This is an exercise for the imagination. While it would help to know how to dance the simplest form of jig and to have the music playing because the dance music helps to make the body light, it doesn't really matter if that isn't possible. The dance can be imagined. Prepare as you would to dance a simple jig. Imagine yourself standing very straight and still and let your body feel very light. Imagine your body becoming weightless. Imagine bouncing up and landing back down on the toe, just lightly enough to spring back up again. Focus on the point where you body feels weightless, just where you imagine yourself springing up and then down. Continue to focus your imagination on making yourself as weightless as possible, until you experience a fresh, heightened awareness of your body. The focus is the key. You will become aware of the field of energy around and through your body. Imagine being held up from the medulla oblongata, at the base of the brain, the first entry of the nervous system into the embryo.

When there is an opportunity to actually dance to the music with someone else, it is really great if both people have done the imagination exercise first. Then, when you move toward the other person in the dance, you will feel their energy touching yours long before you come close to each other. It is a thrilling sensation, to be so sensitive and aware of your body that you actually perceive your energy moving into another person's energy field before you even come close to them.

The ancient Celts promoted that kind of self-knowledge, beginning with consciousness through the body. They believed, "we are all embryonic gods and goddesses." We can achieve god-hood in our lifetime, that is our true purpose, and when we do, "we have a filial duty to assist our kith and kin." It's all about the individual's capacity, no matter which gender, to interpret and develop their own unique sovereign realm of reality.

The Irish concept of 'Anam Chara' (anam cara) describes the way that we can meet another as a 'soul friend'. Anam means 'name' or 'soul' and chara means 'friend'. The concept of 'Anam Chara' means that we can become 'soul friends' by respectful interaction. We can work at refining that communication and melding our being with another in a non-threatening and beautiful way.

Personal sovereignty simply refers to 'my own realm', where I have complete control and autonomy, where I have the final word about defining or interpreting my reality because only I live in it, and it contains the whole universe, as far as I'm concerned. While no other human being can see reality the way that I see it, and that is the fact, the truth, the really important realization is that it takes profound respect to know anyone in a significant way. We reach out to another and we realize that we are here at the threshold of another being's reality, and there is the vast unknown.

G.L. What are the relevant messages for today, from Celtic history?

M.S. Love is made profound by knowledge. I really like the Celtic tradition of emphasizing subtlety over obviousness. The hidden is more important than the revealed in that it has greater prospects for interpretation – hidden possibilities.

G.L. It's interesting that looking through your lyrics I see references to tides, anchors, rocks, boats – one is about movement and the other is secured. In your song, Danu's Land, there is the Celtic mother goddess making a call to heed her ancient song and come out of hiding. Is that a fair understanding of that?

M.S. Yes. That was one of my first poem-prayers.

G.L. In what sense then does this appeal to the feminine principles or reaction against patriarchal religion, i.e., Christianity, Islam, Buddhism, etc. or is it not?

M.S. It tells us to ignore all of that old politics. It tell us we can come out of hiding and not have to pay any attention to superficialities of politics anymore. It suggests that we can set our imagination free and we can become emissaries of peace.

G.L. The meaning of the title song on your CD FOR LOVE'S CARESS seems obvious. "We are daughters of history, mothers of a new world that's dawning, and this great old world can be made new in the name of love's caress."

M.S. The roles of mother and the grandmother are universally understood models of nurturing and justice. Mothers don't compete with their children, they give themselves to their children. Mothering is the best approach to healing on all levels. We have seen enough war and holocaust and genocide to know that it takes a special effort for us to evolve human consciousness. I believe we should remember the mother's way when we try to bring peace and healing to this planet and the lives of everyone we come into contact with, even in small ways, through positive thought projection, dedication, generosity and most ardent love. I want to find people who are dedicated to this effort because they are the ones who approach relationships with the best energy and consciousness. They make the sparks fly for me. They are the ones who know how to laugh and sing and dance for joy – like children.

A collection of Mairéid Sullivan's written works can be read in the 'articles' and 'poetry' pages of her personal website, www.maireid.com.

CELTIC
Women
IN MUSIC

MARY BERGIN
(CENTER WITH DORDÁN)

MÁIRE BRENNAN

SHEILA CHANDRA

DOLORES KEANE

KAREN MATHESON
(WITH CAPERCAILLIE)

MARY BERGIN
(DORDÁN)

BIOGRAPHY

Mary Bergin is a native of Dublin now living in Spiddal, County Galway. She enjoys an outstanding reputation in the world of Irish traditional music and is considered one of Ireland's premier exponents on the tin whistle, having a very distinctive and individual style of playing. Her two solo albums, FEADOGA STÁIN 1 and FEADOGA STÁIN 2, are much sought after, regarded as essential and compelling listening material for those interested in traditional Irish music. Apart from her busy schedule, both as a solo artist and with the group Dordán, Mary also teaches the whistle and is regularly invited to give workshops and master classes both in Ireland and abroad.

INTERVIEW

MAIRÉID SULLIVAN Do you have children, Mary?

MARY BERGIN Yes. Ailbhe, my daughter, is fifteen, and my son, Colm, is seventeen.

M.S. I've spoken to quite a few people who consider you to be their musical hero. There is a consensus, among musicians, that when an artist arrives at the stage of full maturity in their art, their audience is made up of the people who trust them implicitly with the music because they know they are able to 'do it right'.

M.B. I suppose, yes, that's true. For me, it's wonderful at this stage of my life, after playing for so many years, to be acknowledged and recognized as a good musician. I suppose Irish music and musicians are highly thought of around the world, and my experience is that people usually come to a concert because they are really interested in the music. They appreciate if you are playing well. That's great because the amount of time and energy that you would put into getting to that stage takes a lifetime.

At times it can be difficult, but I wouldn't swap it for anything. In particular, early on, when you don't have commitments, it's fine, but when you have a family, it does pull you and draw you in certain directions. It hinders a lot of things that you would take on. I just like the balance of the two things. I wouldn't change anything. The thought of giving up having a family for the sake of music, to me, would be an imbalance in my life. Unfortunately, a lot of women do give up on the music when they get to the stage of having children. I think that's a tragedy.

M.S. Your talent matured while your were still very young. You still had plenty of time to prepare for a normal life, with children and a family life. The fact that traditional music is not about being a star, or a celebrity, but is more focused on community life, would help make it possible to continue to do both. Would your experience confirm that observation?

M.B. Definitely. Yes, it would. Of the many musicians that I know, I don't know one who would set out to learn music or to play music for the glory of it, alone. It just happens when you reach a certain level, you become well known and respected.

When I was young, I just got the bug to play, and there was no stopping me. That was the thing that really drove me on. It's basically a communal thing – sitting in sessions and meeting musicians. Its about 'the craic', and the bond. The bond, I think, is the main thing between traditional musicians. Everything else comes after. They understand in the same way that you understand, and you know that the understanding is there between you. When I started playing, Irish music wasn't a commercial enterprise. Most people would have frowned upon that attitude to music.

M.S. It's a great vehicle for exploring the world – you couldn't be safer.

M.B. Absolutely. I look at it as a passport to the world, with so many wonderful opportunities to play Irish music through the festivals and tours. With a nice handy instrument like mine, the tin whistle, it's physically very easy for traveling.

M.S. You are in a group with three other women now, too. What is that like for you, to be in an all-woman group?

M.B. It's a marvelous experience. The group is called Dordán, and we all live in and around Spiddal, County Galway. We have been together for nine years. We all get on so well, and they are such wonderful musicians. Kathleen Loughnane plays the harp, and is a native of County Tipperary, now living in Galway City. Dearbhaill Standun plays the fiddle and viola and is a native of Spiddal. Martina Goggin sings and plays percussion and is a native of Limerick, now living in Spiddal. I play the whistle and flute and I live in Spiddal, too, though I am originally from Dublin.

M.S. What style of music does the group perform?

M.B. Our music ranges from traditional to baroque. We have three recordings of our music available now, and we will have our fourth launched this year on Narada Records.

M.S. Besides playing with other people, you've recorded two albums on your own.

M.B. They're both called Feadoga Stáin, which means "tin whistles." There's volume one and volume two.

M.S. What are the main facets of your career that stand out for you?

M.B. The traveling and meeting people, and the recognition, I suppose. Being rated highly is an honor. It's wonderful! I don't see it as being really about me, though. It's about my gift. To have the respect of so many top musicians is a great thrill.

M.S. How does that recognition affect your everyday life?

M.B. My everyday life is just getting on with my teaching and my playing, and meeting with the musicians, and the little bit of traveling that I can do at this stage.

M.S. How old were you when you actually started playing?

M.B. I started when I was about eight or nine. I was very lucky, I suppose, because my parents were both musicians. My father played the accordion, so I don't know why I picked the whistle.

M.S. In the seventies the whistle was rated the most popular instrument in Ireland.

M.B. At the time I started, there were very few young people playing the whistle where I lived. We lived out in the country. We didn't get much exposure to music. We were very isolated.

M.S. Where were you in the country?

M.B. We were about twenty miles south of Dublin, and, at that time, it was very remote. I went to Dublin once a year. I wasn't exposed to many musicians at that stage, so I wouldn't have known that the whistle was so popular. I just picked the whistle up, and my father would play the tunes slowly so I could learn them. Then, in my teens, I used to go to sessions and pick up tunes.

We used to enter some of the competitions like the Fleadh Ceoil. They were the festivals of Irish music. The competitions used to be held in these little halls. There was no place for anyone to go away from the main hall, so we would be out in the toilets playing tunes together with all the competitors, all sitting around and sharing the craic, and somebody would yell, "quick, you're on"! and you'd run in and play a tune for the competition. You wouldn't even wait for the results; they were totally irrelevant in those days. The most important thing, for us, was the social side of the gatherings. Nowadays, I think competition is taken much more seriously. We just didn't give a hoot who won. Half the time when we came home from the competition, we wouldn't even know who won. But at the same time it did matter on some levels. Because when you got to senior level, people would look up who won, so they would have an idea who to ask to play at a concert. Then you would get a bit of exposure, and it just rolls from there.

M.S. You made your first album in 1979. How did you get that together? Did Gael Linn invite you?

M.B. Yes, they did.

M.S. Do you improvise at all, or is your repertoire all traditional tunes?

M.B. When I play a tune, it's always my own interpretation. I do it my own way, have my own versions of every tune. I would rarely play a song the same way twice. And it isn't done consciously. Years ago, when I started to teach, I found it very difficult because I would play one way one minute and another the next and the class would be confused. They would say, "You didn't do that before." It's interesting. It's actually made me aware of what was happening in my playing. Most musicians are totally unaware of the little changes they make in the tune as they play it. After learning a new tune they 'settle' into it. And when you settle into it, you sort of make it yours.

In Irish music, they rarely play note for note. Some musicians would learn it note for note, beginning to end, and then after playing it ten or fifteen times, at least a few of the notes would change. The secret in the improvisation of tunes is not to destroy the basic structure of the tune. If you don't understand the subtleties of the ornamentation, you can go overboard and lose the whole skeleton of the tune, and then it's not the same tune at all. It's only with experience that you learn what you can do, or what's right and what's wrong. Sometimes you can overdo it.

M.S. That's what's good about the sessions. They give you the backbone since they give you the structure. I guess the magic would be the improvisation within that structure.

M.B. That's how musicians really appreciate each other. Often in the middle of playing a tune with someone they change a few notes, and that really gives the tune a lift. I feel like going, "wow!" It's brilliant! Even one note can make such a difference. People have shouted at me a couple of times, "Good man, Mary!" (laughs). I would have done something and not even have known it. That's the nice thing about all that, it's the magic of it.

DISCOGRAPHY

FEADOGA STÁIN VOL.2 (1992)
(Gael Linn Records)

FEADOGA STÁIN VOL. 1 (1979)
(Gael Linn Records)

With Dordán

CELTIC AIRE (1999)
(Narada Records)
THE NIGHT BEFORE,
    A CELTIC CHRISTMAS (1997)
(Narada Records)

TRADITIONAL AND BAROQUE
(Gael Linn Records)
JIGS TO THE MOON
(Gael Linn Records)

MÁIRE BRENNAN
(CLANNAD)

BIOGRAPHY

The eldest of nine children, including her celebrated sister Enya, Máire Brennan was born Marie Ní Bhroanain on August 4, 1952. She has been the leader of the band Clannad since they began in 1970. In 1999, they celebrated their twenty-fifth anniversary and won a Grammy for best New Age album of 1998. This group, from Gweedore in County Donegal, Ireland, has successfully crossed the bridge between folk and rock. The word Clannad means 'family' in Gaelic, and the group formed initially to play folk festivals in Ireland. At the time the line-up consisted of three of the Brennan children and two of their uncles.

The group's first successes came in Germany, where they toured in 1975. Clannad initially caught the attention of the wider public in the UK when they recorded the theme tune for television's *Harry's Game* in 1982. The single reached number five in the UK charts and received an Ivor Novello Award. In 1984 they recorded the soundtrack to television's *Robin of Sherwood* and reached the Top 50 in May the same year. The following year the song received a British Academy Award for best soundtrack.

Further chart success followed with the 1986 UK Top 20 hit *In A Lifetime*, on which Máire did a duet with Bono from U2. From their early days, despite establishing themselves into the rock mainstream, Clannad have always retained the Celtic quality in the music.

Máire and her husband Tim have two children, a six-year-old girl, Aisling (Ash-leen), and a five-year-old boy, Paul.

INTERVIEW

MÁIRÉD SULLIVAN What do you think has caused the current wave of interest in Celtic culture?

MÁIRE BRENNAN I believe there is so much interest in Celtic culture because it is so deep. It's quite incredible – and fascinating – that people haven't tired of it yet.

I think it's more than just a phase or a fad because of the ancient aspect attached to it; the treasures attached to it, the origins and the ancestries, and the bonding. There's a bond there that people feel, even people who have no Celtic connections to speak of. There's still a bond, because the Celts have traveled the globe.

The islands have sent a huge population out, all over the world. Ireland itself has a population of four million. You've got families who, up to recently, had nine and ten children. An average family is six children now. So where do they all go? The people are very much spread out.

M.S. When I came to the United States in 1995, I asked the Irish Cultural Center for the population statistics, and they said there are forty million people in the U.S. with direct Celtic roots, and another thirty five million, on top of that, with indirect Celtic roots.

M.B. Really? That is amazing. What has really interested me, too, is the fact that ten percent of the Irish people went out, in the eighth and ninth century, throughout the world. Saint Brendan was supposed to have been in America well before any other Europeans. There are certain roots of the culture planted in places where there wouldn't appear to be any Celtic connections. Why is it that the music is still strong in other cultures and played, interactively, with their own? There isn't a country that doesn't like Irish music.

M.S. The are so many styles of Celtic music, as well as an amazing profusion of literature on Celtic history, available now. For the curious, it's plain to see how uniquely diverse qualities and aspects of the culture have survived, both at home and abroad.

M.B. I think it helps to understand the effect of the great number of people who went out from Ireland, as missionaries, a long time ago, even before the mass immigrations. They were the first to spread Celtic Christianity. It's nearly like a tradition that Ireland has . . . this migration pattern. Emigration has happened en masse because of the famines and the evacuations. But I really think it's always been in the Irish blood to be nomadic. They have planted themselves in distant places we don't even know about, all over the world. Years ago, they traveled by boats, not by land. They were great seamen, and they had the Currachs, which were very strong boats. They were able to survive for great lengths of time at sea. We have proved that was possible, with the re-enactment of Saint Brendan's voyage. So, I really think that's how they had the opportunity to touch people's hearts in far off places.

M.S. When you have a culture whose people are constantly traveling, both willingly and unwillingly, 'longing' becomes a feature of their communal life. Longing for loved ones becomes a focus of the songs and the lifestyle itself. Their longing had no respite and it is still recognizable in the music.

M.B. I think that's because we have an incredible emotion attached to us, that is expressed in this yearning, this longing. The great thing about the Irish people is that we are open people. We're emotional people, and we are not afraid of our emotions. That's one of the aspects that people love about the Irish, their openness, their attitude, their approach to life. My theory is that they have gained a huge sense of hope and encouragement from the development of deep-rooted spirituality.

M.S. Tell me how you describe that spirituality.

M.B. For a long time, I was looking from the outside in, when everybody else seemed to be focusing on Celtic culture. Throughout my twenty-eight years with Clannad I had seen and felt the huge surge of interest in the Celts. Every five years or so something sparks it off, the most recent spark being *Riverdance* and *Lord of the Dance*. You've got three Riverdance and two Lord of the Dance troupes touring the world. They're packed! You can't get in! I've seen it building up: from the first time that we played in small clubs, to return concerts in 2000 seat auditoriums. I also saw that a lot of the interest was leaning towards the Irish mythology, and I love that side myself. I love the folklore stories because I was brought up with them.

But that's not all that Irish and Celtic culture is about: what our ancestors became, where they developed, is what it is also about. It's about the unique way the Celts developed in Ireland; the way they achieved a very strong culture in Ireland; the way education was an important aspect of their culture, long before anywhere else in Europe, with the unbroken tradition of their ancient schools.

All of that is important, but now, for instance, we celebrate St. Patrick's Day all over the world. The whole story about St. Patrick himself is an incredible story. Rather than remembering him with green beer, people should realize who this person really was, and what he did, almost single-handedly, for Ireland.

Patrick was kidnapped into slavery there, he got to know the culture, and then, because of that familiarity, that bond, he returned to Ireland and taught Christianity 'within' the culture. He didn't bring Christianity in, in a ritual form. Reading down through different histories, I have found that our missionaries, who went to different places around the world, in the earliest time, took the same approach. Christianity was passed on without a strict, dogmatic regime in the beginning. The hierarchy came in long afterwards and said, "This is how it should be." Celtic Christianity developed in Ireland long before the hierarchy came in, and it became really rich. When Patrick came into Ireland, slavery was practiced, so there were certain practices within the country that were not in good order. Christianity brought the prospect of goodness into the culture, into the lives of the people. It set new moral standards; it inspired a renaissance, a golden age.

Down through the years, I have often been asked, "What is it about the Irish people, who are such a tragic race, with a history full of sadness and tragedy, that they write so many songs, and that in all these songs there is always an expression of hope?" It is never dark. The reason is, their Christian belief is based upon such great strength and such strong belief. That's why it was very important for me to make an issue of the fact that from the time of our distant ancestors, this is how they lived. They lived with, and they carried with them everywhere, the great strength of a powerful belief.

Today, people come to Ireland and they might visit the Skelligs, where the monasteries were. They may go to see the Celtic crosses or the Book of Kells, but they should realize that all of that history came from Celtic Christianity and not mythology. It became an important matter, to me, when I realized that people weren't seeing all of that as part of the older folklore. Don't get me wrong, I love the folklore. But it is the larger issues, for example, how Tara's Hill became a spiritual place that I think we should be thinking about. I used to hate history and now I find great power in it.

M.S.   What has the power of this knowledge awakened in you?

M.B.   Well, because of my growing understanding, I have become a spiritual person myself. It's really wonderful to feel the power of it. The strength I experienced while making my last album came from that, exactly. I've written words for the songs on PERFECT TIME, and I do know where they came from. I never classed myself as academically inclined, but I have found that there is so much inspiration coming into my spiritual life from gaining a new perspective on the past. There is a lot more in there to be experienced through my inner life. It's full!

We talk about Tir Na Nog but then we can talk about Saint Columba, Saint Brigid, Saint Brendan, Saint Aiden – the stories attached to these people are incredible. Saint Aiden went to Lisdisfarne, in the north of England. Columba went to Iona in Scotland with twelve monks, and that's where Presbyterianism started. While the dark ages were happening right across Europe, including most of England, Ireland became 'the land of saints and scholars'. The Irish enjoyed a golden age.

The miracles around Saint Columba are amazing. He is from Donegal; he was born into a high-middle class family. He was like a Francis of Assisi in Donegal. He loved the earth. He loved the woods. That's why he changed his name to Colmcille. Colum means 'dove' and 'cille' means 'wood'. Derry was once known as Daire Colmcille, meaning 'Derry, the dove of the woods'. There are beautiful, inspirational stories about his life. That treasure is all around us and we seem to glide over certain aspects of it and look at others. I see real strength in the history of the lives of these saints. I'm looking back to about five hundred, seven hundred years, and a thousand years ago, and we're still talking about Christian Ireland. In Irish music, we don't play anything older than 500 years. We are really talking about the hearts of the people, of that time, and their very strong spirituality. They loved the earth; they worshiped God through acknowledging the beauty of the earth.

M.S. Would you say that their highest expression was joy?

M.B. Absolutely! They were very happy and content people. That's how they lived and survived. They were able to see reason in even the saddest things.

M.S. They weren't focused so much on external issues because they were still living in relative peace, politically. They had time to develop a profound understanding of the new meaning that Christianity brought to their lives.

M.B. It's wonderful to take inspiration from those wonderful stories of the lives of the saints. I think Brigid is supposed to have been the daughter of a Chief Druid, who had no problem with her becoming a Christian. Christianity was a new phenomenon. It had just been brought in. It offered something really good, which they recognized.

Now, it is amazing that this country, which has such a magnificently rich Christian heritage, should be split within the Christian community, the Catholics and the Protestants.

M.S. At least we can see what went wrong and there is hope that we can turn it around now.

M.B. I know. But we must first see that the problems arose when people took what Christianity was about and made it their own. In other words, they became possessive with its teachings. If you stop respecting the way others worship, then the hierarchy takes it over and makes it a 'business.' That is very, very unfortunate.

I have been playing in Northern Ireland quite a bit, at various events, and I have found that there are a great many projects, within the communities, which set out to help people reconcile their differences and forget about the political side of it. It's the Christianity side of it that people need to focus on because that is where the heart is. It has given me great strength to have come to realize that this is what the future will be about. The people themselves are going to be reconciled because they will want to focus on binding their children together.

M.S.   The people are going to take matters into their own hands to heal the community.

M.B.   Obviously we need our government bodies, but when it becomes a religious-based political war, that's when it is very sad to see division amongst people.

M.S.   You project a wonderful harmony and a great sense of hope from the perspective you have found on these serious matters.

M.B.   It has completely changed my life. I am a Christian. I believe in the basic Christian themes that we have been given about loving your neighbor and honoring God and praying. That's what I do. First of all, the simplicity I have found in it is amazing, because we have made life seem so complicated. Everybody is out there searching. I have found it in Christianity but that is where my ancestors found it as well. They found strength in knowing that they weren't by themselves. They found a great sense of hope in Christian beliefs.

M.S.   Where do you go to tune in, to pray, to find your inspiration? Do you have a special place that you like to go to?

M.B.   It can be anywhere, but I have to say Donegal has a lot to do with that. I love just being able to walk anywhere in Donegal. There are places there that are just so peaceful.

M.S.   Do you have certain prayers that you like to say?

M.B.   Prayer is just talking to God. I have used samples of Saint Patrick's Breast Plate in one of my songs, which is "Christ with me, Christ on my right, Christ on my left, Christ above me, Christ below me." I meditate on the knowing that God is with me.

M.S.   This is how you reach your bliss, how you reach your maximum joy?

M.B.   Yes, it is. Very, very much so. I feel blessed and very lucky. I don't like to evangelize about my experience too much. Recording PERFECT TIME has made it easier for people to ask me about my insights. I hope people can sense this through my music.

M.S.   How does all of this re-interpret what you have done musically to date? You must look back at the magic of your life and have a new insight into your purpose

M.B.   Yes, I do. I really find it difficult to believe people when they say they aren't looking for something more meaningful in their lives. Material wealth doesn't make you happy – bottom line. You can pretend it makes you happy.

There are a lot of young people, inexperienced with life, who are scared about going into the millennium because they just don't know what's there. Think, if you were young again and starting off in life, it could be overwhelming. They must ask, "What's out there?" because they don't know yet. I went through a bad time when I was younger, I was rocking along and I came to a stop and asked myself, "What's going on? I'm not happy." I wanted to search. I was brought up as a Catholic so I started to pray for guidance and then I met my husband, Tim, who is a Christian. Between us, we've learnt an awful lot from our differences because he was brought up Protestant in England. What we learnt was a very important aspect of what we're about now. The pieces fit together like a jigsaw. We realize that there was something in our history that was greater that we ever realized. Even our writers – Joyce, Yeats, Shaw – debated from within their spirituality. You can see it in their writing. It made them better writers. We are close to losing that; we seem to think that it's cooler not to be thinking of wanting something more in our lives, a spiritual being or a spiritual focus.

M.S.   Over the last few years, I've noticed that it is much easier to talk about personal spiritual life without it becoming political or controversial in some way.

M.B.   That's what I love to see.

M.S.   There's a greater prospect of our not competing with each other when we are more spiritually attuned.

M.B.   Why should we be ashamed to talk about our spirituality? Those people who left on those boats long ago had such a powerful welling up of the spiritual inspiration in their breasts. Their vision gave them enough courage and inspiration to carry them on, to the ends of the earth. To be able to express this feeling musically is tremendous.

DISCOGRAPHY

PERFECT TIME (1999)   MÁIRE

MISTY EYED ADVENTURES (1994)

With Clannad

LANDMARKS (1998)

AN DIOLAIM (1998)

CELTIC COLLECTIONS (1997)

ROGHA: THE BEST OF 1982-89 (1997)

ROGHA – BEST OF 1982-89 (1997)

LORE (1996)

CLANNAD THEMES (1995)

BANBA (1993)

ANAM (1990)

PASTPRESENT (1989)

SIRIUS (1987)

MACALLA (1985)

LEGEND (1984)

MAGICAL RING (1982)

FUAIM (1982)

CRANN ULL (1980)

IN CONCERT

DULAMAN

CLANNAD 2

Website: http://www.jtwinc.com/clannad/clanhome.htm

sheila chandra

biography

$\mathbb{S}$heila Chandra was born in 1965, in London, England, of Indian parentage. She was enrolled at the Italia Conti stage school at the age of eleven. The school's preoccupation with show tunes did not correspond with her interest in jazz, soul, and gospel music, but the school allowed her to record an audition tape for Hansa Records which was passed to songwriter and producer Steve Coe. He was developing a new group, Monsoon, to fuse pop music with Indian classical structures, such as fixed note scales. Sheila's heritage made her the perfect choice as singer, and three months before she left the Conti school she had become Monsoon's full-time vocalist.

After releasing an independent EP, the group was signed to Phonogram Records, and their debut single, *Ever So Lonely*, was a UK Top 10 success in 1982. Sheila had suddenly become Britain's first mainstream Asian pop star at the age of seventeen. However, following disagreements between artist and record company, Monsoon disbanded at the end of the year.

Sheila spent the next two years furthering her studies into Indian and Asian music, which resulted in her debut solo album in 1984. Both this and a follow-up collection, also released in that year, demonstrated her growing technique and fascination with vocal experimentation. QUIET was the first record to include her own compositions, and in 1985 she recorded two more studio collections. THE STRUGGLE was firmly song based, leaning towards the pop dance culture she had known as a child, while NADA BRAHMA was a more experimental song cycle, absorbing influences from the East and Afro-Caribbean music (notably the raga-tinged title-track).

Five years preceded the release of her fifth album, ROOTS & WINGS. This accentuated the Indian tradition of 'drone' music, while also continuing to highlight her fascination with cross-matching cultures. She stated: 'I am often unaware of the precise joining point between two styles of vocal from different traditions, it seems so natural to slip from one to the other.' In 1991 she signed to Real World Records, through her own production company Moonsong, and recorded WEAVING MY ANCESTORS' VOICES. A year later she made her live performance debut at the Spanish WOMAD Festival. 1994's THE ZEN KISS was inspired jointly by the spirituality implicit in its title and her newfound passion for live performance.

interview

maíréd sullivan I thought your story would be perfectly set, Sheila, in this collection of profiles on Celtic women in music because you sing the Irish traditional songs so truly. Since both ancient Vedic Indian and ancient Celtic European cultures came from Indo-European roots, its great to hear the joining of old traditions that you have created. You have bridged the deep emotional currents of very ancient singing traditions.

sheila chandra Yes. It really all started to come forth for me in 1989, when I was singing *Lament of the McCrimmon, Song of the Banshee*. I came across this fantastic lament, written in 1745 by McCrimmon as he was about to go out to battle on the front lines. He knew he would be slaughtered, and had to write his own lament because, being the best piper in Scotland and Ireland at the time, there was no one else to write it for him. I thought the idea of having to write your own lament was incredible! You know you're going to die! It was written in a very stoic pentatonic scale, and I wanted to put the feminine depth in. So I was emulating an instrument that is played at funerals and weddings, the shehnai, which has a very reedy, slurring sound. I think it's the closest approximation to human wailing, to keening. So I started to compose melodies based around that emotion for *Lament of the McCrimmon*, and it became *Lament of the McCrimmon, Song of the Banshee* which appeared on the 1990 album, ROOTS AND WINGS.

That became a seminal track for the trilogy that I've done on Real World, which is all voice and drone. That was the beginning of my folk – Celtic adventure. I had studied a lot of vocal techniques, but up till that point with Monsoon, etc., everything I had done was based around pop vocals and instruments, and Asian vocal and percussion obviously were starting to be absorbed. *Lament of the McCrimmon* was really the leaving off point for me. It was great to be able to contrast a very Eastern sound, being a melancholic scale, with this very stoic pentatonic scale the lament was holding up. You try to be stoic and you break down again. That became the dynamic of the song.

It was really a seminal point also, in that I decided that for the first time in ten years, instead of being a studio based musician, I would start playing live. I thought this was a perfect opportunity. If I could just go out on stage with a drone and make it as long as I wanted to, and weave vocal techniques from around the world together just using my voice . . . one voice, one mind that would be the ultimate for me. That's why I wrote WEAVING MY ANCESTORS' VOICES, THE ZEN KISS, and ABONECRONEDRONE.

People called me an Indo-Celtic artist. I'm sure you know it's so difficult to draw a technical boundary when you're between Islamic, Indian, Turkish, Arabic, Bulgarian, Gregorian chant, Celtic music, and then on into Soul music. All those ornaments have commonalities. Vocal styles also lead into one another, via trills and arpeggios and things that are common to all of them. Throughout time, all over the world, the voice is the only instrument that remains the same. It's obviously going to have a common ground. Monks kept it as a primary instrument and the Asian tradition regards voice as the ultimate instrument. Celtic tradition does that too because it's kept the concept of unaccompanied voice, within a strong melodic tradition. I feel that's why whenever I have played in Ireland the understanding coming from the audience has been so great. There are fundamentals that make the Celtic tradition very similar to the Asian tradition.

M.S. It must be really interesting for the Irish to hear you coming in with that, because they had never had a real influx of Indian culture, in any of the Islands, before the expansion of the British Empire. It's refreshing. It's stimulating!

S.C. I think that, in a way, they've got their own version. They've kept voice as a central part of their tradition, and so many traditions have forgotten that. They've gone off into chords and orchestras.

For the last four to five hundred years there has been a general cultural deviation, but the Irish tradition seems to have stayed true to the voice as its primary instrument. It seems to have maintained similar structures and a similar reverence for melody and for the vocal line, and for the eminence of the singer and the superiority of the expressive powers of the voice. That is something that is very obvious to see when comparing the Celtic tradition and the Asian tradition.

M.S. Do you like to study history, in terms of social and cultural connections?

S.C. I haven't got time. (Laughter) I've been so busy being a singer. I don't go out reading about the social contexts and history, and structures of music. The songs come to me purely because their beauty attracts me. That's really what happened. I became very attracted by Irish music just because it has such a fantastic sense of melody. I just completely fell in love with some of those melodies and what I could do with them. The first really strong Irish song I came across was *Donalogue*, and there is a version of on WEAVING MY ANCESTORS' VOICES. It's a gorgeous song, and it's supposed to be a thousand years old, and somebody just sang it to me. I just thought it was one of the most fantastic melodies I had ever heard. I had heard several translations of it when I decided to put in this Islamic section to describe this woman's feeling. Also, because I found my voice very naturally taking off from the third line in the verse up till the Islamic style vocals, and then coming back down again without a break, I was able to go between Irish and the Islamic tradition pretty seamlessly. I found out later from one of the translations that there is a suggestion that Donalogue rejects the young woman who is singing this song because she is a gypsy. It's almost like these connections are just completely written in on a kind of cellular level, and anybody who sings those songs gets the feel for the original intention that they were written with.

It was another instance where I could contrast, because the melody is written on a specific scale. Then the melody that I added, which I call Dhyana, meaning compassion, was much more melancholic, much more wild, saying, "I'm just crazy about this person and he won't even look at me." The new scale expressed that kind of wildness.

M.S. Do you find the scale in retrospect?

S.C. It just came out of my mouth. Often that's what happens with me. I don't sit around saying "Moorish people, and Celtic music and Indian music all have something in common." There's a Spanish lullaby on WEAVING MY ANCESTORS' VOICES, which is probably an original Moorish traditional lullaby. It was sung to Manuel De Falla by his nurse when he was a young boy, and he later arranged it for piano and voice. Plummy operatic voices usually sing it. It certainly doesn't get sung to a drone, but I happened to know it. One day I had my drone tapes on, which are set to around sixty-nine minutes long, and I was letting my voice go. It came out, and worked perfectly over the drone. My voice discovers for me, my body discovers for me, rather than anything I think up as any kind of clever intellectual style.

M.S. You must feel fortunate for having this opportunity to explore with your voice. You obviously had a room that had a good echo earlier on in life.

S.C. (Laughs) I had the family stairwell which was uncarpeted, and fortunately the house next door was being done up when I was fourteen, so there was nobody there to mind me singing in the evenings.

M.S. How did your family feel about your singing? They must have loved it.

S.C. I didn't think they took it very seriously. They thought of it as this weird thing Sheila does. She goes off into the night for hours and sings in the stairwell.

M.S. Could they hear you singing?

S.C. They probably could. I had a measure of privacy, but I don't think they seriously considered that it was a direction that I would pursue. My musical freedom is something that I've had to fight for. I've had to make certain specific decisions, and sometimes sacrifices, to make sure that my musical integrity is preserved. I had a hit with Monsoon in the early eighties. My family understood me being a artist, as long as I was that kind of glamorized pop star and accessible on the box every night. When I said I wanted to make solo albums and not release singles, and that I wanted to explore various musical terrains, they were not happy. In fact, they were extremely unhappy with that.

The decision to split up Monsoon was necessary. We were being pushed into toning down our music. I fought for my freedom, because that kind of wide, deep, lateral musical apprenticeship and exploration was very important to me. I haven't released a single since. Real World has understood that and has been very good to work with.

M.S. It must have been nice to have found kindred spirits there?

S.C. Yes, absolutely. I don't think they've always understood exactly what it was I was aiming for, but they've supported it, and they've understood how important it has been for me in not having any interference. I own the copyrights and recordings. They license them on a one-off basis. They've been willing for me to do that. It puts a record company in a slightly insecure position when they don't have an option on the next piece of product. But they've been willing to do that, because they see that it's important to me.

M.S. You're a very strong woman to have been able to manage the business like this.

S.C. I was fortunate because the person I write with, Steve Coe, who has produced for me ever since Monsoon, when I was making my first five solo albums, handled the business side then. He did all the business so I could concentrate on learning my craft, and learning all the technical stuff in the studio that I needed to know, to get the sound I wanted. I absolutely trusted him. But he hates doing business. So, as of 1990, he said, "How about if you do this now"? He only did it because he was part of the writing team, and he wanted to protect the music as much as I did. I have found that I actually like to do it. I don't hate business the way he does. I formed my own production company and publishing company, and I've gone on from there. There are times when I really have to shut Real World out and not talk to them because I'm crafting something very vulnerable and unfinished and delicate. I really can't have any kind of business energy around at that time. They understand that. They know I'll go to them when I'm ready, and they know that I keep my word. I promise that I'll chat to them later on about the project, and I will. It all works because there is a trust.

M.S. I wanted to draw out more on your emotional sense in singing and exploring your voice. You've developed a range of explorations and have been innovative with your own voice. What do you feel when you are exploring a new sound combination?

S.C. It's a personal and intimate experience for me. Sometimes it gets to the point where I feel like I'm being sung, where something is coming through me, that it's not really to do with my own intelligence. It's not something that the clever part of me could cobble together. I find myself singing things that I later edit down and put into a piece, and then four or five months later I discover the other levels and meanings that are already woven into them which I didn't see at the time. It really feels as though something more is moving through me. There are also times when I hear things in a drone. I hear almost full-blown performances of things that are far beyond my skills, that I wish I could sing, so other people could hear what I'm hearing in the drone. I really feel guided, as if the songs exist as entities and are just waiting for me to make contact. It's a great feeling, because otherwise, a song could just be like a crossword puzzle that doesn't have a set of answers. A song can be an emotional technical problem that you can't necessarily solve. If you feel it has a personality and it's already talking to you, then eventually you're going to unravel it. It will give you enough information to blurt it through into some kind of concrete reality. So, I became obsessed with finding out about exploring various ways of expressing emotion in the voice.

Singing can get very stylized, and I wanted to know how other people, through various vocal traditions, had expressed the same emotions, despair and joy and all that. Because when you are in joy or when you are in despair, your feeling affects your vocal chords, it literally biologically affects the way your vocal chords work and the way that you sound. That's the only instrument on which that is possible. I just spend my time building the number of techniques I have at my disposal. Whether it's just for use as a solo voice over a drone or whether it's as lots and lots of layered voices, for example on ROOTS AND WINGS, where there's sometimes twenty-three voices doing different things, all my voice, layered up to produce a certain emotional effect. QUIET, my second solo album where I started to write, had no lyrics and was all about vocal cyclic riffs and things, where I could explore some of these ways of transmitting emotion through the voice.

M.S. Externally, people look and say, "hey, that's kind of like a yoga practice in a way," or it's one of the ancient ways of going into yourself. You've learned to loosen up your limitations and peel back the layers.

S.C. I find that psychologically there is a glass ceiling on what I think I can do. I hear people who have been studying ornaments in a vocal tradition for twenty years, and think, "Oh God! I could never do that!" In fact, when I just let go, and let the sound come through me, I would often find myself singing those things perfectly. Then I would seize up again and get all nervous as to whether I could ever repeat that. Part of it was learning to physically free up. I did the Alexander technique and I found that it helped a lot, and I concentrated on that, so that it became much easier for me to let the ornamentation come through. In a way, it keeps that inner critic quiet because it gives the inner critic something to do. When I do get sung, or played like a flute, as I mentioned before, I get carried away. When I'm on stage and that happens, the audience gets that twinkle in their eye. What do you go and see a live performance for? It's not to see a technically brilliant performance, or a technically perfect performance. It's that spark of connection I think a performer is able to channel and the gift that the performer gives; once the performer is in contact with that higher intelligence, the audience starts to contact it as well. I found much later, after I started to naturally do this, that, in fact, that was the reason why music and dance were first performed in temples. In a way, the dancer or the singer was praying, was contacting that higher intelligence for the congregation.

M.S. Like a shaman?

S.C. Exactly, a shaman. That's what we still want to see performers and entertainers do for us.

M.S. What about that concept of entertainer?

S.C. When powerful self-knowledge is suppressed, what better thing to do than to hide it under trivia? Entertainment is never going to die. People are always going to want to be entertained. It's one of the safest hiding places. Entertainers by virtue of what they have to do, by virtue of the discipline of singing or dancing, take people more deeply into themselves. If they go far enough into their craft, they will, because they are involving their bodies, stumble onto this knowledge. It is knowledge that cannot be lost. It is cellular. I believe it really is. It will arise. It's the perfect hiding place. It doesn't matter that it's covered in trivia.

M.S. How do you prepare for the stage?

S.C. I try to get calm and get quiet. I do my warm-up singing exercises and breathing exercises. I'm lucky. I find that when I start singing I don't have any other chatter in my head. I can simply sing a scale and just be so in love with the way the notes sound against the drone. It's because that's where the interest is when you're dealing with drone music. They counterpoint the form of harmony between the melody notes and the drone notes. I am very fortunate that it is an automatic reaction with me. That's where my ear goes and that's where my interest goes.

I have been aware recently that I didn't learn stagecraft very well. I went to a theater art school when I was growing up and I learned a very disempowered form of stagecraft which I think unfortunately a lot of people get. It's that "the show must go on," it doesn't matter how you feel instead of using your gut emotions and reactions as the fuel for what you should be doing on stage. Sometimes it is right to walk off, or it is right to get the security guards and say, take that guy in the front row out. It is honoring your feelings as a performer. I was taught in the old way, to stuff your feelings down and the show must go on. That's something I'm starting to get around by exploring sacred clowning, and feeling empowered on stage. It is a very powerful thing to go out on stage completely alone for forty-five minutes and not bring on a band half way through. The audience is with you because they know how vulnerable it is. At the same time, it takes massive amounts of concentration and energy because you're painting this huge bubble, you have to paint the entire atmosphere of the song with a single voice. Sometimes there's not enough energy for you to be able to fight off all those conflicting emotions about where you are and how safe you are, and how good the sound is, and all that. I think there are definitely other ways of approaching it.

M.S.   How do you feel when you walk into the studio? Do you have a problem recreating your sacred space?

S.C.   No, absolutely not. Partly because I started with the studio – Monsoon was a studio-based band. We didn't play live. I learned a lot about my craft in the studio. To me the studio is a kind of sacred box where you can create your own world. You can be completely in control. It's a wonderful peaceful space where no one may intrude unless you give them permission. You can go over things as many times as you like. You can go for exactly the sound you want, unlike when you play live, and repeat yourself night after night. You go in to do something new and something delicate and something vulnerable and fresh every single time. I learned, from some very good old-school engineers, how to clear the space so they could work, when to be quiet, when to interject, when to make sure the session keeps going on track.

I'm also very fortunate because Steve Coe, whom I mentioned before, who produced all my music and co-wrote with me, started out as a piano player, but got increasingly interested in voice because of what I was doing. It got to the point where he no longer writes music on the piano. He's very much my cohort in creating that space where the finest nuances of the performance come through. When he mixes all the tracks on recordings, such as WEAVING MY ANCESTORS' VOICES, he'll spend sixteen hours on the voice alone. That's completely unheard of in the average pop production where you spend sixteen hours on the drum sound and you have a half hour left for the voice because you are running out of time and money. Steve has a huge silence in which to paint the subtlest nuances. It becomes a challenge for the mixing engineer, and it becomes a challenge for the producer. You know it's not going to be covered up by guitars and bass and piano. The spectrum is not going to be eaten up by other sounds.

M.S. Do you plan to have children?

S.C. No, my albums are my children. They take a hell of a lot of energy. I think I'm far too selfish about music to have children.

discography

MOONSUNG (1999)	STRUGGLE (1985)
(Real World)	(Indipop)
ABONECRONEDRONE (1996)	NADA BRAHMA (1985)
(Real World)	(Indipop)
ZEN KISS (1994)	QUIET! (1984)
(Real World)	(Indipop)
WEAVING MY ANCESTORS' VOICES (1992)	OUT ON MY OWN (1984)
(Real World)	(Indipop)
ROOTS & WINGS (1990)	
(Indipop)	

With Monsoon

MONSOON (1982)
(Phonogram Records)

Compilations

BLISS (1998)	VOL. 1 – BRIEF HISTORY
(Real World)	OF AMBIENT (1994)
VOL. 2 – TRANCE PLANET (1995)	SILK (1991)
(Triloka)	(Shanachie)

MARY COUGHLAN

BIOGRAPHY

Previously a drinking and smoking chanteuse, there is an impression of Mary Coughlan as the embodiment of the self-destructive female jazz/blues singer. It's an image that is almost true, but in the best tradition of myth-making, there is a gap between what appears to be and what is actually the truth. The really interesting aspect of Mary Coughlan is that, through her many fine song interpretations, she blurs the line between the two.

Born in Galway, Ireland, in 1956, Mary Coughlan is the eldest of five children. Mary's father was a soldier from Donegal, her mother a hard-working housewife from Connemara. Reared far from the lap of luxury, Mary's first memory of singing in front of an audience was with her sister in an officer's mess at the age of four. "The song was Bridie Gallagher's *Two Little Orphans*," she recalls. "My mother had us primed for it – it was the only song we knew. I didn't sing in public again until I was twenty-eight."

In her teenage years she opted for rebellion over compliance. She became a hippie, sewing Ban The Bomb signs on her flares and peace signs on an old army bag, two anti-authoritarian tactics that ensured the wrath of her father. She would sneak out to see folk and rock bands playing in Galway, the late nights clashing with early mornings for school in the local Presentation Convent. She stopped going to church around this time, too, spending Sunday afternoons drinking with her gang of underage school friends. She also experimented with drugs and by the age of fifteen had overdosed on pills, slashed her wrists and spent six weeks at a psychiatric hospital. At seventeen, she left home, qualified academically, but yearning for freedom from what she viewed as unnecessary restrictions.

She went through many varied jobs, from nude modelling to sweeping roads in London. Eventually, Mary returned to Galway with her new boyfriend, a Galway man she met in London. They married in 1975, and Mary gave birth to her first child, Aoife, a year later. Two more children followed, but the marriage broke up after six years.

While living in a house with a motley collection of people, Mary met Dutchman Erik Visser, a classical guitarist. Erik had come to Galway to study the work of Ireland's most famous harpist, O'Carolan, and has been a creative, instinctive thread running through Mary's life ever since. "Erik knew I could sing," explains Mary, "I made a demo of a song called *The Beach* for his record company. They weren't interested, but Erik reckoned he could do something with it." She recorded her first album, TIRED AND EMOTIONAL, in 1985, followed by seven more before releasing AFTER THE FALL in 1997 on the Big Cat/V2 label.

interview

mairéid sullivan You've been through the whole issue of the legality of divorce in Ireland. What impact did it have on you?

mary coughlan I have campaigned for Legalization of Divorce since 1987. I did gigs for the divorce action group. I was active in demonstrations. It was a bit of a relief when it came through.

m.s. I guess you have some pretty interesting opinions about all that?

m.c. I do indeed, the abortion thing is still a problem here, and so the two issues went hand in hand. Women can travel to England for abortions, and thousands and thousands of them do every year.

m.s. Have you heard of the book on the *New York Times* bestseller list called *Are you Somebody?* by Nuala O'Faolain.

m.c. Oh yes, I've read it. She's very honest in her writing. Maybe a bit too honest, because her parents are still alive. The whole thing about alcoholism and abuse is hurtful. It's very blaming. I've been through all that myself, and you learn not to blame. It's hard to carry all that stuff around.

m.s. Your music must be a wonderful expression, even a release, for you.

m.c. I find it healthy to sing. I find it cathartic. I love singing now more than I've ever done. I do communicate very well with people when I sing.

I used to be embarrassed about it. People would tell me it was great, but I never appreciated it. There is definitely something that gets communicated. It's the emotion, the feelings. A lot of women come back after a concert and tell me I sang something that means a lot to them and they cry.

M.S.   Do you write your own songs, too?

M.C.   I just started writing, and I co-wrote a couple of the songs on the last album. I scribble around constantly, and a friend of mine, Ritchie Buckley, an excellent saxophone player, and I are starting to sit around and write together. He's been working with me for nine years, so he's close to me.

M.S.   That must be quite an exploration. What are you talking about in your new songs?

M.C.   Trying to put the past into perspective, and things like that. It's hard to do it without being too personal. I don't want everyone to know exactly what I'm talking about. I'm desperately in need of a funny song, so we're doing a 'pick-up' song. However, mostly we're doing songs about the past.

M.S.   Is your repertoire a good mixture of up-tempo as well as slow songs?

M.C.   I can really never find enough fast ones, and I don't think it matters because the kind of stuff I do is songs where people listen to the words more than anything else. I do have a few good funny ones, very tongue-in-cheek. There's one about the Bishop of Galway. The story is about a Bishop who banned two-piece swimming costumes years ago. Apparently, he saw a woman wearing a bikini on the beach one Sunday morning and he said, "Excuse me, my dear, those things are banned." So, she says, "Which piece do you want me to take off?" A friend of mine wrote a song about that called *The Beach*, and there's an old Leon Redbone song called *I Want To Be Seduced*. We change the words around all the time to fit in with what's going on politically in the country. It's funny to hear a woman singing those songs.

M.S.   Have you recorded any of that?

M.C.   Oh yes, they're all recorded.

M.S.   Do you perform live a lot, or is it mostly recording?

M.C.   I perform about nine months of the year. I released an album in 1997 called AFTER THE FALL, and it's a fairly autobiographical album of an alcoholic. I was an alcoholic, and I've been five years sober now. So, I wrote a couple of the songs about people who had been in a similar situation.

M.S.   When did you start singing?

M.C.   When I was thirty. I'm forty-two now. I had my first gin and tonic when I was thirty-one. I took to it like a duck to water. It got progressively worse, until about six years ago, when I decided to try to get help. The Irish people don't handle alcohol well.

M.S.   What are your favorite themes from the songs?

M.C.   I've sung every theme under the sun. I like to tell stories in songs.

One song is called the *Magdalene Laundry*, which is about a place women who were pregnant in Ireland were sent to. That was a very powerful song, and the subject of three television documentaries, one by Channel 4, one by the BBC, and one by a big French Television company. It sparked off a huge controversy in this country back in 1989. A lot of women came out and spoke about their own personal experiences. It's been a very huge song for me. I tend to be controversial. I'm not afraid to sing about what I feel strongly about.

M.S. I'm really glad to be talking to you because you're talking about what is really happening in Ireland in your songs.

M.C. You know Christy Moore wrote songs about the political side of things. I've always written songs about things that have directly affected me and affect women. I do a song called *My Land Is Too Green* which has become very controversial. It's about being bogged down with religious tradition and oppression by the government. Traditional singers sing folk songs, and folk songs by nature talk about things that are happening now. Everybody likes to sing songs about love, but what about things like the drug situation now in Ireland, and what it's like. I have one song called *The Ice Cream Man*. It's about a man who was arrested as a felon for selling ice cream to children and heroin to their mothers, from the back of one of those neighborhood ice cream trucks. I've had a lot of criticism for doing that sort of thing.

M.S. I'm sure you must have a pretty strong audience since you talk and sing about these important issues.

M.C. I have a strong and loyal following that I've built up over the past twelve years. The last album I did on a new label V2, Richard Branson's (Virgin Records) label. It was the first one released on V2 in New Zealand, Australia, Japan, and America, so people are beginning to find out about me. I may never make million seller albums, but the people that buy them like the music, and that's what counts. I think I was the first artist that the label signed in 1997.

M.S. Since you're involved in so many controversial issues, how do the people in the Church treat you?

M.C. I've been lambasted for being so outspoken. It was just the time in Ireland, during the late eighties, when all the scandals started to come out about the Catholic Church. People try to cover it over. The Catholic Church in Ireland educated the people; if it weren't for the priests and the nuns, very many of us wouldn't have any education. The thing that bugs me the most is that they never actually said they were sorry about the destructive things they have done. They just try to deny it and hide it. When the cases come up in court, they say, well "We'll do something about it," but they don't. I think a lot of people have actually begun to sue the Church for stuff that happened in orphanages and homes. In the last ten years a lot of priests in Ireland have been leaving the clergy because they haven't been able to toe the line on issues like contraception, abortion, and divorce. A lot of people find that they can't talk to priests anymore because they just don't know what they're talking about when it comes to the real life of the people. They're not changing with the times.

M.S. You're talking about what is really happening in society, and I think it's the artist's role to be brave enough to expose it, as you have done.

M.C. I think so. I'm very angry about a lot of things in this country at the moment. I feel it's important to face the issues. A lot of people think it shouldn't be said in music, but I think it should. Like blues and good folk music that tells what's going on; people like Dylan and Woody Guthrie. It's an important thing for me to say these things.

M.S. Did you have any trepidation when you first started twelve years ago?

M.C. I don't go around shouting about it all the time, but I certainly talk about it when I'm asked. I speak openly about my marriage breakup and issues of alcoholism and abortion in this country. People appreciate it. I like to be open and honest about my life. People like to go around digging up dirt. My family has been a bit concerned that I say too much some times, but they accept it because it's the truth, and the truth wins out.

M.S. Beginning your singing career at thirty is surprisingly late. How come you began then?

M.C. I was busy being a mother. I have a friend, Erik Visser, whom I've known for twenty-five years. He's a musician from Holland. He wrote a piece of music for my first daughter when she was born. It was number one on the Dutch charts for almost a year. When he became rich and famous in the mid-eighties, he said, "We should really do something about this career of yours." He actually paid for my first album. I was twenty-nine going on thirty when we went into the studio. The album was sort of an overnight sensation. It went to the top of the charts in Ireland, and I became a rock star (laughs) at the age of thirty. It changed my life . . . so that's how it all started.

M.S. How did that affect you? It obviously gave you more strength.

M.C. Well, before that, I was cleaning offices three nights a week, and my uncle was a painter, so I was his assistant. When the singing career started, it was wonderful because I'm doing what I really want to do. In the beginning there was a lot of guilt. I was thinking that I should be home with my kids, and I never spent a night away from home until my son Owen, who is eighteen now, was seven. My parents were very supportive and looked after them when I had to be away. I think the guilt of leaving them home made me drink a lot. I've come to terms with all that now, and it's okay. I'm a mother as well as a musician. I combine them and do what has to be done.

M.S. How about your musical background? What was that like?

M.C. Nobody in my family is very musical. My mother sang around the house, and we had a record player. She would listen to Guy Mitchell and Andy Williams and some American stuff. There was no tradition of music in the family. I just started listening to records that were in the house. I think a lot of Irish kids that grew up when I was a teenager rebelled against the Irish language and music, and thought it was like living in the dark ages. Now I think of the Irish traditional music as being like the blues. It's a music that developed from repression and story telling and I think sean-nos singing is like the blues . . . roots music.

M.S. What do you think about the growing interest in Celtic culture?

M.C. I suppose *Riverdance* and things like that have contributed to a lot of people wanting to find out about Irish culture. It's made it more popular. People are asking questions about where it comes from, and the traditions in it. Personally, I think it makes the whole thing very pretty. I think they miss out on a bit of the tradition. It was a very strict tradition that was looked at as an art. There was a lot more to the dance. It meant something . . . it was a celebration that didn't happen very often. It was mainly for special occasions. Now it just splatters all over the television and it's pretty. It's commercialized and desensitized.

M.S. What makes you laugh in your career? Where do you find delight?

M.C. I get a lot of enjoyment from my children. The way they perceive my career. Especially my two-year-old who can't understand how I can be sitting in the room and I'm on television at the same time. Things like that. I just did a big concert for the school which my daughter, Clare, attends. It's one of the only non-denominational schools in Dublin. They don't get any funding from the government, so we have to raise the money ourselves. I do a concert every year for them. My daughter gets such a thrill out of that because everyone talks to her about it. Her schoolmates are all age seven and eight. They can't believe that it's me.

M.S. It must mean a lot for her self esteem as a seven-year-old.

M.C. It does, and she loves that I'm doing it for the school. Everyone at the school really appreciates it.

M.S. How many children do you have and do any of them play music?

M.C. I have five children. My twenty-three-year-old daughter, Aoife, is a photographer. My twenty-one-year-old daughter, Olwen, is a multimedia artist. My youngest son, Cian, is two years old. My youngest daughter, Clare, is seven, and my eldest son, Eoin, is nineteen. He plays the guitar and bass. He also has his own fully equipped studio here at the house, where he records dance music with his friends.

M.S. Do they enjoy your career?

M.C.   They do, yes. They say a lot about it. I've brought all of them on tour at one time or another, Finland, Norway, America, and they have a great time.

Discography

AFTER THE FALL (1997)
(Big Cat/V2)

LIVE IN GALWAY (1996)
(Big Cat)

LOVE ME OR LEAVE ME,
   THE BEST OF (1994)
(EastWest)

LOVE FOR SALE (1993)
(Demon)

SENTIMENTAL KILLER (1992)

UNCERTAIN PLEASURES (1990)
(WEA)

UNDER THE INFLUENCE (1987)
(WEA)

ANCIENT RAIN (1986)
(WEA)

TIRED AND EMOTIONAL (1985)
(Mystery/ WEA)

CONNIE DOVER

BIOGRAPHY

Vocalist Connie Dover is an accomplished interpreter of the traditional music of Great Britain and Ireland. Her soaring, crystal clear voice displays a depth and breadth of range that have earned her a place among the world's best Celtic singers, a distinction all the more remarkable as she comes from the American Midwest. Her three solo recordings firmly established Connie's reputation as a world-class vocalist, and have sold over 100,000 copies, garnering rave reviews from around the world. All three albums were produced by Silly Wizard alumnus Phil Cunningham, and were recorded in Scotland with instrumentation by some of Scotland and Ireland's finest musicians.

Born in Arkansas and raised in Missouri, Connie Dover is of English, Cherokee, Mexican, and Scots/Irish descent. She discovered the wealth of the Celtic music tradition as a teenager, and began a search, which continues to this day: researching songs, collecting and composing music and studying traditional singing styles.

Connie's diverse background, which includes undergraduate study at Oxford University, a history degree earned from William Jewell College, and her work as a trail cook on a Wyoming cattle ranch, reflects the depth and richness of her approach to traditional music. The theme, which runs through her work, is the exploration of the common ground between

British Isles and American folk music. Her style is innovative in its synthesis of tradition, yet always respectful of that legacy. She has recorded three solo albums while also appearing on several compilations from Narada, CELTIC ODYSSEY and CELTIC SPIRIT.

INTERVIEW

MAIRÉID SULLIVAN How are your views on the world at large shaped by your musical career?

CONNIE DOVER I think it would be more accurate to say that my views on the world at large are shaping my musical career. My own world view, or my "values," determine the songs I choose, the subject matter about which I write, how I approach the business of music, how I interact with audiences, and most of all, what I hope to communicate to listeners.

I find myself being educated by my listeners, by the people who respond to my music, and I am learning that music reaches out to people in ways I'd never dreamed were possible. We all crave beauty, and many of us are searching for some true expression of how we feel about our lives and the world around us. I believe that we are also trying to connect with each other in a meaningful way. This music can be a conduit for that expression. Quite often, listeners contact me to tell me how a particular song has affected them. They communicate with me about what moves them and about ways in which certain songs affect them on an emotional level. It's their heartfelt response that is a revelation to me. Because most of these people have never met me, their willingness to share with me on this level is very courageous, which is very humbling to me. I see over and over again that music can break down conventional barriers and provide us with a new medium of understanding, empathy, and communication.

M.S. Do you have a personal 'Mission Statement'?

C.D. My musical mission statement, and I'm loosely paraphrasing the great Bill Monroe, is this: "I just want the song to go from my heart to yours, and may nothing get in the way."

M.S. Tell us about your own philosophy and your personal lifestyle, how you like to live.

C.D. My approach to music is shaped by my view of life. Instinctively, I find myself always moving toward creating and maintaining balance and harmony, in my environment, in my relationships, and as part of my inward journey. My music is just one manifestation of this.

Kindness, tolerance, charity, patience – these are qualities I try to cultivate within myself and to practice each day. To experience and appreciate beauty, to live in and appreciate every moment, no matter what that moment may bring, is the method of living I aspire toward. This is a discipline that requires recommitment every day. I try to put this same mindfulness into my music. I select a song for both its beauty and for the integrity of its message. Each song I choose to sing, whether in performance or in the recording studio, is a unique expression of some human experience. Sometimes there is a lesson to be learned, a story to be told, and a passion or yearning to be shared. Each song offers its own unique emotional experience that transcends cultural boundaries. It is a powerful means to connect with people, and it goes beyond convention-al modes of expression that can be so limiting to our imaginations and our communication with each other.

I live in rural Northwestern Missouri, on the edge of the Kansas prairie. Being in the open spaces, and being able to enjoy the view of rolling hills and fields, is a luxury, and is very sustaining. I treasure every moment of it. Although I'm a very social person, it is this solitude, plus daily contact with trees, grass, and sky, the true physical world, not the man-made "environ-ment" of 20th-century urban America, that keeps me centered.

I also live and work in Wyoming for at least part of each summer. For the past seven years, I have worked on ranches as a cook, both in guest lodges and on the trail during ranch cattle drives. Cooking outdoors over an open fire, hauling water, living 'in the weather', riding horses and feel-ing nature all around me puts life in a truer perspective, at its most ele-mental, and helps to remind me that I am part of a living planet. It also keeps me aware that playing music is only part of what I do in life, and is only one expression of who I am. This serves as my "retreat" and my place for balancing out.

It is also my inspiration. These beautiful places, 'out West', where I've lived and worked, in the high country of the Rockies, sleeping under the stars on the open prairie, in deep forests, among the elk and other wildlife, watching a storm blow in from the Bighorns – these are the views that my mind's eye sees when I sing. I store them in my heart, and when it is time to make music, I take them out again, no matter where I am.

m.s. Tell us your favorite themes and passages from the traditional songs and from the original songs you sing.

c.d. One of my favorite passages is from the song *Ned Of The Hill*, named after Irish patriot Edmund Ryan. The words have great passion and lyrical beauty – they describe not only Ryan's experience as an Irish 'outlaw' dur-ing English occupation, but also express his own yearning to be with his beloved, from whom he is separated (translation from Gaelic by Barbara Cartwheel):

My darling, my beloved,
We will go off together for a while
To forests of fragrant fruit trees,
And the blackbird in his nest,
The deer and the buck calling,
Sweet little birds singing on branches
And the little cuckoo on top of the green yew tree,
Forever, forever, death will not come near us
In the middle of our fragrant forest.

This verse is typical of what draws me to traditional Celtic songs – the lyrics have enough power to reach across centuries and draw in the modern listener by connecting with universal human experience, in this instance, feelings of love and desire.

I was inspired to write the words to the song *Who Will Comfort Me* by my great love for the American West and my sadness at observing how much its landscapes have been ravaged, even during my own lifetime. Here is the chorus to that song:

When the boundless spirit has no place to roam,
The heart will sadly whisper this world is not my home,
When the sweep of wind along the grass bows down to destiny,
When the last bright star has fallen, Lord, who will comfort me?

m.s. What are some of your other interests, your intellectual pursuits, responsibilities, etc.?

c.d. I own and operate a record label called Taylor Park Music, which I formed in order to release my own albums. For the first several years, I handled all of the marketing, distribution, foreign licensing, advertising and promotion of my releases. Fortunately, I now have a wonderful office staff, which allows me the freedom to spend more time with my music.

When I first started in the record business, a number of people told me, you can either be a record label or you can be an artist, but you can't be both. Well, I'm here to tell you, it can be done, you just have to be prepared to wear a lot of hats. To make all of the work worthwhile, you must believe in your product and yourself. This is another reason I've not signed with a label. For me, music is a form of self-expression. If I allow the songs I record to be chosen by someone other than myself, I've lost that self-expression and traded my own vision for someone else's.

When I started Taylor Park Music almost ten years ago, there were very few American women who were making a full-time professional career singing traditional Scots and Irish music. Certainly, record labels were puzzled about how to market a woman from Kansas City who sang Celtic music. Once I had become more established and had received some great publicity and good record sales, the same record labels who wouldn't return my calls in the beginning were calling me up to see if they could "help" me. It was then that I made the decision that, at least for the time being, I wouldn't sign with anyone. By that time, my auton-omy, and the freedom to decide what songs I would record, and when and where, had become too precious to relinquish. I'm not saying that it's something I would never consider doing, but I love having control over every part of the process.

For recreation and relaxation, when I'm not in Wyoming, I enjoy spending time with my horses and working outside. I have learned that nothing rejuvenates me more and takes me out of being "too much inside my own head" than being out of doors and doing hard physical work. So much of the work that I do is cerebral, both with regard to working on music and running my record label. Getting outside and working until I'm physically exhausted is very refreshing to me. I run three miles a day in a nearby state park. I also love reading history, as I enjoy trying to piece together social and historical contexts for songs.

M.S. Why did you come to your musical career?

C.D. I have a degree in history, and had every intention of becoming a teacher. I've always sung 'along the way', as a child and through school and college, just for my own pleasure, and because I was so captivated by this music. It became clear to me over time that I could have the oppor-tunity of choosing music as my career, and so it's the path I've taken, but it is a path that I choose and rededicate myself to over and over again. I never considered myself to be an 'artist', though. I just like to sing!

M.S. Tell us how you came to your own musical style.

C.D. My style is simply a reflection of my taste. It's a combination of what moves me on an emotional level, what pleases me aesthetically, a song that has a meaningful cultural or historical context, lyrics that speak to me in a direct way and which I hope will speak to others.

M.S. Can you trace your musical background influences for us?

C.D. I was not raised in an Irish-American or Scots community. I was born in Arkansas. My father's family comes from rural northeast Arkansas. There was music in his family, and in my mother's as well. I happened on to the old folk ballads as a teenager. Imagine my delight when I discov-ered that my Grandmother Dover in West Ridge, Arkansas knew some of these same old songs. I felt like there was a real link between me and this music and its history, that I wasn't just on the outside looking in.

M.S. Who are or were your mentors?

C.D. My mentors are all of the people in my life, family and friends, who have encouraged and supported me. Musically, I am truly inspired by the work of Phil Cunningham, who has produced all of my albums. He has been at the forefront of traditional music since he burst on the scene in the 1970s with the great Scots band Silly Wizard. Phil's expressiveness and creativity go far beyond mere technical prowess. He is a truly talented multi-instrumentalist who is not only an incredible player, but who is also gifted with the ability to capture the spirit of the tunes he plays.

M.S.   Did you get a special 'big break' as a professional musician?

C.D.   When I released my first recording, SOMEBODY: SONGS OF SCOTLAND IRELAND AND EARLY AMERICA, I was interviewed by Scott Simon, host of NPR's *Weekend Edition Saturday*. The combination of conversation, a little live performance, playing tracks from the album gave me some great instant national exposure. What I really appreciated about Scott and the producers of the program was that they did not feel that my 'American-ness' was something that they would have to 'overlook'. We were actually able to explore why Celtic music is our music too, and I think this touched a nerve with many listeners.

M.S.   Do you like touring and what kinds of venues do you prefer?

C.D.   I enjoy being able to travel and to share this music with audiences in new places. I love to sing in churches. The acoustics are usually live and brilliant, and many of them were designed for solo voice, without a sound system. At one point I would have said that I preferred an intimate venue, and I suppose I do, but I think intimacy, a kind of one-on-one relationship between the singer and each member of the audience, can be achieved even in a large hall.

M.S.   How do your travels influence your music?

C.D.   My travels have really influenced and shape the music I do. I feel that I've been blessed with a unique perspective: growing up in the American Midwest, studying at Oxford University in England, recording albums in Scotland, and working on Wyoming ranches have given me a birds'-eye view of the music of all of those places. It also has helped me to see how connected they truly are. I'm also particularly moved by the landscape of these beautiful areas, and they always provide a visual inspiration for my music.

M.S.   What do you think are the reasons for the overwhelming popularity of Celtic music now?

C.D.   Speaking from an American perspective, I think we are hungry for beauty and for meaning. As a result of urban and suburban growth, changing technology, and the pervasiveness of the media in our lives, our brains are over stimulated by a lot of external sources that are not necessarily of our own choosing. Traffic, strip malls, noise pollution, and countless other kind of uninvited sensory input assault us on a daily basis. We find ourselves either needing to escape from it or to find an antidote to it. Music can be one of these antidotes. Celtic music is new to many contemporary American listeners, and it offers us music that is both substantive and pleasing to the ear. The melodies in Scots and Irish traditional music have a rare and unusual beauty that stand out in the midst of what we're generally offered by way of 'popular' music.

M.S. What do you think is the essence of the genre?

C.D. The heart of this music lays in its capacity to capture the listener on an emotional level and draw us into an experience that is both meaningful and aesthetically pleasing.

Celtic music has the power to transport us, to temporarily lift us out of our daily cares, our surroundings and ourselves. As we near the end of the 20th century, we are, in a manner of speaking, starving to death, we are cut off from our past, from our ancestors, from many of the traditions that made us feel as if we were a part of a human continuum. On its most profound level, Celtic music comforts and soothes us as only music can do, but it also elevates us. It is more than a window to the past, it spans oceans, time and cultural boundaries, and for many of us, gives voice to that deep inexpressible part within each of us that, without it, would not have a voice.

Discography

IF EVER I RETURN (1997)
(Taylor Park Music)
THE WISHING WELL (1994)
(Taylor Park Music)

SOMEBODY (1991)
(Taylor Park Music)

Guest Artist

ROGER LANDES, DRAGON REELS (1998)

JOHN WHELAN,
FLIRTING WITH THE EDGE (1998)

Narada Compilations

CELTIC ODYSSEY
CELTIC SPIRIT
HEART OF THE CELTS

CELTIC VOICES
NARADA WORLD

Ann Heymann

Biography

Ann was born on May 7, 1951 in Minneapolis, Minnesota, and married Charlie Heymann in 1976. They have two daughters: Orlaith, age ten, and Honor, age seven. From the mystical strains of music to harp repertoire found in lute and bagpipe manuscripts, from laoidh to amhran, from the European court dances of Cormac MacDermott and the compositions of Turlough O'Carolan to contemporary gigs and reels, Ann Heymann illuminates the dark nooks and crannies of another age. With Charlie Heymann contributing on vocals, guitar, cittern, button accordion and bodhran, Ann's clàrsach (KLAR-shuk) transports audiences to sonic realms unvisited by modern ears.

Ann's book *Secrets of the Gaelic Harp*, an instructional method based upon the first tunes once taught to Gaelic harpers, has become the instrument's 'bible'. She has served on the faculty of the Historical Harp Conference & Workshop, Amherst Early Music, the Edinburgh Harp Festival, the World Harp Festival, and the Oberlin College Scottish Harp School. Ann has also led master classes and workshops at numerous institutions and organizations, including Comhaltas Ceoltoiri Eireann, the American Harp Society, Cairde na Cruite, Comunn na Clàrsaich and the School of Scottish Studies.

interview

mairéid sullivan How did you become so deeply involved with the wire-strung harp?

ann heymann Well, to understand me, you must first become acquainted with my instrument, if only because, of the two of us, she has the stronger character! The Gaelic harp, my chosen instrument, is temperamental, robust, and profound, and to me, she is the perfect musical archetype for 'Celtic woman'.

Known as "clàirseach" (KLAR-shuk) (Irish) or "clàrsach" (Scots), which means literally "female sound board or trough," this brass-strung harp was intimately connected with magic and the otherworld. Its voice was silenced 200 years ago and the three mystical musics – goltraighe, (GOLE-tree), gentraighe, (GON-tree), and suantraighe, (SOON-tree), literally crying-strain, laughing-strain, and sleeping-strain – were carried away by the winds of time.

I'm often asked, "What's a 'Scandahoovian' from Minnesota doing playing the Irish harp?" This tactless and all too frequently asked question never fails to stun me. Even though my categorical and honest response is, "I fell in love with it. It is the realization of the music I was searching for," the issue is so complex that even I am not sure of the real answer!

m.s. You seem to know quite a bit about the history of the harp. Can you tell us some more?

a.h. In olden times, it was an instrument of ceremony and ritual that was used to accompany the chanting of syllabic poetry and clan genealogy. The decline of the filidh (poets) and clairseoirs (harpers) began with the demise of the old Gaelic way of life in the 1500s. By the end of the 1700s, this thousand-year-old oral tradition had faded into silence, but not before some of the music and traditions were collected from the last of the clairseoirs. Their legacy provides us with a way to hear the voice of the legendary clàrsach, but today's commonly played instrument is the lever harp, which with its gut or nylon strings bears only a superficial resemblance to the ancient harp of the Gael and cannot hope to represent its music.

m.s. What did you do before you became a musician?

a.h. I was a professional horse trainer and riding instructor who became enamored with Irish music. Having received a pennywhistle as a gift, I proceeded to teach myself to play and soon began 'moonlighting' as a charter member of a local ceilidh band. A fortuitous reading of historical accounts regarding the ancient harp of Ireland and Highland Scotland piqued an interest that soon gave way to total fascination. In 1974, after three years of searching, I found a copy of the Castle Otway harp made by master harpmaker Jay Witcher. Sounding the brass strings with finger-nails especially nurtured for such an occasion, I heard the bell-like voice of the clàrsach for the first time, and with the financial assistance of my future husband, Charlie Heymann, I made the purchase.

Five years earlier, at eighteen years of age, I'd quit playing piano and pipe organ, but it is likely that this musical background helped to prepare me for the task of dealing with this notoriously difficult instrument. There were no teachers, tutors, arrangements, or recordings. Oddly enough, I hadn't yet heard of Alan Stivell. Armed with my knowledge of tradition-al music and Edward Bunting's *Ancient Music of Ireland*, music and tradi-tions collected from the last of the clarseoirs, I began my quest. Charlie was always there with his exceptional musicianship and extraordinary understanding of the clàrsach. The clàrsach was my actual teacher. It murmured or rang out in approval when I was correct, but clashed testily and assaulted me with vertigo-inspiring cacophony when I was wrong.

M.S. What inspired you to pursue further research?

A.H. A continual source of inspiration has been Gaelic mythology and lore, which, when finally connected with elements of the clàrsach tradi-tion, has provided me with a very special insight. It happened on a day when I was down with a fever, which I took for an opportunity to finally read the music section of Eugene O'Curry's lectures series, *Manners and Customs of the Ancient Irish*. While reading a section about the Dagda and his crot-player, Uaithne, (OON-yeh) in the "Cath Maige Tuired" (Kah Moy Cheerid), I was struck by a lightening bolt of understanding! Momentarily so clear, the 'gods-eye' view that was offered me was fleeting, and by the time I'd run from my bed to the next floor with O'Curry in hand, I could barely communicate my revelation to Charlie. He listened patiently, read the significant portions, and bit by bit, he helped me recon-struct the thought form that had been so generously offered by my muse.

M.S. How did you interpret this revelation?

A.H. What had been revealed to me were the symbolic attributes of the clàrsach. Embodied within the framework of the instrument are three very basic principles: female, male, and androgens/neuter, creating a Celtic ver-sion of a yin-yang symbol. The soundbox, with it's mortise, or concavity, at each end, is the female part of the instrument equating with belly or womb. The forepillar, with a tenon, projection, at each end, is the male segment synonymous with phallus. And the harmonic curve, with both a mortise and tenon, represents the spiritual union of male and female. An essential part of the human psyche and the universe at large, these three aspects are reflected in our Indo-European languages with feminine, mas-culine, and neuter references like he/she/it. This same trinity can be observed in the three mystical musics: the female goltraigh, nurturing music for the crying of women in labor or men injured on the battlefield; the masculine gentraighe, music of laughter and vitality, such as love and war; and the sacred/androgenous suantraighe, sleeping music of death and the otherworld. Likewise, these three aspects are symbolic of the cycles of life, birth/life/death, which highlights the importance of having a Gaelic harp at seasonal festivities and, of course, at rites of passage such as births, weddings, and funerals.

M.S. Do these three forms suggest different tunings, or playing styles?

A.h. Yes, the traditional tuning of the clàrsach, with two consecutive tenor G strings, known in English as "the sisters" are called "na comhluighe" (na-COW-lee) in Gaelic, which means literally "lying together"– conjugally. It was from these two strings that the rest of the harp was tuned, a practice first evidenced in the 1100s and surviving to the end of the tradition in the 1700s. The playing of the Gaelic and Welsh harps on the left shoulder, with the left hand taking the treble strings is also symbolically connected to the gendered principle, left being female, right male. Vestiges of this widespread concept can be seen at weddings, where family and friends of the bride are seated on the left and those of the groom on the right. The clàrsach was sometimes referred to as "the harper's wife," probably for this very reason, as it lay on the player's left shoulder.

M.S. How did this revelation affect your playing style?

A.h. Six years ago I had a major musical breakthrough. I was continuing my search for the clàrsach's lost repertoire of "ceol mor" (kyole-more, Gaelic for great music), now played on the bagpipe as "piobaireachd" (PEE-bruk). I had yet to find a way to adequately express it on the clàrsach. All of a sudden, miraculously, I began to play in a whole new way! Ceol mor began to spring forth from my hands, and I subsequently recorded my solo CD QUEEN OF HARPS, which included a thirty-two minute composition entitled *Lament for the Harp*.

M.S. That must have been quite a breakthrough!

A.h. It was indeed . . . with this piece I accomplished my life's work. I felt as if I'd completed my 'mission'. Anything else that I could do in the future would be simply 'icing on the cake'. Five years later, I continue to feel this way, and I have never enjoyed playing more. I'm still discovering facets of this new system, with the alternating right and left hands, that I have now named 'coupled hands'. Hindsight tells me that this musical breakthrough was a long time coming; that I had unwittingly trained my hands through the frequent playing of *Burn's March*, the fourth tune traditionally taught student clairseoirs back in the 1600s and 1700s. This is just one example of how the past can inspire creativity. I liken it to driving a car: one travels into the future while keeping an eye on the rearview mirror. Whether we accept it or not, our lives and creations are intrinsically linked to the past and they cannot exist without each other. Many musicians imagine themselves as rule-breaking innovators, refusing to acknowledge any ties to ancient practice, when they are doing something so musically determining as tuning their instrument!

M.S. What message do you feel people get from Celtic music today?

A.H. Celtic music speaks to people in many ways. Its soul has a timelessness that breaks through our desensitized techno-industrial senses to reveal our humanness in its full glory. People are embracing the trinity within themselves, their feminine, masculine and spiritual/androgynous aspects, and perhaps that is why they are drawn to the music of the Gaelic harp – a veritable Triple Goddess. I think that its music is so subtle that it can surround an aura, reveal its shape, and even gently caress it. Perhaps this is why people can perceive the same piece of music in different ways. Probably the most rewarding experience has been when people told me about their use of my *Lament for the Harp*. I know of at least three women who chose it to be their birthing music. A man in Northern Ireland used it as a meditation for peace the entire month prior to the Peace Agreement. And a woman with terminal cancer used it to prepare for death. In addition, a number of writers and artists have told me that it enhances their creative process. Four years after recording this thirty-two minute piece, I was finally asked to perform it at the 1998 Edinburgh International Festival!

M.S. Do you ever miss your career with the horses?

A.H. I have no regrets, although one of the hardest things I have ever done was to give up my horse career, which was necessary when I married Charlie in 1976. Charlie and I and another couple took to the road, all fitting into a Volvo stationwagon, along with instruments, luggage, and sound system. After two years the band broke up, and Charlie and I decided to play as a duo before we 'settled down'. For nearly twelve years we shared a dufflebag, driving from one side of the U.S. to the other, playing in Irish bars, oftentimes five nights a week, folk clubs, festivals, and occasionally doing college concerts. We made enough money for an annual trip to Ireland and eventually Scotland. Through the years we have met the most wonderful people and amazing characters. The fabulous sessions and all-night kitchen music becomes a blur of late nights, drinking, and traveling. We never took pictures or kept a journal because the ever-changing environment made us live for (and in) the moment. A wonderful book, *Last Night's Fun* by Kieran Carson, provides a glimpse of this 'craic'!

M.S. How did your music career affect your family life?

A.H. Our first daughter, Orlaith, was born on New Year's Day, 1989, and in 1992, Honor came along. Both girls love to sing, and Orla does Irish dancing. They have added immeasurable dimension to our lives. We now live in our own home and try to juggle the demands of parenthood with a career that has no job description, and still make time for horse riding!

M.S. What are your plans for the future?

A.H. Musically, we've been very excited about our combination of the clàrsach with the chanting of Gaelic syllabic poetry. Future projects include a long overdue Carolan recording – though plenty of people have made lovely renditions of his music, it is important to me that I play them in an authentic style, largely because I'm on the 'correct' instrument, and I finally feel convinced of my interpretations! Among other things, it is also important to me that I continue to compose new music for the clàrsach. So much to do and so little time! Our BIG dream is to create a center for the Gaelic harp in Ireland – for it is still quite neglected and organizations who should be remedying the situation haven't yet taken up the cause. I don't yet know how it will happen, but that is the direction in which we wish to proceed.

So, why is this "Scandihoovian from Minnesota" championing the clàrsach? Back in 1983, Charlie and I followed a trail of Gaelic harp clues to Scotland. It was my playing of the *MacDonald Clan March* that instigated THE HARPER'S LAND collaboration with Alison Kinnaird. But it wasn't until seven years later that Keith Sanger (Scottish scholar and co-author of *The Tree of Strings*) found this amazing historical information: In 1731, at the end of the clàrsach tradition, the widow of Neil MacShennoig, clan harpers to the MacDonalds, Lord of the Isles from the 1400s, inherited the last of Scotland's harpers' lands (harper's lands were large land holdings granted to clan harpers) and her name was Ann Heymann! Since Heymann is a German surname, and my husband's name, we never expected to come across it in Ireland or Scotland, much less intimately connected to the clàrsach tradition. Ann Heymann is my married name, but I use these amazing coincidences to assure myself that I am on the right path; that I'm following my destiny; that I am doing what I was fated to do. Perhaps "Ann" had to be coupled with "Heymann" to provide the necessary 'magic' to resurrect the music of the clàrsach!

Discography

QUEEN OF HARPS

HARPER'S LAND
   with Alison Kinnaird

HÉMAN UBH

ANN'S HARP

LET ERIN REMEMBER
   with husband Charlie

CHRISTMAS IN THE KING'S COURT

Compilations

HARPISTRY

eileen ivers

biography

Riverdance star Eileen Ivers came into the world in 1965, the daughter of John and Annie, who came to the Woodlawn Heights section of Bronx, New York from County Mayo, Ireland. Eileen and her sister Maureen were encouraged by their parents to become Irish dancers. However, after six dancing lessons, Eileen realized that she was destined to focus her attention on another Irish art form. Within a year she had picked up the bow and has wowed the world with her fiddle playing for the past twenty-three years.

If anyone asks Eileen Ivers where her original inspiration to play the violin came from, she will probably show her beautiful smile and quickly reply, *Hee Haw*, the popular American Country and Western comedy/music television show. However, it was while the family was in Ireland that Eileen asked her mother if she could take violin lessons. At the age of nine, in Buncrana, Donegal, Eileen earned her first all-Ireland medal (Banjo). Through the years she has accumulated an incredible total of 35 All-Ireland titles, combining eight solo All-Ireland titles on her fiddle, six for slow air playing, and the remaining medals for duets, banjo, and trios playing.

After her college graduation, where she received a degree in mathematics, she played with the great musicians Mick Moloney and Seamus Egan. Moloney formed Green Fields of America with Eileen as a member.

She later worked with Luka Bloom, and was recognized by Daryl Hall and John Oates producer T-bone Wolk, who recommended that Eileen record and tour with the rock duo.

On returning to New York, Eileen played with such notable musicians as John Doyle and Kimati Dinizulu, before joining the band Paddy A Go Go, begun by Black 47's Chris Byrne, and featuring former Speir Mor lead singer, Pat Maguire. With Joanie Madden, she co-founded the group Cherish the Ladies, then met Irish composer Bill Whelan when he needed a fiddle player to play the score he was writing for Leon Uris's best-selling book, *Trinity*. And so it was that when Maire Bhreathnach left *Riverdance*, Eileen Ivers was chosen to join the show.

interview

Mairéid Sullivan Are you still touring with *Riverdance*?

Eileen Ivers Not much in the past year. I've been taking time off to finish my own recording, which was actually completed last week. It's called CROSSING THE BRIDGE.

M.S. Why did you choose that title?

E.I. Actually, Sony Classical picked that title.

M.S. You recorded it on Sony?

E.I. Yes, I finished the deal I had with Green Linnet Records, and my producer suggested we see if there was some interest from other labels. As you know, it's the time right now for Celtic instrumentalists and everything Celtic ... it's just booming. I was really impressed with Sony Classical. I met the president and a few of the people over there and we had a great meeting. I'm really excited. Hopefully, it's one of many records I'll do with them.

M.S. This is a great break, but then Cherish the Ladies was also. When did that start by the way?

E.I. That was around ten years ago. Joanie Madden and I co-founded the group. The basis of that was women playing Irish music, the brainchild of Mick Maloney. That was a lot of fun being in that group for a couple of years.

M.S. Wasn't that an interesting time in music? It wasn't so much a focus on the Celtic genre as it was a focus on the women who were such brilliant instrumentalists.

E.I. I think for a lot of us, we don't realize, "This is a woman playing music." For myself personally, I consider myself a musician, working on my instrument, hopefully learning and growing day by day. It was interesting that somebody just said, "Let's create a group of women musicians." That was fun.

I did that for a couple of years, and other musical projects just kind of came up. I toured with Hall and Oates for about a year. I took it as a learning experience. It was a nice initiation to touring. It was rough but I got into it after a while.

M.S. How is all this nurturing your soul and giving you confidence to be yourself? In terms of your experience as an artist, do you feel that you are broadening your own expectations of a more beautiful experience with your work and that you are blossoming more in your confidence?

e.i. Oh yes, absolutely. I really believe that everything in life is a growing experience. Everyday is a learning experience, whether it's your career or your musical point of view. We all strive towards being better people and getting along better together, and I think that's very important. In my own music, I always try harder to perfect my skill. As you get older you learn things, you pick up things through life, and it's a very cathartic experience. I keep looking ahead and moving on, but I think it's good to stop every now and then and look at what you're doing in retrospect. You learn a lot. In that looking back you can see that everything was done for a reason. For example, playing with Hall & Oates opened up a lot of new doors for me. In the R & B world I had to approach the violin as a different instrument, compared to its role in Irish music. After that I was involved with a more alternative pop band in New York, called "eo". It was a great band. I worked with them for a few years, and we had a seven-record deal on Arista Records. We started making the first album but we had a rough disbanding before anything happened. Again, you look at why, or what caused that to happen. During those years I started playing a lot of electric fiddle, and I learned to use the instrument more like a lead guitarist would. It became a different voice. I learned a lot more about the instrument I was playing.

M.S. How did you feel to be moving into that electric sound? Coming from the traditional music, you know how the traditional scholars are so sensitive about doing anything different with the traditional music. Was it liberating for you to not have to worry about stretching that?

e.i. Absolutely. For so much of my life I spent a great deal of time doing my homework, as we all have to do in traditional music. You know, getting the recordings of the older traditional players and learning them exactly. You know, the way they played certain settings, going through that, going to the Irish competitions every year, it was something you had to do as a traditional player. When I left that part of my life, it was very liberating, as you said. I did my last competition when I was eighteen.

M.S. It's like Picasso, for example, he had to become a master of the old school of art before he could experiment. Once he became an acknowledged master, he could do anything he wanted.

e.i. That's a very good analogy. Beautiful!

m.s. We need to know those things. We need precedents.

e.i. That really sums it up. Especially in music, the violin is next to the human voice in expressing emotion and what you can do with that instrument. Obviously I'm biased, but I feel that your personality can come through the instrument because it is such an expressive instrument.

m.s. I want to ask you something about that specifically. The violin was introduced to the Irish tradition in the seventeen hundreds or somewhere around that time. I know it was strong at that time in Scotland. I don't know how early it came to Ireland. It took the traditional music, the harp music, which was traditionally very slow, into the fast dance tempo.

e.i. I think it's a great instrument because you can be so rhythmic on it. You can play the dance tunes; and you can also be very melancholy. You can play the laments; you can express anger or joy. It is that kind of an instrument.

m.s. Before the folk revival in the late fifties, early sixties, the singers were into singing very slow songs. It was all about the slow easy feel. Do you like playing that on the violin?

e.i. I love it. That's a whole other part of it.

m.s. What's your favorite pre-occupation at the moment?

e.i. I feel very happy in life right now. I feel very fortunate. I've had a lot of great opportunities come my way in the last few years. When I left college, I was just six credits from getting a Master's degree, which I will one day complete. I studied mathematics and that is something that I really love. It's something that I'd like to get back to.

m.s. Do you like physics too?

e.i. You know I like physics, but I didn't touch that in college. I find that math is really fascinating. I think math and music really do go hand in hand in so many ways. The overall structure of math, when you talk theoretically, is like music. It is all about forms, how, for instance, a counter melody may support a melody. Pieces which all fit together. That is really fascinating to me.

m.s. Wouldn't the antidote to the chaos of the touring, professional lifestyle be to seek out concepts of order? You're expressing the music, but in your mind you want to see order.

e.i. It's interesting. There is room for order and disorder in life. Sometimes I think disorder is fun and appropriate. So many times when I'm playing, and I feel like I'm playing well, or I'm playing with great musicians that I have a great deal of respect for, when we're really connecting and listening, and speaking back and forth musically, it's the best feeling in the world. Then you're really living in the moment . . . you're going with your thoughts in the moment. That, to me, is really the ultimate musical experience.

Hopefully, that translates into the audience so they know that you are giving of yourself 'right now', in the present. You're not going through the motions of just playing a tune. You're not just backing a song.

M.S. The person listening in the audience longs for the artist to open up other dimensions of experience.

E.I. I try to always approach live playing in that way. To be real, and to be sincere. Audiences are very smart and I believe they pick up on things like this and that's exactly why I took a break from *Riverdance*. It's certainly not putting anything down, but I found myself gradually not giving myself fully to the music. After eight shows a week for three years, I began to see that I wasn't thinking fully about what I was playing. When I had the featured solo spots, I would be giving it everything, but on the band numbers I was beginning to space out and that's not fair because many of the people are coming for the first time. As it's their first time experiencing the whole thing, I just felt it wasn't fair to me, to the audience, to the show. I just thought, hey, I need a break! The Riverdance production office has been very understanding. They said, "Look, go out, take a break, do a gig with your band, do what you need to do." They said, "You're always welcome and just let us know when you want to pop back in." I couldn't ask for a better scenario. It's healthy; you come back in and you're excited to play again. I have a band now that I put together. We're performing and it's a lot of fun.

DISCOGRAPHY

CROSSING THE BRIDGE (1999)
(Sony Classical)
SO FAR: THE COLLECTION
 1979-1995 (1997)
(Green Linnet)
WILD BLUE (1996)
(Green Linnet)

TRADITIONAL IRISH MUSIC (1994)
(Green Linnet)
EILEEN IVERS (1992)
(Green Linnet)

With Other Artists

HER INFINITE VARIETY:
 CELTIC WOMEN (1998)
ROOTS OF RIVERDANCE (1997)
 with Bill Whelan
CELTIC MUSIC TODAY (1997)
CELTIC LOVE SONGS [CELTOPHILE] (1997)

HOME AWAY FROM HOME (1994)
 with Andy Cooney
HEALTH & HAPPINESS
 SHOW TONIC (1993)
STRAIGHT OUTTA IRELAND (1993)
 with Straight Outta Ireland

CELTIC MAGIC:
   11 IRISH INSTRUMENTALS (1997)
TASTE OF IRELAND:
   IRISH TRADITIONAL (1997)
SEASON OF MISTS:
   COLLECTION OF CELT (1997)
JIGS & REELS:
   DANCE MUSIC OF IRELAND (1997)
LAUGHING MAN (1996)
   with Yazbek
CELTIC WOMAN (1996)
SOME MOTHER'S SON (1996)
   with Bill Whelan
GREEN LINNET
   20TH ANNIVERSARY COLLECTION (1996)
GONE AGAIN (1996)
   with Patti Smith
SONG OF THE IRISH WHISTLE (1996)
   with Joanie Madden
OUT OF IRELAND [O.S.T.] (1995)
RIVERDANCE (1995)
   with Bill Whelan
WHISTLE ON THE WIND (1994)
   with Joanie Madden
HOME OF THE BRAVE (1994)
   with Black Forty-Seven
22 BRIDES (1994)
   with Twenty Two Brides
HARBINGER (1994)
   with Paula Cole

DEAR OLD ERIN'S ISLE (1992)
WHERE IN THE WORLD
   IS CARMEN SANDY (1992)
MY LOVE IS IN AMERICA BOSTON
   COLLEGE IRISH FIDDLE FESTIVAL (1991)
RIGHTS OF MAN:
   CONCERT FOR JOE DOHERTY (1991)
CELTS RISE AGAIN (1990)
   with Celts Rise Again
WEEK IN JANUARY (1990)
   with Seamus Egan
WHAT IT'S LIKE (1990)
   with John McCutcheon
CHANGE OF SEASON (1990)
   with Hall & Oates
RIVERSIDE (1990)
   with Luka Bloom
PLAYING WITH FIRE:
   CELTIC FIDDLE COMPILATION (1989)
LOVE OF THE LAND (1989)
   with Robbie O'Connell
LIVE IN CONCERT (1989)
   with Green Fields of America
BIG SQUEEZE (1988)
INVASION (1987)
   with Jerry O'Sullivan
FRESH TAKES (1987)
   with John Whelan

Website: http://historyoftheworld.com/music/blue/home/ivers.htm

ÐOLORES KEANE

BiOGRAPhy

Dolores was born on September 26,1953, in Caherlistrane, County Galway, Ireland. A former member of Irish folk group, DeDannan, her first solo album, which received a gold disc, was produced by ex-Silly Wizard member Phil Cunningham and included the Si Kahn classic *Aragon Mill*, Kate and Anna McGarrigle's much covered *Heart Like A Wheel* and, most surprisingly, Marlene Dietrich's *Lili Marlene*. FAREWELL TO EIRINN, which included John Faulkner and Eamonn Curran, featured songs describing the story of the Irish immigration to America from1845 to1855, when nearly two million people (or twenty-five percent of the population) left Ireland. LION IN A CAGE remained in the contemporary setting, with songs by Chris Rea, Paul Brady, and Kieran Halpin. The title track was a reference to Nelson Mandela, who was still a political prisoner in South Africa at the time. Despite the freeing of Mandela, *Lion in A Cage* remains a powerful song, and one of the better of the genre. Dolores participated in the television series *Bringing It All Back Home* in 1991, performing with Mary Black and Emmylou Harris in a band comprised of John Faulkner, Daragh Connelly (keyboards), Liam Bradley (drums/vocals), and Eddie Lee (bass).

ɪɴᴛᴇʀᴠɪᴇᴡ

ᴍᴀɪʀᴇ́ᴅ ꜱᴜʟʟɪᴠᴀɴ How old are your children now, Dolores?

ᴅᴏʟᴏʀᴇꜱ ᴋᴇᴀɴᴇ Joseph is twelve, and Tara is five.

ᴍ.ꜱ. Have they expressed an interest in music yet?

ᴅ.ᴋ. When you ask what kind of music they're interested in, they pull back. But they're interested in everything that is going on. You know how kids are. It could be Boys of the Lough today, Spice Girls tomorrow, and some folk song the next day. Tommy Sands brought out a children's tape a few years ago, and I got them a copy of that. Joseph was mad about it! Tommy sings all kinds of songs on the tape and tells stories, and they just loved it.

ᴍ.ꜱ. You're trying to give them the options, so their horizons will broaden a bit.

ᴅ.ᴋ. I would hate to start buying them instruments; I would prefer that they made their own minds up about all of that when they're ready. We have music sessions here in the house with all kinds of instruments being played, and we take them out to sessions. They know it's live, and it's happening, and it's not just something they see on the television or whatever. They're being exposed to a lot of new music.

ᴍ.ꜱ. Do they dance?

ᴅ.ᴋ. Oh, Tara is mad for dancing! She loves to hop around the floor. She knows the basic steps.

ᴍ.ꜱ. You've been playing out for quite a long time. Do you remember when you first started singing?

ᴅ.ᴋ. The RTE presenter, Cierán Mac Mathúna taped me when I was around four or five. He worked for radio and television. He used to travel around the country with a mobile recorder and tape people, collecting songs for his programs. That was back in the late 1950s. He used to come twice a year to Rita and Sarah's house, my two aunts. He would come to record them, and I was there once when he came over, and he recorded me.

ᴍ.ꜱ. So you knew songs then?

ᴅ.ᴋ. I knew bits of songs and I loved to sing. I did sing a bit of a song for Cierán. That encouraged me, from then on, to learn and sing songs.

ᴍ.ꜱ. You did the rounds at the competitions, too, when you were young? A lot of people I've talked to say how important they were to them in terms of giving them self-confidence and a forum when they were very young.

ᴅ.ᴋ. They were great. Once you were singing in a competition, then you knew you were going to the Fleadh as well, and it was wonderful to get away for a weekend. When I was going to secondary school, all the girls would stay in the convents when we traveled to the Fleadh. The girls were madly into pop music and, obviously, I was. But my first love was for traditional and folk music, and I didn't really say that much about it when I was in school. Even when I was on television, I didn't mention it, because it was considered very old fashioned and behind the times.

When I was growing up, there was very little to do around home, especially in the countryside. If you lived in a town, there would be a youth club or something like that. When we went to a Fleadh, not only did we mix with our own age group, but with adults as well. All the age groups were there, together, enjoying themselves. You never felt left out, whereas, when you came back home again, our parents would go out on weekends, but you were left at home.

M.S. Did you go to sessions much?

D.K. Yes. When I went to sessions, I played the whistle and the flute, so I was singing and playing as well. I always played the flute in sessions, in whatever tunes that I knew. I was always picking up tunes as well, and learning new ones.

M.S. Do you do that still?

D.K. I do, oh yes!

M.S. When you became an adult, an independent person, was it obvious that music was taking over your life?

D.K. Not really. I never got that feeling. Even now, people ask me about when I decided to go professional? The only answer I can come up with is that I don't think I ever did. It's obviously something that I do, but I never see it as something that encroached upon my life. I'm quite lucky. I've been able to do lots of other things as well. For example, I'm able to have the children and be at home with them. I suppose I see the children more than anyone with a nine-to-five job would. I go on tours and come back and I'm home for three or four weeks, and then I leave again, maybe for a weekend or week, and then I'm back again.

M.S. Have you ever taken your children with you?

D.K. Yes, lots of times, but I wouldn't take them abroad now. They're too young. It's too early. It would be too hard for them. On tour, you get up in the morning, you get in the car and you drive to the next venue, you go to the sound check, you go and have dinner – if you have time, then you're back, and you're up on stage. There's nothing there that would be enjoyable for the kids. Tara doesn't mind the traveling, but Joseph gets mad with long journeys in cars. He loves to get in an airplane, and say, "Oh! I'm in an airplane," but then he falls asleep. Three weeks ago I was presenting a television program with my brother, Sean, and I brought the children along. We were out on location and the weather was really cold. I felt bad because they were back in the hotel and it was a bit too cold to go over on the town and look at shops, etc. They had the television and video to occupy them, and seemed to be happy enough, but I just feel sad about it. I realized this wasn't a good idea. In the summertime it's much easier.

M.S. You've traveled a lot, you're a seasoned traveler now. Have you been all over the globe?

D.K. I've been to Australia, New Zealand, Canada, America, and different parts of Europe.

M.S. Have you gone to Asian countries?

D.K. No, but I would love to, well, actually I was in Hong Kong in June, and I've done a few concerts in Bahrain in the Middle East. Europe is great. I did a lot of work in Germany a few years ago. The Germans are incredible. I love the festivals in the States.

M.S. When you first started out, traveling the world, it must have been a real eye-opener for you, a real education.

D.K. It was fabulous. It's a brilliant education to go and hear different languages and eat different food, see a different culture. It's great because it broadens the mind. You tend to draw parallels between how they are living, and how you are living. We're very lucky to be musicians, to be able to do all that. Other people pay thousands and thousands of pounds to go on holiday, and we get paid to do it. I'll be visiting Norway again soon, it's fabulous.

M.S. Do you spend extra time exploring when you're traveling? Do you take a few extra days?

D.K. If we can, we always do, depending on how things are going. Right now, I'd just love to go over to London and just have a day off, just to see a bit of it again. It's changing all the time.

M.S. You live outside Galway. How is it there these days?

D.K. Galway is really going through changes! It's a boomtown. There are huge hotels going up all over the place. There have been awful changes. I would like to see it slow down. There are an awful lot of people from outside of Galway, and outside of the County, coming in to stay and building all kinds of developments. We live eighteen miles northeast of Galway, near the town of Headford.

M.S. There are a lot of musicians from that area.

D.K. There's a lot of good music happening around here. The Saw Doctors come from Tuam. They are all very good friends of ours. We have sessions together all the time.

M.S. Are you interested in history? Do you study the Irish history?

D.K. I'm interested, but I didn't have a lot of time for that since I was so busy with music. I know the contemporary history. You notice that there is a change of attitude, even with the younger people in Ireland. When *Riverdance* started, or when Phillip King did *Bringing it all Back Home*. That brought out the history of the music, and what Irish people had achieved abroad, and suddenly the world became smaller. I think since then people are more interested in listening to different types of Irish music and other music styles as well. If they have a hardanger fiddler, or an old timey fiddle player, they'd be more inclined to listen to it now, rather than saying, "That has nothing to do with us, we don't know anything about that." Now they listen and they say, "One of our lads heard the tune, and that's his version of it."

People are much more open now. The songs now, as well, are coming away from themes of the troubles. At one time, say with the Wolf Tones, we'd be waving banners and saying free the Irish people! What we're talking about now in songs, and what the writers are doing is saying, "Hey look, either keep it or give it away. Do what you like with it, but don't be killing people in the process." It's not the people who are at fault here. It's the authorities. They are the people making these decisions, to set one group of people up against another.

Because everyone now has a television, they are able to see it all. Just a few years ago, you'd see the politicians shouting, up in the local Parish Church, and gathering the people around. They'd be telling them what was right and what was wrong, saying, "Vote for me," and then they'd go off and do the opposite. Nowadays, we actually see all the ministers on the television, the whole lot, in their own building shouting across at each other. We're getting a closer look at them all the time. A lot more people are aware, and they know a lot more now. It's not just the troubles in the North that people are informed about.

Sean and I went to Omagh, in Northern Ireland, to turn on the Christmas lights, and they were symbolic of peace lights. Everyone had candles and it was just an incredible experience. It was outdoors, and thousands of people turned out. There was a beautiful choir on stage. The different Bishops, Catholics and Protestants, and whoever else, were all there. Sean and I did a song written by Tommy Sands, *Like the First Time, its Christmas Time*, about the peace process.

Like the first time,
it's Christmas time,
Standing by your side.
Singing with the Children,
Silent Night

We sang the first part and then a choir came in, it was lovely.
M.S.   That's what I've been hearing is happening up there. People are actually taking it into themselves now, not focusing on the politics so

much, but really looking at the community.

Ꝋ.K.   That was the point I was telling you about. People are beginning to see now, and say, "Hold on a second, this has been going on for too long. Let's make proper decisions here ourselves."

Ꝋ.S.   In Ireland, the musician and the poet has always had a leadership role in the community. Today, you can see yourself, you as a singer, being put in a leadership position because there's no controversy there, you are trusted by everyone. You are a leader because the arts can draw people's attention and focus, and give it back to them in a way that unites them. When you're bringing people together in a concert situation, it is thrilling, but when you're doing it as a political statement, it must be incredible for you to experience that. How do you carry that responsibility?

Ꝋ.K.   I think because the people would listen to me, that when I get up on a stage, and basically the stage is mine for however long, I have to be very, very careful about what I say, especially in singing the kind of songs that I sing. Now, with the peace process in motion, it gets a bit easier. Years ago when I would sing a political song, they were in a peace mode as well, but you had to be very careful. You don't want to give the wrong impression to people either. You have to get them to resonate with each other. The one thing I never did, and I made this decision years ago, was never to take sides on anything, because I was brought up as a singer, and I'm a singer of songs. I want to sing any kind of song as long as it's a good song. I've always made that point very clear.

Ꝋ.S.   Are you getting enough good songs right now?

Ꝋ.K.   Well, there are a lot of people writing songs and some very good songs among them. But to find a song that has a tune that appeals to me, along with lyrics that I feel I want to be identified with, really isn't that easy. We usually accumulate a whole box of 'demo' tapes during the course of the year or so, between recording new albums, and then have a blitz of listening to them and trying them out with the band, etc., and it's usually less than one percent make it to the studio. So, it's both a yes and a no answer to your question. There are certainly good songs and songwriters about, but getting the right one at the right time is something else!

DISCOGRAPHY

NIGHT OWL (1998)

BEST OF DOLORES KEANE (1997)

SOLID GROUND (1993)

A WOMAN'S HEART (1992)

LION IN A CAGE (1989)

DOLORES KEANE (1988)

SAIL OG RUA with John Faulkner (1983)

FAREWELL TO EIRINN
with John Faulkner (1980)

BROKEN HEARTED I'LL WANDER
with John Faulkner (1979)

THERE WAS A MAID (1978)

With DeDannan

BALLROOM (1987)

ANTHEM (1985)

THE GREAT STORM IS OVER (1985)

DEDANNAN (1975)

Compilations & Guest Artist

THE MAN FROM GOD KNOWS WHERE
with Tom Russell (1999)

CELTIC GRACES (1999)

THOUSANDS ARE SAILING (1999)

OTHER VOICES TOO
with Nanci Griffith (1998)

DANCING AT LUGHNASA (1998)
with Bill Whelan

LIKE THE FIRST TIME IT'S CHRISTMAS
with Seàn Keane (1998)

CELTIC AURA (1998)

WHERE HAVE ALL THE FLOWERS GONE . . .
SONGS OF PETE SEEGER (1998)

HOLDING UP HALF THE SKY VOL. 1 –
COLLECTION – WOMENS VOICE (1997)

TIDELINE with Rita Eriksen (1996)

CELTIC TAPESTRY (1996)

A WOMAN'S HEART 2 (1994 -1997)

ALL HEART NO ROSES
with Seàn Keane (1993)

WAKE UP SLEEPING
with the Saw Doctors (1993)

A WOMAN'S HEART (1992)

NOMADS/FANAITHE
with John Faulkner (1992)

THE REHEARSAL
with Christie Hennessy (1991)

SONNY with Emmylou Harris
& Mary Black (1991)

BRINGING IT ALL BACK HOME (1991)

ALL I REMEMBER
with Mick Hanley (1989)

REEFER & THE MODEL
with Johnny Duhan (1987)

MUINTIR CATHAIN
with the Keane Family (1985)

FOLK FRIENDS 2 (1981)

THE CHIEFTAINS 6 – BONAPARTE'S
RETREAT (1976)

Alison Kinnaird

Biography

Alison Kinnaird has been a leader in the revival of the harp in Scotland, and is one of its foremost players. She plays both gut-strung Scottish harp and wire-strung clàrsach (harp) using the very different techniques appropriate to each. She was the first player to make a study of the lost repertoire of the Scottish harp, and in 1978 she brought out the first record of Scottish harp music, THE HARP KEY, on Temple Records, produced by her husband, Robin Morton. She has published a number of her arrangements of harp tunes in her book *The Harp Key*. In 1992 she was co-author with Keith Sanger of the first history of the harp in Scotland, *Tree of Strings*, which brought to light much new information on the subject.

Her other recordings, THE HARPER'S GALLERY and THE HARPER'S LAND with Ann Heymann, which brought together for the first time the sound of the gut and wire-strung harps, and as part of the Gaelic group Mac-talla, have all been critically acclaimed. For a number of years, she and Christine Primrose have performed together in concert, and have toured widely in Europe, the U.S.A., and Canada. They recorded their album THE QUIET TRADITION OF GAELIC SONG AND SCOTTISH HARP MUSIC together in 1990.

Alison is also a highly respected teacher, holding regular classes on the Isle of Lewis and in Dingwall for students who travel great distances for their monthly lessons. She teaches at a number of Feisean and at the

Gaelic College in Skye. She has been a visiting lecturer/performer at courses held by the Scottish Harp Society of America at Oberlin College and also at Amherst College. She has developed her own oral methods of teaching traditional-style harp music. She has served on the BBC Broadcasting Council for Scotland and on the Scottish Arts Council. In 1997 she was awarded the M B E for services to music and art.

interview

mairéid Sullivan You have written in your book, *The Tree of Strings*, that when you were investigating the origins of the harp, you found that the triangular harps appear inscribed on the standing-stones of Eastern Scotland, two to three hundred years before the Irish examples.

Alison Kinnaird That's right and it surprised us.

m.S. When were they discovered?

A.K. They had been known about for quite some time, but the myth was so firmly fixed in everybody's mind that the harp came from Ireland through Scotland. It never occurred to anybody to question it. When we started looking at the dating of the stones, we discovered they might be earlier than we had previously thought. Then we looked at the Irish ones. We all knew there were harps in the old Irish stones, but when you look at them, they're all quadrangular harps or lyre type instruments.

m.S. When did you do this investigation into the age of the stones?

A.K. Keith Sanger did the research with me. We published our book to coincide with the Bicentenary Belfast Harp Festival that year, 1992. We were the first people to actually put it into print, and describe what it meant to us.

m.S. The consequence of that information must be to have put a fire under the Scottish people's appreciation of their own history.

A.K. Well, yes, I think that some people appreciate it. It's funny how people don't like to change their ideas. It's really difficult when people have an idea ingrained deep in their minds. They really don't appreciate somebody changing it for them. I think it takes a while for people to get used to the idea.

m.S. So the researcher does have a large responsibility as an educator?

A.K. Yes, and you have to be realistic about what you're suggesting. We say this is a hypothesis, and we have evidence to support our thesis. We're going by the primary evidence that we have. The conclusions we draw are the result of a great deal of research.

m.S. It's been seven years since you published your research, and now, in hindsight, how does it look?

A.K.   Keith and I were searching, in our own separate ways, fifteen years before that. My research began when I was trying to find a repertoire for the Scottish harp. I couldn't believe that there was nothing left for this instrument, that one couldn't play again in a traditional way. When you hear an old melody, obviously nobody knows how it was harmonized and exactly what they did long ago. There were a lot of different versions of tunes, so there were obviously lots of versions extant in the first place. People played their own versions of melodies. So, I was researching the harp from the point of view of the music, getting drawn into all the historical background that way. Keith is actually a piper himself. He plays Highland pipes. He started researching pipes, and kept tripping over harp references and realized that he was becoming fascinated with that side of things. He does fantastic historical research. He reads everything and remembers everything. He's got a wonderful way with lateral thinking. When we pooled our information, we managed to come up with some things that were really important for the harp.

M.S.   It must have been interesting for you to be using your lateral thinking to piece the information together.

A.K.   Absolutely! It's important for people to have an open mind. I learned so much doing this and writing the book with Keith. It pushed me into taking up the wire-strung harp. That was the other thing that we found … that there were two harps running parallel in Scotland.

M.S.   That's a point I wanted to talk about, too. Did you also find that there were different melodies from each side of the country that could be traced to the two types of harp?

A.K.   The harp melodies that have survived are all associated with the wire-strung harp. We can see which area they came from. The gut-strung harp, the small harp, as a folk instrument, died out in Scotland around 1600. At that point people carried on playing what we now consider 'early music', the classical repertoire. So there were various harps played throughout history. As a traditional instrument, the wire-strung harp survived in the Highlands much longer, until the end of the eighteenth century.

M.S.   The Highlands and the Lowlands had a different cultural orientation. The Lowlands were more connected to the English, and the Highlands were more connected with Europe, France in particular.

A.K.   Yes, they certainly have a different culture. They have a different language. The whole of Scotland really has quite close connections with Europe. Scotland has always had ties with France, the Netherlands, and Scandinavia because of the sea connection. It's easier to get to any of those places by sea than traveling by land down to England. Obviously the Lowlands had quite close ties with England, whereas the highlands tended not to, just because of geography. Many Scots, both Highlanders and

Lowlanders, would often have gone to France or the continent for their education, rather than to England.

The Scottish Gaelic is the Highland language. These days, 'Scots' refers to the language, which like English, is descended from Germanic roots, and is spoken on the East Coast and in the Lowlands. The way we refer to it is quite specific now. Scottish, as a word, could cover the whole country. But 'Scots' is something you would actually refer to as being from the Lowlands or East Coast. But the Gaels, when they first came over from Ireland long ago, were called 'Scots'. It's confusing. So when you're talking about unifying the Picts and the 'Scots' of old, the Picts were from the East Coast and the Gaels/Scots were from the West Coast at that point in time. Nowadays, 'Scots' is definitely East Coast and Lowland.

M.S. Isn't it fascinating how that turned around? Do you know when it turned around?

A.K. I don't really know. Actually that would be a good topic to research.

M.S. It seems that the only way now to find the distinguishing features of the culture is to focus on the arts. You can't even put your finger on a particular event or reason why the focus on the arts and the history is happening so strongly right now.

A.K. That is quite true, but the move towards political independence in Scotland has encouraged interest and enthusiasm for all aspects of our own culture.

M.S. I wanted to ask about what was going on in Scotland, at the time historians say Ireland was experiencing its Golden Age, when Europe, and parts of England, were going through the Dark Ages. The Irish took on Christianity without the over-seeing ritual of the Roman Catholic hierarchy, and they were able to take it in as a cultural renaissance, rather than a dogmatic intrusion on their familiar life-style. They didn't have political wars outside the country to interrupt them. Would Scotland have gone through some of that renaissance as well?

A.K. I don't think anything quite as obvious happened in Scotland. The influences were coming from different directions at that point. There were the Norsemen in the north, and the Angles pushing up from Northumbria into the south of Scotland. I think there were distractions in Scotland that didn't happen in Ireland during that period. Christianity came over from Ireland at that point, and also up from Northumberland. I don't think it was as obvious a flowering as they experienced in Ireland, although Iona was a very important center, and the Book of Kells is supposed to have been created there. Scotland had waves of cultural flowering, which happened in the late fifteenth and sixteenth centuries, and later, in the eighteenth century.

M.S. In an earlier conversation you mentioned that Scotland has two of everything, two pipes, two harps, and two languages.

A.K. We haven't got two fiddles. (Laughs) Well, there's the Hardanger fiddle that crept in, but that is a Scandinavian import.

M.S. Earlier, we were discussing lateral thinking, which brings in ideas from different sources and correlates them. It must have been thrilling to apply those skills to your research.

A.K. Yes, it is actually a thrill in many ways because I've been looking at the tunes for a long time and playing them, and putting them back into playable form. There are many that work very well on either harp, but since I took up the wire-strung harp, I would play a tune that I've played a number of times on the gut-strung harp. The experience was so different that I found myself thinking, "That's what it's supposed to sound like! That's the instrument it was created for!" The melody possesses the character of the instrument, just because of the way the phrase is built up and the way the notes ring against each other. I don't try to play the songs as they were played originally. That's quite a different attitude. In contrast, any clues that you can get from the past can help you express the music more accurately, and that is wonderful.

Some people think of traditional as being only tunes carried by the continuous oral tradition. That's not so. It's more the character of the music, which has been carried by the oral tradition. You know when you've actually found the heart of that particular piece of music, and sometimes it takes a long time. I find that I really like to play important tunes for a year before I feel comfortable with what I'm doing with it.

M.S. Have you recorded with both harps?

A.K. I'm just in the process of doing a new album now where I'm using both harps. This has been in the works for about three years. It's a bit, as we say in Scotland, "the Cobbler's bairns are the last shod" because we have our own studio in the house, but I'm the last to get using it. We've had the Battlefield Band in here recording for the past three weeks, so the project is on the shelf again until that project is complete.

M.S. If you've played those old melodies on a gut-strung harp and then you play them on a wire-strung harp, I imagine it must take a while to get a feel for that. Is that true?

A.K. That's true. I try not to transfer them. If I've been playing them on the gut-strung harp, that's the way I hear them. If I'm looking for a new tune, or there's one that I've had in the back of my mind for a while, I decide which harp I think would suit it best, then I'll try it on that harp first.

M.S. What about the songs that you discover later, that were played on the wire-strung harp?

A.K. The harp music that has survived is almost all wire-strung harp music. That instrument still was played within living memory when the collectors started writing things down. That's really the problem. No harpers ever wrote anything down themselves in Ireland or Scotland. Scotland actually has some of the earliest actual manuscripts of harp tunes, which date back to the beginning of the seventeenth century. Lute players wrote them down. Lute players took an interest in harp music during that period. They found that the melodies suited their instruments as well.

M.S. Transcriptions of the Irish harper Turlough O'Carolan are supposed to be the foundation of the music, but he was transcribed by a classical musician.

A.K. Yes, that's true, and I think that Carolan's playing was in that idiom, in many ways. You can hear it in some of his tunes. He knew the old tradition as well, especially the slow airs. That's where I hear the stronger tradition coming out. It got sidetracked a bit because Carolan was such a fashionable player and was taken up with delight by the whole society. A lot of people copied his style and forgot the earlier, older styles of harp playing, which would have given a lot of variety to the music. You still got that in O'Hempsey's playing. He actually lived to be one hundred and eighteen years old. He was in his nineties at the famous Belfast Harp Festival of 1792. He crossed that whole period, you see. He also married when he was in his eighties, and fathered a daughter. He was the last player who played in the old style. He was asked to play some of the old tunes, and he refused. He said nobody would understand them. He really did see himself as the end of an era. He was very significant. He also traveled in Scotland, so there was a lot of exchange.

M.S. Has any of his work been notated or written down?

A.K. Gráinne Yeats and Ann Heymann have been doing a lot of research into that. His harp survived, and it has been copied. Ann has a copy of it. Edward Bunting also wrote down a lot of O'Hempsey's tunes, but Bunting, being a classical musician, an organist, could never be relied on for taking it down exactly the way it was played. He really didn't understand the technique or the style of music. On the other hand, it's better than nothing. We should be grateful that people did hire Bunting to do the job.

M.S. If the tune is original and you're playing it on the instrument it was intended to be played on, then maybe you have a chance of getting very close to how it was played?

A.K. You can certainly do a good job in expressing the tune, but I'm not really aiming at playing it in an 'authentic' older style; there isn't enough evidence to do that. It would have changed over two hundred years. If it came down through the hands of direct oral tradition, it still would have changed. One shouldn't be too worried about that. You can't get too bound up. You have to feel, and want to express beautiful music. If I'm arranging a tune – and because I'm steeped in traditional music, whatever I do will be traditional sounding – it may not be the way people listen to it now. When I perform, some people say, this isn't what we expect traditional music to be, because they're not used to hearing tunes like these. These tunes are not simple tunes. They are part of a very sophisticated and developed ancient tradition.

M.S.   What context would they be performed in during ancient times?

A.K.   It was very formal music. The harp was a professional's instrument, an instrument of the aristocracy. It wasn't a folk instrument in the way that fiddle and pipes were, although they too had a formal role at times. Professionals would have played it in a high-class setting. It would have been in the households of the Chieftains in the Highlands, or the big houses of the nobles, kings, and rulers. It was formal music, and they were expected to accompany the Bards when they were doing formal poetry, and to accompany singers. They were expected to compose tunes for important occasions, like eulogies. A lot of the harpers would have been based in one household for long periods of time. They were happy doing that because even these days, carting a harp around is very difficult. I can't imagine what it was like when they were traveling around on horses. Women didn't play in a professional context because women did not have professions. Women didn't work. We've only found the name of one woman as a harper in Scotland, and that was in Aberdeen. It wasn't regarded as a woman's instrument, where now it is. It was a man's profession.

M.S.   Don't you think the masculine approach to it then would be more dynamic, instead of the Victorian parlor image that we've come to associate with the harp?

A.K.   A lot of the music you tend to hear played on harp is very 'tinkly', and that's one of the problems with it, the classical, Victorian, and feminine imagery. The tunes themselves are quite often strong, and you have to make them strong. Although it has a different character than something like the bagpipe, it's still a dignified and majestic instrument. You can't put strength into your playing. You have to touch the metal strings very lightly with your nails. It's very much a chamber instrument. The whole character of traditional music is different. It doesn't call for filling in harmonies to maintain interest; the interest is done by melodic variation. It's the melody that's the strong feature. When you start doing little arpeggios and glissandos, and twiddles underneath a tune, it becomes 'tinkly'. You have busy music going on, busy sound going on the whole time. I think the wire-strung harp particularly demands space. Each note is much more important because you have to decide when to play it, and you have to decide when it stops. It's much more in tune with the character of Gaelic music than what you often hear as harp music.

m.s.   You are a musician, on a very deep level, and you also have an incredibly magnificent craft in your glass engraving, which can be found in many museums, including the Victoria & Albert Museum. Those are two extremely strong streams of vocation.

A.K.   Well, a lot of people say to me that it's unusual to have two talents, and it's not. They quite often go together. You'll find that musicians are artistic or artists are musicians in their spare time. The only unusual thing, perhaps, is that I've run the two parallel, partly because I tend to do unusual facets of both. Luckily for me, both were in demand, so people kept asking me to do one or the other. They both developed into equally important careers for me.

ɒiscoGRApḫɥ

THE HARP KEY (1978)
(Temple Records)

With Ann Heymann

THE HARPER'S GALLERY   THE HARPER'S LAND
(Temple Records)   (Temple Records)

With Christine Primrose

THE QUIET TRADITION (1990)
(Temple Records)

mary jane Lamond

Biography

With her stunning release SUAS E! (su-ess-ay), Mary Jane Lamond has emerged at the vanguard of a Celtic cultural renaissance, successfully reclaiming and reinterpreting an age-old tradition. Singing exclusively in Scottish Gaelic, Lamond simultaneously fuses pop and funk, with hand-made percussion, Highland bagpipes, Irish bodhran, and cello. The result is a meeting of two distinct and dynamic musical cultures. The effect is nothing short of stirring. Mary Jane is a rising star in the Canadian music scene with three ECMA nominations, a Juno nomination (Roots and Traditional Album: Solo), a headline performance at Celtic Connections in Scotland, a featured performance on *From Canada With Love: An Olympic Salute*, a performance on CBC's *Celtic Electric*, and a six-week run as a featured performer in the Toronto musical production of *Needfire*.

The East Coast and Cape Breton region of Canada Mary Jane now calls home has yielded a wide and rich musical palate, with artists ranging from stalwart traditionalists Rita MacNeil and Anne Murray to new Celtic performers Ashley MacIsaac and Nathalie McMaster. It was there that she first remembers hearing Gaelic songs at a "milling frolic," where a heavy woolen cloth is repeatedly beaten against a table and people gather to sing and rhythmically keep time. The power of that experience and the music that emanated captured Lamond's imagination. "I was so taken by it, I became determined to learn and sing Gaelic myself," Lamond recalls.

Before Lamond graduated in Celtic Studies from Antigonish's Saint Francis Xavier University, she had released her first album, the beautiful BHO THIR NAN CRAOBH (From the Land of the Trees). It consists entirely of traditional material and also features a young, and at the time, little known, Ashley MacIsaac. Unbeknownst to both, this was to be the beginning of a highly creative professional collaboration. Lamond hit the road with MacIsaac and The Kitchen Devils as they toured with Melissa Etheridge, The Chieftains, and Crash Test Dummies.

Mary Jane's affection, understanding, and deep regard for the people and culture of Cape Breton are evident in every aspect of SUAS E! She has burst onto the world stage at a time when audiophiles hunger for 'new' music and pundits yearn for the values of days gone by. On SUAS E! Lamond integrates both a formidable spirit of innovation and a deep respect for the rich heritage of the Gaelic culture.

INTERVIEW

MAIRÉID SULLIVAN   Where do you go to restore your energy, to tune in to your artistic muse?

MARY JANE LAMOND   Definitely it's here in Cape Breton, and not just in my own house. The whole environment inspires me. Singing is my source of inspiration. I love the traditional songs from this part of the world. Some, I sing very traditionally, and some are done with more modern accompaniment. What I do is very much tied to this place because this is where I learned the songs. I really have to live here in order to do what I'm doing because otherwise I would be completely out of touch with the music that I sing, and I think that would be impossible to live with. I live in a rural area, so I can go down the road and hear a Gaelic storyteller, or go down the road and sing Gaelic songs with a very traditional singer.

M.S.   That's great! So you have a lot of the traditional performers in the area?

M.J.L.   Well, not as many as eight years ago, but they're still there.

M.S.   What happened in the last eight years?

M.J.L.   People got older very quickly. Since I started seriously investigating around eight years ago a lot of the people that I spent time with have passed away. However, we're getting more singers coming up, and there's a lot of interest among the young people. I was out yesterday, and a neighbor commented that it's too bad we don't have more of the older people to teach it to the school children. The woman is a teacher, and she said she was very limited as to what she could teach them because she only knows a few songs. The Department of Education is currently working on a curriculum for the Gaelic Culture.

Between the late 1700s and the mid-1830s, tens of thousands of Gaelic speaking people came here. Even though now we're in the fifth generation, there are still Gaelic speakers around. People say that at the turn of the century there were probably over 80,000 Gaelic speakers in the eastern parts of Nova Scotia.

My people come from North Uist; it's an island in the Outer Hebrides. The worst clearings happened in North Uist in the 1850s, and my family had already been over here around thirty years by then. More than just the physical clearances, there were the subsequent economic pressures that caused people to migrate. When we think of the clearances, we think of people being burned out of their homes. People were forced off their land and weren't able to make a living. They were forced to leave.

M.S. I wasn't aware that the population that migrated there were mostly Scottish.

M.J.L. A great number of Irish came to New Brunswick as well, and some settled in Nova Scotia and on Cape Breton Island.

M.S. Eight years ago you had a redirection or change in focus. What were you doing before that?

M.J.L. I did a lot of different things. I hadn't really decided what I was going to do with my life. I grew up in Ontario, and Nova Scotia, and Quebec, but my family is from here. I moved back to Nova Scotia around 1990 and discovered the Gaelic songs that were sung here. I learned a couple phonetically. I became so fascinated that I decided I had to explore the tradition more deeply and learn Gaelic. So I went back to school part time, and started learning Gaelic. Then I did the degree studies and got the degree. Really, I came to it very gradually. Over that time I just started learning more and more songs.

M.S. Do you ever go back to Scotland to study the tradition?

M.J.L. Well, I studied in Nova Scotia. It's the same tradition; it's very strong here. I've never studied in Scotland. I've been there to perform. I've also been to Scotland and the Hebrides several times.

M.S. When you look back at the Celtic history, you realize it's not centralized. Language and philosophy united all these nation states, but they still were separate, and they were moving cultures. In a sense that's in keeping with the tradition of the people.

M.J.L. I think any culture, which is based on an oral tradition, like the Celts', there is a great deal of emphasis placed on having things exactly like they were handed down from your grandmother or grandfather. That's what's considered to be the criterion for a good singer or storyteller. It's so different than Western society today. To be considered a good artist or artisan you have to be good at what people consider innovation. Being innovative is what is considered to be artistic today.

m.s. There's such a fine line between innovation and making a song your own.

m.j.l. Making a song your own isn't really a part of an oral tradition. You would consider it to be your own in that you learned it, but the idea is that you have things exactly the way they've always been which is why these cultures survive.

m.s. There is a debate amongst people about the preservation of the culture and the introduction of new instruments and new styles. We look back at the recordings and see the different trends. We see the contemporary folk groups of the seventies taking the old music and introducing foreign instruments and presenting that as the culture. What do you think about all that?

m.j.l. Well, the traditional culture was probably so evident twenty years ago that people thought that it would never go, that they would never lose that. Where I personally stand on it is that I grew up with Scottish-Gaelic speaking grandparents, but was never taught the language. I grew up in a world where I listened to all kinds of things. As a teenager I was listening to contemporary rock music, all different kinds of music.

m.s. What decade are you referring to?

m.j.l. I was born in 1960, so this was the mid-seventies. I was listening to the Sex Pistols, and Iggy Pop, and whatever I could find that was alternative, but somewhere in this upbringing there was a definite emphasis on roots. Even though we moved around, my parents always referred to Nova Scotia as their home. I grew up in a world where innovation was considered to be artistic, but I have a great deal of respect for tradition. If I record the songs, say with electric guitar, then the approach I take to all that is that if you took away all those instruments, and just listen to my vocals, the vocals should still sound like a traditional Gaelic song. I don't let the instrumentation dictate the voice of the song. The song dictates the arrangement. It's a very simple thing, but it works. I think you have to maintain respect for the tradition. I've heard other people arranging Gaelic songs, and I think, "Gee, who do you think you are?" I'm sure there are some people who object to what I do, but I'm comfortable about it.

m.s. It is those who are doing the explorations and experiments that have the trouble with the purists.

m.j.l. Tradition is such an important part of what the culture is. It's something we all have to think about. I just don't mean the dancing and playing and singing. I mean the whole culture. How are we going to reconcile these cultures to the 21st century? We have to figure out how we're going to do it. Things change so much more quickly now than they ever did in the past and it's increasingly difficult for people to understand, to keep it alive. You have to make it relevant to people.

M.S. Some of those songs have such fundamental attraction that I think people enjoy them just the way they are. When they are performed in the traditional way, as part of the general lifestyle in the home and in the community, they will be preserved because they are so deeply ingrained, by osmosis, from early childhood. It's when people approach the tradition for the first time as adults that the music is learned superficially because the music has not been ingrained from their formative years. I think there are enough people who are experiencing the tradition as children that they carry it with them into adulthood.

In this recent resurgence of interest in the roots of music, there are more singers being given voice than ever before because the music is moving beyond the dance music. There's something new being appreciated in what the singers have to present.

M.J.L. There is a new generation that is going to take more interest in the songs; they just haven't been exposed to it enough yet.

The poetry is so important in the Gaelic songs. The history of Gaelic society is told through poetry. The ballads are certainly not like English ballads where they start with; 'the year was such and such and we did this and that'. They are much more abstract than that. This is a huge part of who the people were. It's told through their songs, and so, to me, if people really want to appreciate the songs, they have to understand the language to a certain extent. I know there are people buying my albums who don't understand any Scottish Gaelic.

M.S. That's another interesting point. Some of the singers have told me that they would be in concert, for instance, in Japan, and people in the audience would be weeping, while they have no idea what the singer is singing about in the Gaelic songs.

M.J.L. Yes, absolutely. I was in Japan, and a couple of people who had my first record came up to me and told me how beautiful they thought the songs were. I am interested in all types of world music. I like listening to Pakistani singing, for example. I feel I can understand, to a certain extent, what that's about. It's about people relating to traditional music. Traditional music like that, or Portuguese Fado singing, expresses the most basic human emotions through the melody and the rhythm of the words. I think that's why world music is becoming so much more popular. People relate to music that is strongly rooted in community. It gives people something you don't get from a homogenous culture.

M.S. I think more people want to listen to music that recalls harmonious and gentle feelings. These songs carry with them an emotional memory that does not have nationalistic borders.

m.j.L. I think that's true for people who can get beyond the resistance to foreign experience, and not everyone can do that. A big part of people's non-acceptance of other cultures comes from not understanding their own.

There is a huge pride in being a Scottish Gael and at the same time there is a resistance to it as well. For example, five years ago the Education Department here wouldn't even look at having Gaelic in the schools. Now, because we have had a few festivals that have brought a thousand people into these very small communities, some with populations of a hundred or two hundred people, there is a greater interest in doing something about reclaiming the tradition. The new attitude is that we should get this back into our schools, so that we can sustain it, because it is one of our cultural resources and, potentially, an economic asset.

m.S. Self esteem is the fundamental thing in creating a strong community. Once its been wiped out by the destruction of the traditional culture, it seems to me, the way to restore it is by the reclamation of the traditional culture.

m.j.L. That is influenced by the re-evaluation of the old cultural traditions in other communities. If others, in the wider communities, value cultural tradition, then everyone gains something. That is what I see as the benefit, ultimately, of the resurgence of interest in Celtic culture worldwide.

Discography

BHO THIR NAN CRAOBH (1995)
(Independent)

SUAS E! (1997)
(turtlemusik/Universal)

TALITHA MACKENZIE

BIOGRAPHY

Talitha MacKenzie has been singing all of her life, whistling and singing by the age of five months and first performing at a family wedding a week before her third birthday. Trained as a concert pianist from the age of four, she was teaching piano at thirteen. Having first heard Gaelic song at the age of seven, she was in her teens when she became enthralled with the old-style traditional singing. With nothing but a *Teach Yourself Gaelic* textbook and a handful of field recordings, she began the arduous task of learning the language in order to perform the songs that she loved.

Throughout the 1970s, she was involved in a number of specialist dance ensembles (including Renaissance/Baroque, Balkan, and Celtic). This, along with her work as shantyman and deckhand on tall ships, gave her a unique insight into the organic rhythms of movement-related music. Beginning as a Russian major at Connecticut College, she graduated from the New England Conservatory of Music with a degree in Music History/Ethnomusicology.

By the mid-1980s she had recorded an album with Boston-Irish group St. James Gate and her first solo album, SHANTYMAN! After several years of touring America and performing mouth music with Scottish dance bands, Talitha moved to Scotland in 1987. There she began work with the folk ensemble Drumalban, while continuing in a transAtlantic a cappella duo with singing partner Anne Goodwin. In 1988, Talitha began to work with Martin Swan in an effort to get traditional Gaelic song into the mainstream. Two years later, as the duo Mouth Music, their contemporary World Music arrangements were released on an eponymous album which topped the charts and received international critical acclaim. When Swan left to work on other projects (still using the Mouth Music name), Talitha continued the original Mouth Music project under her own name, releasing a second solo album, SÒLAS (solace), in 1993.

Supporting Run Rig on their Amazing Things tour, Talitha and her band have also performed throughout Europe and North America. In 1995, a role in the Gaelic play *Reiteach* took her on tour to Scotland's main cities, Highlands, and Islands. Later that year, she signed a contract with Shanachie Entertainment, recording her third solo album, SPIORAD (spirit), in France, with producer Chris Birkett (whose credits include Sinéad O' Connor and Buffy Sainte-Marie).

interview

MAIRÉID SULLIVAN   How are your views on the world shaped by your musical career?

TALITHA MACKENZIE   For me, music is the language through which I understand the world. It is straightforward, without guile, just as I was when I went from music student to professional musician. I prefer to view the planet as a single positive entity, not divided into Old World, New World, and Third World.

M.S.   Do you have a personal philosophy?

T.M.   To be honest with myself and true to my songs, to be honorable and fulfill commitments, to promote nurturing, avoid ill-feeling, and to find the right balance between work and home life. When I first came to live in Scotland, my mission was to bring Gaelic music into the mainstream and to promote a more powerful vocal style for women, singing in a natural register, not up in the stratosphere, with more breath than pitch. Now I feel driven to change the infrastructure of the music business, so that all those with talent and determination can make a decent living, not just the small percentage of people at the top of the pyramid.

M.S.   How does your philosophy shape your music and your personal lifestyle?

T.M.   My motto is, "All that is worth doing, do well." Coming from a long line of workaholic perfectionists, I spend a lot of time going over and over things until they are just right. An agnostic pragmatist, I like to 'walk the mystical path with practical feet.'

When I lived in America, I attempted to cram as much as possible into each day, living in a constant state of frantic agitation; after ten years in Scotland, with my husband, Ian, I have grown to appreciate the benefits of living on Highland Time, doing very little, very slowly.

M.S. Tell us your favorite themes and passages in the songs that you sing.

T.M. Water is a recurring motif, but the theme of injustice is showing up more in my recent work. A lot of my songs deal with the search for emotional strength in situations of adversity, as in *Owen's Boat*:

> You've got your hand on the tiller,
> but no control of wind or weather
> Don't wait for a sign of what's to be,
> you can hold the lines of your Destiny
> And when you find you're on dry land,
> rebuild your ship and put to sea again
> There will come a time when you will see
> that what seemed such a crime, was meant to be.

I wrote this when my business partner walked out, just before a coast-to-coast American tour. He left Mouth Music, but kept using the name: first carrying on performing our arrangements without me, then using the name for other projects that had nothing to do with Mouth Music. Our album had been a success, but I never got the opportunity to promote it; instead, I had to watch another group travel the world with my material. I was so distraught, I had worked so hard for so long, only to have the rug pulled out from under me; I became ill and wasted away, until I received a greater shock to my system. With news that my ten-year-old son, Owen, was in intensive care, in Boston, I took the next flight out, not knowing if he would be alive when I arrived. Owen did pull through and recovered more quickly than expected. It was his optimism and strength that helped me out of my purgatory and inspired me to compose again.

M.S. What are some of your other interests?

T.M. I'm a 'clothoholic', a purist, when it comes to natural fibers, and love to knit, sew, embroider. I read a lot of self-improvement and religious books and share my father's interest in genealogy, especially since I found that we're descended from Kenneth MacAlpin, Eochaid I, and Alfred the Great. Taking my role as tradition-bearer very seriously, I enjoy baking my grandmother's holiday recipes, wishing on eyelashes, and not telling dreams before breakfast. I keep up my languages by helping my son, Ross, with his Gaelic-Medium homework and singing with the women's a cappella group, Sedenka.

M.S. Why do you think that you chose a musical career?

T.M.   It chose me. As a child, I imagined myself touring the world as a classical pianist, but gave up that idea when I began singing full-time at Mystic Seaport.

M.S.   Tell us how you came to your own musical style.

T.M.   In 1986, I had a 'Road to Damascus' experience. A dyed-in-the-wool purist, I used to perform Gaelic songs either a cappella or with clàrsach, (harp) and wearing a homespun drugget skirt.

Looking for a way to celebrate Oidhche Shamhna (Hallowe'en), I visited a local clàrsach-player who was also a medium. During trance-channeling, I was told that, in order for Celtic music to retain its power, it needed to be flexible, to flow with the times – not to be played just as it had been, two or three hundred years ago, because my audience was not of that time period.

Shortly after that, with guidance from Tríona ní Dhomhnaill, I bought my first electric piano and never looked back. I moved to Scotland, co-founded the duo Mouth Music, and I carried that contemporary sound with me when I returned to my solo career.

M.S.   What are your musical influences?

T.M.   My parents raised me on Broadway musicals and the multi-lingual songs of Harry Belafonte. My mother had a good repertoire of lullabies, and my father's booming baritone could be heard throughout the house. My brother taught me to play boogie-woogie piano; my sister helped me to pick out harmonies in pop songs. I had my classical favorites, especially the Slavic, Spanish, and French composers.

I quote from Ravel's *Le Tombeau de Couperin* in SPIORAD. My album collection is pretty diverse, from medieval to rap. When I started writing, my favorite artists were Joni Mitchell, Hedge & Donna, The Incredible String Band, and Stevie Wonder, but when it comes to singing in Gaelic, my biggest influence is Mary Morrison, from the Isle of Barra. Her vocal timbre is totally compelling and nothing can compare to the virtuosity of her piping imitation.

M.S.   Who are your mentors and how do they inspire you?

T.M.   My classical music mentor was my piano teacher, Avraham Sternklar, who used to say: "The notes may not all be there, but the spirit is there." He introduced me to Albeniz and Ravel and showed me how to teach myself, to create exercises out of the music and to practice slowly and methodically, so that my fingers wouldn't run away with themselves. He taught me to isolate difficult passages, analyze them, break them down, and eliminate the difficulty, all this with unlimited patience. I consider myself fortunate to be able to apply his pearls of wisdom to many areas of my life, not just to music.

My mentor in Scotland is the Gaelic scholar John MacInnes. One of those rare academics who is both collector and informant, his knowledge is immeasurable, yet he is always willing to share it. He has been of tremendous importance to me, in my work.

My children, however, are my greatest inspiration. My younger son is my biggest fan and my older one my most severe critic. My husband keeps me on track and gives me feedback and support when I most need it.

M.S. Did you get a special 'big break' as a professional musician?

T.M. My 'biggest break', as it happened, was also my greatest downfall. It was a peculiar situation, having a number one album in *Billboard's* World Music Chart, but no opportunity to perform for the fans who had bought it. It was difficult coming to terms with the fact that I would probably never receive any money from sales of MOUTH MUSIC, that the record company considered me to be irrelevant. I try not to be bitter, but it's not easy. Being blocked from touring America, with Mouth Music, was very hard on me. Recording SÒLAS was a great help, but it took two years before I had the strength to do that.

M.S. Do you like touring? What type of venues do you prefer?

T.M. I love to tour and will perform almost anywhere. I enjoy large stages, with room to dance, but they make it harder to keep eye contact with backing musicians. Intimate venues have their appeal: if you're close enough and the lighting permits, you can get feedback from facial expressions. All things considered, I prefer venues with good sound. I love to sing a cappella in a large hall with natural acoustics, or out of doors, overlooking a body of water. Toronto's Harbourfront is great for that. I also get a thrill singing from the tops'l yard of a beautiful square-rigged ship. My husband says, "If you want Talitha to sing, just drop a hat . . ."

M.S. How do you feel about live performance and how do you prepare for the stage?

T.M. I love the stage, it gives me the opportunity to channel my songs in the way that I feel they want to be heard. *Fear a' Bhàta*, for instance, is usually bound in a homogenous waltz, but if you've ever lived the words, you know that they need to be free of those restrictions. I love to let them go and watch them fly.

I try to warm up, in a quiet smoke-free dressing room, with plenty of drinking water. I do deep breathing, sometimes with a crystal, and say a prayer called "The Remover of Difficulties," then do some vocal exercises. I check my props, instruments, handkerchief, watch, copy of the set list, Fisherman's Friends, bottle of water, and, just before going on, I try to acknowledge the people with me, including technicians. If I have the chance to go through my rituals, I am much more likely to achieve 'caoineadh' onstage. Caoineadh is like mojo; it involves the merging of musician with music, the melting away of personal identity and the expansion of spirit consciousness. It was Belle Stewart who first spoke to me about this. She said to me, "You have the caoineadh, promise me that you will never, never let it go." More commonly used to mean 'keening', which is weeping, wailing, lamenting, the word is associated with a trance-like state. Only when I have the full transcendental experience do I feel that my performance is complete. No amount of applause can fill the void if this does not occur.

M.S.   How do you feel about singing in the recording studio?

T.M.   I love working in the studio, as long as I have the opportunity to keep the quality control to a high standard.

M.S.   Do your travels influence your music?

T.M.   I wrote *Tortola* in the Caribbean, *Owen's Boat* in Boston, and *The Intelligent Dilettante* in New York City. A lot of the material on SPIORAD came together while I was recording in France. Now I'm working on a track called *Songlines*. I'd love to go to Australia for inspiration. Hearing other languages and getting other people's take on the world is invaluable.

M.S.   What are your future hopes and plans?

T.M.   After I get to grips with my new software upgrade, I plan to finish the demos for my Worldbeat album GLOBAL SEQUENCE, then record it and go on a promotional tour. I'm hoping to get to the West Coast of America this time, and would love to tour Australia and the Far East; return to the Caribbean and cover more of Europe, East and West. I also have material for a more personal album, JUPITER RETURN, and dozens of projects on the back burner: a Celtic lullaby album, a World Music Christmas/Winter Solstice album, a multi-media Gaelic childlore project, a screenplay and soundtrack for a feature film, a Celtic music/dance extravaganza, a CD-ROM Gaelic textbook, and a black grouse project, since both the bird and folkdance are endangered species. I have a lot of ideas, but funding is a problem.

M.S.   What do you think is the essence of Celtic music?

T.M.   Western music tends to be very angular, full of I-IV-V-I progressions that are box-like in structure. Celtic music, however, has more options, more modes, not just major and minor. Often not ending on the tonic, tunes have a more circular feel. There are a wider variety of musical stresses and fewer restrictions on phrase length, which gives more freedom to the composer/arranger and opens up the musical horizon for the listener.

M.S.   Do you think that there is a growing interest in ancient Celtic culture?

T.M.   Not in ancient Celtic culture, per se. Medieval and Renaissance Celtic culture, for example, the Arthurian legends have been popular for centuries, but there is much confusion regarding what is ancient and what is Celtic. Misconceptions about pre-Celtic standing stones have led to the popularity of Stonehenge and Callanish. On the other hand, many things considered ancient, in fact, are much more recent. 'Family tartans', for example, were a Victorian invention, but this does not sit well with many who enjoy clan stalls at Highland games. That bagpipes were never banned, that the finger position in Highland dancing is not in imitation of stags' antlers, but a vestige of snapping fingers, that the drugget skirt, not the kilt, is the traditional dress for Highland women, is information unwanted by many who purport to have an interest in Celtic culture. People seem to prefer the myths to the truth.

M.S. What do you think is the most relevant message from Celtic history?

T.M. Perhaps that if your cultural identity is in tact, you are more likely to survive any onslaught, be it martial, political, or economic. Ireland seems to have succeeded in prioritizing its cultural identity, taking practical measures, like lowering airfares for touring musicians. In Scotland, however, the government have not done as much to ensure that musicians can earn enough to survive, or that music will remain in the school curriculum. Positive steps have been taken recently. For example, the Musicians' Union have acknowledged a new Folk, Roots & Traditional category, the Scottish Arts Council have supported a new Scottish traditional arts committee, and the current government, after much pressure, have pledged money to improve music tuition in schools.

There is, currently, a lack of distinction between what is traditional and what is conventional in Scottish music and dance. Consequently, a lot of the heart and soul, so vivid in field recordings of the 1950s, is lost in contemporary renditions. Women have been encouraged to sing as much as an octave higher than their counterparts of two generations ago. Rough edges and idiosyncrasies have been ironed out, unusual stresses have been made to follow predictable patterns. The once all-pervasive Highland folkdance, recorded by Flett & Flett in TRADITIONAL DANCING IN SCOTLAND, has all but disappeared, supplanted by stylized exhibition dancing, or nineteenth-century ballroom dances, which now make up most of the ceilidh dance repertoire. The spontaneous improvisation of everything from setting steps to piping ornamentation has been stifled by copious rules and regulations.

M.S. What is the funniest thing that has happened to you since you began performing professionally?

T.M. To end a festival, Johnny Cunningham hosted a massed round robin and I was asked to sing between his fiddle solo and two Irish pipers. I had left my son, Owen, then a toddler in nappies, in the front row, but he crawled up the backstage steps and fell asleep. Lifting him into my arms as the frenzied audience called for an encore, I returned to the stage, complete with sleeping bundle. I could feel the audience holding their breath, all eyes on Owen, just inches away from the Irish pipes, as I finished my second turn. However, as the drones sounded, there was a conspicuous lack of movement in my arms. He did not stir, but remained sound asleep! When I try to rouse him for school, I often think of that night – he's still impossible to wake!

Discography

SPIORAD (SPIRIT) (1996)
(Shanachie)
SÒLAS (SOLACE) (1993)
(Riverboat)
MOUTH MUSIC (1990)
(Triple Earth)
SHANTYMAN! (1986)
(Islander)
ST JAMES GATE (1985)
(Kells)

SEA SONGS: HEARTY RENDITIONS OF
    TRADITIONAL SONGS & CHANTEYS
    SUNG AT THE NEWPORT CHANTEY
    FESTIVAL (1980)
AMERICAN ACADEMY OF ARTS
    & LETTERS AWARD RECORD (1979)
(Folkways)

Compilations

BARRACHASH THE MODERN MYTH
    OF CELTIC VOICES (1998)
CELTIC ANGELS (1997)
ONE VOICE: VOCAL MUSIC FROM
    AROUND THE WORLD (1997)
(World Music Network)
HOLDING UP HALF THE SKY,
    VOICES OF CELTIC WOMEN (1997)
(Shanachie)
A CELTIC TAPESTRY, VOL. 2 (1997)
CELTIC MOUTH MUSIC (1997)
(Ellipsis Arts)
HER SONG: EXOTIC WOMEN
    FROM AROUND THE WORLD (1996)
(Shanachie)
CELTIC TWILIGHT 3, LULLABIES (1996)
(Hearts of Space)
THE ROUGH GUIDE TO
    SCOTTISH MUSIC (1996)
(World Music Network)
TROUBADOURS OF
    BRITISH FOLK, VOL. 3 (1996)
(Rhino)

GLOBAL PARTNERSHIP II, VOL. 2 (1995)
(World Music Network)
CELTIC TWILIGHT 2 (1995)
(Hearts of Space)
CELTIC LEGACY:
    A GLOBAL CELTIC JOURNEY (1995)
TRIPLE J EARTHCORE (1994)
(Worldbeat Dance Music ABC/EMI)
THE ROUGH GUIDE TO WORLD MUSIC,
    CATALOGUE 1 (1994)
(World Music Network)
WORLDS COLLIDE, REMARKABLE MUSIC
    THAT YOU CAN'T CATEGORIZE
    SAMPLER (1991)
(Rykodisc)
THE CAVA SESSIONS,
    BEST NEW MUSIC IN SCOTLAND (1989)
(Tennents Live!)
REAL MUSIC ON A REEL (1989)

KAREN MATHESON
(CAPERCAILLIE)

BIOGRAPHY

Scottish actor and political activist Sean Connery has exclaimed, "Karen Matheson has a throat that is surely touched by God." She has been called "the finest Gaelic singer alive today." This reputation has been earned in a career which began with her performing in local ceilidhs when she was a child and progressed to her winning the silver pendant for best singer at the MOD – a gathering of Gaelic culture from all over the world.

One of the founders of the band Capercaillie as a student at Oban High School on the West Coast of Scotland, Karen learned from her grandmother, a singer from the island of Barra in the Outer Hebrides, many of the traditional songs that have been the backbone of Capercaillie's material over the years. Capercaillie released their first album in 1984 while still at school, and over the following eight albums have established themselves as "the most exciting and vibrant band in the field of Celtic music today," according to *Billboard* magazine. They have sold many hundreds of thousands of albums across the world, and played in over twenty-five countries, including ground-breaking tours of South America, The Middle East, and Eastern Europe, receiving enthusiastic response in every country. Karen Matheson released her long anticipated first solo album in the U.S. in October 1996, featuring an amazing line-up of musicians and Karen's stunning vocal talent.

interview

máiréíð sullivan   When was the band Capercaille formed?

karen matheson   We began the band fourteen years ago. We were actually in high school when we first got going. We were influenced at that stage by the huge Irish resurgence that was going on. Planxty and The Bothy Band were far more influential than anything that was going on in Scotland. There wasn't anything exciting coming out of Scotland at the time. There were exceptions, like Silly Wizard and the Tannahill Weavers, but not in the area we wanted to get involved in, which was more contemporary, not using so much of the traditional aspect. Fusing it more, cross-pollinating it, which is what we were always more interested in.

m.s.   I think it's amazing that you were into that in your teenage years.

k.m.   Absolutely. The first track that we ever recorded was with a synthesizer, a Prophet V. That really hadn't been explored much at all. It had only been done in Ireland. I suppose it was very Clannadesque, using lots of voices and very ethereal sounds.

m.s.   That part doesn't surprise me so much, it's that you were into that and also into the tradition.

k.m.   It was a case of taking what you know and what you feel you're good at, and fusing it with all the good contemporary sounds. There was an element of growing up in a small community and finding your contemporaries going out and listening to the pop scene at the time. It was considered slightly strange to be playing Celtic music. It's not like everybody played Celtic music. It was a small pocket of musicians who supported it. A lot of our contemporaries were saying, "What the hell are you doing playing this rubbish?" So we had to break through that as well. It was obviously definitely not cool when we started doing it.

m.s.   I've seen videos of your work and you did it in such a cool way.

k.m.   Yeah, we like to think so. It's become so much more cool now. There's a different approach all together now in it. It's become much more accessible and hip.

m.s.   How long did it take before you were able to get a really good staging of your music with dramatic lighting and sound?

k.m.   Just a few years. In the early years we actually came to the States quite a lot and did it very cheaply. It was trudging around for bread and butter. It was quite a while before we were able to get a good stage show with lights. We still go out and tour without all that stuff. It's like stripping back, and that's equally exciting, just being there on the stage without all the tricks. That's the beauty of traditional music. You can do that.

The kind of music we play has heart and soul. It can stand up on its own without all the theater.

M.S. Was it exciting when you got all the lights and everything?

K.M. Absolutely! We thought we were the Beatles or something. It's a very exciting thing to have a big crowd and the lights and effects. Again the kind of thing, when you're young that you imagine you can never do with traditional music. In the early days we were playing at the local ceilidh where the audience was much older because they were the ones who were the most interested in the traditional music. Younger people weren't that interested. So to actually arrive at the time when we were able to look out at the audience and see people that were our own age was really exciting. It's fabulous.

M.S. What an affirmation! Do you tour much now?

K.M. We do. We've been very busy touring for the past two years. It's been a whirlwind! We've toured Australia, America, Europe, and an awful lot in Spain. Celtic music has had a real resurgence in Spain. The audience is very young there, and it's a real kind of hip, cool festival type scene. Because of the weather, they have open-air concerts, and it's great.

M.S. Do you think the people there are referring to their old Celt-Iberian roots?

K.M. I think they are. When we tour there, we do quite a lot in the north of the country, the more Celtic areas, but it's now progressed right down. We recorded our last album in the south of Spain. We took our gear over and recorded in a villa down there. We could see that the interest in the music has crossed all boundaries now. We don't just have to go to these wee Celtic pockets for people to come out to hear you. They have festivals all over the country now.

M.S. That's wonderful.

K.M. It is. It's a huge inspiration to us, having done this for fourteen, fifteen years. When we started there just wasn't the platform for it that there is now.

M.S. Do you sometimes have an insight into where this trend is going to go in the future?

K.M. I think it's going through a fashionable phase, and I'm quite sure that like every other form of music it will dwindle in time. But I think the very nature of the music, the fact that it comes from people having a good time basically, having sessions, being so much a part of the culture that it is a way of life, will mean that it will always be there. It's not like a pop song that's popular for a short time and then it disappears out of sight. I think the fashion will go full circle. It comes in and out and in again. That's a healthy thing, I think. There have been very dangerous things that have happened in the last few years because it has become so popular. You know, the record companies are tagging on and releasing all these dreadful compilation albums. There are some good ones, but there's a lot of diluting of the standards, which is disheartening. But that is the bad side of what happens when something becomes fashionable. However, fortunately, the good side of the whole phenomenon is far stronger, making it more accessible. Everybody is now aware of what Celtic music is.

M.S.   It is a good thing for us to see the exploitation because we know it is there, and it's everywhere in life anyway. I think its good for us to see it for what it is. Then we can get on with expressing our true values and ignoring the consumer mentality. You know, you go to the supermarket and see all that junk food and you realize it's there because people buy it because it's been well packaged and marketed, but if you know what's in it, you can make informed choices.

K.M.   Absolutely! I totally agree.

M.S.   It's great that we can see in our culture the model for the higher standards. It's an educational process. We don't want to be slaves to commercialism. There are enough excellent musicians presenting their work with integrity that, I believe, will save the day. It's good for people to be learning to say, "I know the difference." We've got to see the positive side too; or else we'll get depressed. You know I've heard someone say, a couple of years ago, "Celtic, give me a break." They are feeling pinned to the wall, with no break from all the hype!

K.M.   That's inevitable really, isn't it?

M.S.   So, with that, I'd like to talk about your own personal interests. Where have your interests been developing personally?

K.M.   It's made a huge impact on me as a person. Because I come from a small community on the West Coast of Scotland, I grew up in a place where people often don't move away from home. They stay there, they marry and have children there, they put back into the community. I would probably have done that had it not been for the fact that I started to sing at a very early age and got the opportunity to travel. I think that has allowed me to develop as a person, and I am hugely grateful for that. Just being able to travel and meet people and open up my whole outlook on life had been an extremely valuable thing. So I would credit purely the music. It had been such a growth-promoting thing; I feel I have been educated via travel more than I have in any other area of life.

M.S.   Well, it's a new phenomenon that the Scottish people and the Welsh and the Irish have been able to stay at home. They haven't been forced out or transported against their will recently.

K.M.   That's true. My mother grew up through the whole era of being ridiculed for being a Gaelic speaker. She wasn't allowed to speak Gaelic when she came from the island to the mainland.

M.S. Which island do you come from?

K.M. Barra.

M.S. You're from Barra, too? Do you know Flora MacNeil?

K.M. Yes. She is wonderful. She has been a huge influence to me. She is one of the real pioneers of Gaelic music. In my mother's and also Flora's generation, it was very much frowned upon. It was considered very slovenly if you spoke Gaelic when you came to the mainland. In most work environments, especially in places like hotels, they were forbidden to speak Gaelic at all. You know that creates a whole psychological block, where you are ashamed of your own culture.

M.S. Now, we are living in a transition time.

K.M. Yes! Now everyone wants to speak Gaelic, everyone wants to sing and play the music. That is just so brilliant! People like my mother, in her lifetime, have seen the full circle. She sees what we've done with the music and she is so delighted.

M.S. Do you still go up to the islands to play music?

K.M. Yes, but not as the whole band all the time. We go up home and we play at ceilidhs and for the odd charity event.

M.S. Where are the other members of the band from?

K.M. They are quite scattered really. Manus Lunny is from Ireland, he's Donal's brother. He lives in Donegal. He is the bouzouki player. Our bass player, Ewen Vernal, lives down in Troon, on the water, here in Scotland. Charley lives up in the East Coast, near Elgin, which has another, different style of fiddle playing, very different from the West Coast style. He injects a different style altogether with his playing. Our drummer and percussion players, Chimp and Wilf Taylor, both live in Glasgow. And Donald and I live in Glasgow. Our base is here in Glasgow. Our studio is here. We are quite scattered and we just get together before a tour and we rehearse and go on tour together.

M.S. In the fourteen years that the band has been playing, you have been there to see Glasgow go through its renaissance. It turned itself around and became one of the top cultural centers of Europe by promoting the arts.

K.M. Absolutely.

M.S. I've seen the poster!

K.M. Did you? (Laughs) We were influenced a lot, when we first moved to Glasgow, by the scene here. The bands that were coming out of Glasgow at the time were getting a lot of recognition. It was very inspiring to see that people were sitting up and listening to the music of all those bands. Although it wasn't Celtic music, it was music from Scotland. Scottish musicians who were into rock music. That gave us a huge boost, to see it being so accepted.

M.S. I want to get back to the development of your own personal outlook, having had a chance to broaden your horizons and learn about the world from first hand experience. I am wondering if you can remember the way you were in the beginning and whether you have noticed a difference in the way that you, as they say these days, find your muse? Whether you feel more expansive in yourself because of it, whether you feel like you can take a deeper breath and express yourself more fully and freely?

K.M. Definitely! Definitely! Without a doubt. It is a very spiritual thing. It's very hard to put into words, to explain. Traveling just broadens your horizons so much. Meeting people of varying cultures. We've been to the far corners of the world. We've toured in Iraq, we were in Egypt, the Sudan, and on every continent. We are exposed to so many different lifestyles and so many cultures. The experience can't be compared to anything else. We've met musicians in all the different countries we've toured.

M.S. Did you jam with many musicians from those exotic places?

K.M. We had people come up on stage with us in Brazil and in Baghdad. We played at the Hanging Gardens of Babylon, which is so fabulous. We invited local musicians to come up, and it is such a spiritually uplifting experience to meet people and share their music. Music is such a universal language; you don't have to be able to speak their language to play with them.

M.S. Do you write poetry or songs?

K.M. I write poetry for myself. I don't write professionally. There are too many good writers in the band, and I work with a couple of writers here in Glasgow. I am working at the moment with a man named James Grant. He played with the band Love and Money. When you get involved with people like that who have been doing it for a long time, you tend to shy away into the background. Usually when I'm angst ridden, or when I'm down about something, when I can't see the light . . . I write poetry. I write melodies. They come into my head and I set them to poems sometimes. I like setting them to Gaelic poetry.

M.S. How do you feel about the exploration of the voice, when you're taking a poem that is already set, and you can't change the words, so you've got to move your voice around?

K.M. I'm big on experimenting and trying out different styles. It's very important to stretch yourself. It's so easy to become blasé about what you do, and you think, 'I'm really quite good in this area so I'll just stick to that'. I think that's dangerous. You've got to keep moving all the time to keep fresh, and to keep yourself inspired. I think I'm a very down to earth person. I think Celtic music is very much a part of me, very much a part of my soul. It will always be with me. With all the other forms of music I experiment within, the force of the Celtic influence always comes through. It is a comforting instinct.

M.S. Any future plans?

K.M. I'm just about to start work on a new album, and in fact I'm recording right now. The boys are in the studio waiting for me. We're working with new ideas with James, the songwriter, and an incredible piper, Michael McGoldrick, who's been working with Capercaille for the past year. He's injected a huge amount of new energy into the band. He plays uilleann pipes and flute. I love the bittersweet sound you get with strings and pipes. I've been working with these great string players, the BT Ensemble. They are a well-known classical ensemble in Glasgow. To have that fusion is very sweet. The combination of the strings and the pipes is incredible.

DISCOGRAPHY

DELIRIUM (1996)

With Capercaillie

BEAUTIFUL WASTELAND (1998) GET OUT (1992)

TO THE MOON (1997) SIDEWAULK (1989)

SECRET PEOPLE (1993) CROSSWINDS (1986)

Website: http://www.capercaillie.co.uk/

Eileen McGann

Biography

Eileen McGann has been called "Canada's folk music voice to the world" and "one of Canada's most distinguished cultural exports." Born in Toronto, Eileen is one of four children, including her older sister, Mary Elizabeth Lauzon, a published poet. Her mother was born in Wales to parents from Cork, her father was born in Dublin. Besides being a singer-songwriter, Eileen is also a painter, in watercolor and acrylics. Her academic background includes four university degrees, in philosophy and history, education, theater and medieval studies. For a number of years she was also a semi-professional sword fighter and fight director. Rapier and dagger were her specialty.

Eileen McGann represents the best of the Celtic singing tradition, together with the best of Canadian contemporary songwriting. Add to this a dynamic performance style, an infectious sense of humor and a singing voice variously described as "magnificent," "stunning," and "hauntingly beautiful," and you have an artist not to be missed.

Eileen has produced four solo recordings, all of which have received five-star reviews. She has toured across Canada, the United States, Great Britain, and Ireland, and has become a favorite at festivals, clubs, and on radio shows on both sides of the ocean. Eileen is also one-third of the renowned vocal group Trilogy, along with Cathy Miller and David K, with whom she performs the acclaimed stage show *Two Thousand Years of Christmas* every winter. She has recorded four solo albums on the Dragonwing label.

interview

mairéio sullivan Where are the places that are most important to you?

eileen mcgann I live in Calgary, Alberta, at present, in the foothills of the Rocky Mountains. My house is in a valley, near the Bow River, and I am a block from a park that encompasses a couple of miles of riverbank, as well as a large pond and winding lagoon. I find that trees have always been very important to me, and the park is the place I like to walk, if I can't make it out to the mountains.

I also love the Canadian west coast, especially Vancouver Island, and plan to live there some day, surrounded by big trees. At home, my special room is where I paint, which has a window looking out on my tiny perennial garden. I have a 'sitting chair' in that room, for just thinking. Because I live on the road much of the year, I really value my brief times at home. While traveling, it is important to me to make sure I take some time each day to get centered, and try to make my heart's home be wherever I am. I find that I write my best songs when I am walking or paddling a canoe, filled by the sounds of the natural world.

m.s. What are some of your favorite themes from the songs you sing?

e.m. There are so many favorites, it's difficult to choose! One of the traditional songs that has always moved me is an Irish song called *The Parting*. I recorded it on my TURN IT AROUND CD, and it has continued to be a powerful song to sing live. It is a song of emigration – a lover bidding farewell to a loved one going overseas. The thing what is most striking – and perhaps most characteristically Irish – about it is the imagery that connects the heart to the things of the natural world, as if they were in one clear continuum. The second verse runs:

> When my love and I parted, we shed no tears
> Though I knew that between us lay weary years
> For a bird was singing upon a tree
> And a beam of sunlight lay on the sea.

The song ends:

> No fate can sever my love from me,
> For his heart is the river and mine, the sea.

Show me a pop song that comes even close to the power of that! Especially when it is combined with an incredibly haunting Irish melody. It is meant to be sung a cappella, and works best that way, the song needs nothing but itself.

My own songs range from very contemporary and political to some that sound and feel very like the traditional. Of course, singing political songs is very much a part of the Celtic tradition, as I learned from an early age. Other songs deal with the human condition, or tell stories based on ancient legends, or on the lives of people that I encounter in my travels. There's also the occasional humorous song, usually with a point to be made, such as *The Feminist Movement Is Dead* or *Too Stupid For Democracy*.

M.S. Why do you think you chose a musical career?

E.M. I think it chose me, actually. I have always loved to sing. My parents tell me that I used to sing myself to sleep from a very early age, and I remember 'making up' songs while sitting on the backyard swing at the age of about five. The thought of making a living in music seemed a pipe dream when I was a teenager, especially since I was so shy, and I only very gradually got drawn into performing in public. It still sometimes seems very wonderful that I get paid for doing the most joyful thing possible – singing songs. Now, it seems clear to me that making, writing and sharing music is part of my larger life-purpose. I feel that this kind of music draws people together in a way that is desperately needed in these splintered and violent times.

We need to sing together and think and dream and encounter beauty, not just for the intrinsic benefits of these things, but to help us fight back against the negativity of our general culture. It helps to keep us alive and connected with each other to hear each other's stories and see the world from someone else's point of view. This kind of music also encourages people to make music themselves, and not just listen to others making it. The ancient songs help connect us with our past, and help us think about our future as a race in a context of past centuries. Modern western culture is very 'now-oriented'. The past is ignored or denigrated, the future is projected no further than tomorrow or next year. Business decisions are made on the basis of this quarter's profits, and little thought is taken for long-term consequences, and the future generations are no longer a factor in our relationship with the planet. I am not saying that traditional and acoustic music will solve any of these problems. In a small way, I think it helps to keep us connected with our ancestors and our planet, and puts us in a context that joins us, as music-making, story-telling humans, with all our brothers and sisters now, in the past, and in the future.

M.S. Tell us how you came to your own musical style.

E.M. I began my professional career as a singer of Irish traditional music in my late teens. I had been writing songs for many years, but I rarely sang them for anyone. At my very first large festival, I was placed in a workshop for which one of my own songs was just right, so I sang it. I was amazed at the response from people who wanted to hear more of my writing, and within a year or two, I was being billed as a "singer-songwriter" instead of a traditional singer at many venues. My musical style is a mixture of the Celtic traditional influences and the very strong Canadian tradition of songwriting.

m.S. Can you trace your musical background influences for us?

e.m. My parents are Irish and played a lot of recorded Irish music in our house when I was growing up. I remember especially liking Irish rebel songs, since they were fun and lively and rhythmic – I had very little idea of the politics surrounding them, of course. When traveling through Ireland a couple of years back, we passed through many towns with songs about them, and I was amazed at how many of these songs I remembered, in their entirety, from my own childhood. I also listened to many of the singer-songwriters of the day, like Gordon Lightfoot, Joni Mitchell, Harry Chapin, and Jim Croce, and loved how they used words.

m.S. Who are or were your mentors and how have they inspired you?

e.m. Aside from Irish and Scottish traditional music, I was influenced by a number of singers who also wrote and sang contemporary songs out of that tradition, such as Archie Fisher, Stan Rogers, Ewan MacColl, and Dick Gaughan. The world of the Celtic and folk musician is a very friendly one – I can't count the number of musicians who have directly helped or encouraged or inspired me over the years. There is a powerful sense of common goals and a love, which leads to a kind of sharing and fellowship that, I think, is very rare in the larger music business. I believe this shows in the power of the music that is made in this community.

m.S. Do you like touring and what kinds of venues do you prefer?

e.m. I love to sing for people, and have them sing with me. I don't know if I have a preference of type of venue – each size and kind of performance space has its own particular ambiance and advantages. I love festivals, especially having the chance to meet and play with other musicians whom I may not otherwise see from year to year. The interaction at Canadian festivals in particular, where 'workshops' are set up to encourage such spontaneous jams, is a special delight and results in memorable once-in-a-lifetime performances for the audiences and performers. I also love intimate venues, like folk clubs and even house concerts, where the audience interaction is very informal and direct. Large halls have an amazing energy of their own.

m.S. How do you prepare for a performance?

e.m. I always try to do vocal warm-ups before going on stage – it makes a big difference in the resilience of my voice over the course of an evening. If there is a lot of chaos surrounding the set-up and sound check, then I will also try to find a quiet place to center myself and make sure that I begin the show with calm and positive energy.

m.s.   How do you feel about singing in the recording studio?

e.m.   The recording studio is a different kind of challenge in that you are singing in a bare room, to no one. I generally close my eyes and picture an audience there.

m.s.   How about your travels? Do they influence your music?

e.m.   I have been on the road most of the time for about the last twelve years, and I think the best part of that is the fact that I meet so many wonderful, warm people, who love the music and are seeking for beauty in their lives. I see a lot of beautiful places – and many places that are appalling. Differences in politics and culture and assumptions and living conditions from country to country tell a lot about who we are as humans. It certainly helps my understanding of the world, and this can't help but influence the music. My songwriting reflects some of the stories and people that I encounter, and my choice of traditional songs to add to my performing repertoire is also influenced by relevance of the songs to the feelings and situations that are part of my own experience.

m.s.   Could you tell a little about your future hopes and plans?

e.m.   I have my next four albums planned already – as always, mixtures of contemporary and traditional music – it's simply a matter of finding the time between tours to get the albums recorded and designed. I would also like to find more time for songwriting and for painting. In the last few years I have been asked to teach at a number of music camps around the country, and have enjoyed this tremendously – I'd like to do more of that too, and, of course, I will keep on touring and singing as much as possible.

m.s.   What do you think are the reasons for the overwhelming popularity of Celtic music now?

e.m.   With the advent of the 'music video', pop music has become even more about image and flash, and less about good music, well sung. I think many people are tiring of this and are searching for music that comes from the heart. Celtic music has such depth and authenticity, both in the instrumental and the singing tradition, that it is a natural choice in this context. It must also be said that the big record companies have jumped on the bandwagon and been pushing Celtic and 'Celtoid' music in a way that it has never been pushed before, bringing it into the public eye on a huge scale. The best side of this phenomenon is that it may lead people to explore beyond what the big labels are selling to find the authentic music at the grassroots level, to find and support their local folk or Celtic music venue, and maybe to pick up an instrument themselves.

DISCOGRAPHY

ELEMENTS
(Dragonwing Music)
TURN IT AROUND
(Dragonwing Music)

JOURNEYS
(Dragonwing Music)
HERITAGE
(Dragonwing Music)

With Trilogy

TWO THOUSAND YEARS OF CHRISTMAS
(Dragonwing Music)

Website: http://www.canuck.com/~jscown/mcgann

LOREENA MCKENNITT

BIOGRAPHY

Self-managed, self-produced, and the head of her own Quinlan Road label, singer and composer Loreena McKennitt has sold over nine million records in over forty territories around the world. THE BOOK OF SECRETS, her seventh album, is her most acclaimed and commercially successful release to date. McKennitt has twice been honored with a Juno, the Canadian music industry's annual award, and was given the Billboard International Achievement Award in 1997.

Born and raised in Morden, Manitoba, she moved to Stratford, Ontario, home of Canada's renowned Shakespeare Festival, in the 1980s. As an actor, composer, and musician, she was featured in a number of Festival productions, including *The Tempest* (1982) and *The Two Gentlemen of Verona* (1984). In 1985, with the release of ELEMENTAL on her own label, Quinlan Road, she began her career as a recording artist, selling the cassettes from her car while meeting the public on the street, as a busker and in cafés and bookshops.

McKennitt followed ELEMENTAL by cutting a seasonal perennial in the Christmas carols of TO DRIVE THE COLD WINTER AWAY (1987) and made her first steps towards cross-cultural fertilization in the subsequent PARALLEL DREAMS (1989). She's particularly proud of tracking down *Bonny Portmore*, included on THE VISIT (1992), an obscure ballad mourning the loss of ancient British stands of oak, once worshiped by pre-Christian tribes, which has a contemporary relevance to today's fight to save old-growth forests.

A pivotal moment for Loreena McKennitt's evolution occurred in 1991 in Venice, Italy, at the largest ever exhibition and collection of international Celtic artifacts. "Until I went to that exhibition. I thought that Celts were people who came from Ireland, Scotland, Wales, and Brittany," recalls McKennitt. Seeing the unimagined riches and variety in the centuries of Celtic art gathered from as far afield as Hungary, Ukraine, Spain, and Asia Minor, she recalls, "I felt exhilarated. It was like thinking that all there is to your family are your parents, brothers and sisters, and then you realize there's a whole stretch of history that is an extension of who you are." That epiphany transformed McKennitt's music.

Interview

MAIRÉID SULLIVAN   Where did you grow up, Loreena?

LOREENA MCKENNITT   I grew up on a farm in Morden, Manitoba, a small prairie community about 80 miles from Winnipeg. It was an interesting community to grow up in. It was comprised of a mixture of Mennonites, Anglo Saxons, a mix of Icelandic people, and Ukrainians. The lifestyle was quiet and simple. My father was a livestock dealer and my mother was a nurse. My mother is retired now, and my father has passed away. I think growing up in that rural environment, on the farm, inspired a deep-rooted reverence for the land and the countryside, and I sometimes yearn to keep that connection. I currently live in a wonderful old stone farmhouse built around 1830, which is about 10 miles away from Stratford, a little town in southern Ontario.

M.S.   Why do you think you chose a career in music?

L.M.   Well, I studied classical voice for five years and classical piano for about ten years. I wasn't all that enamored with the classical repertoire, but I found that it did ingrain in me a strong sense of dynamics, technique, and musical theory that has contributed to my current forms of musical expression.

M.S.   How about your travels? Do they influence your music?

L.M.   As I travel more, I find that I'm constantly redefining my sense of home. I'm referring to the term "home" not just as a physical house. Home, for me, is definitely a community of family and friends, kindred spirits. My house is a place that allows me to engage in the natural world in ways that I like and feel comfortable with in many ways. There is a wonderful old Chinese proverb that I love, "A good traveler has no fixed plans and is not intent on arriving." I think about my personal approach to musical projects much like a travel writer might approach the preparation for a book. You latch on to a certain theme or historical event and follow that into the unknown, while, at the same time, expanding on those themes.

M.S. Why do you think there is a growing interest in ancient Celtic culture?

L.M. For me, it's always been difficult to articulate exactly what it is within Irish/Scots/Welsh music, what we identify as Celtic music, that attracts people. It seems to operate in a very instinctive primal way, and for a lot of people, including myself, I think that there is something in the older structure of the music, the rhythmic patterns, which is very inviting.

I first became exposed to Celtic music at a folk club in Winnipeg in the late seventies. Several members of the club hailed from Ireland and England, and through them I learned a lot of the traditional repertoire. Also, the way the music was performed impressed me. The club was a very casual place, everybody took a turn playing songs, and people would sit in and play along. When I visited Ireland, I saw this very relaxed extension of people's self-expression. The music wasn't just relegated to a more formal concert atmosphere, which psychologically changes the whole experience.

Until the early nineties, I was under the impression that the Celts were this mad collection of anarchists from Ireland, Scotland, and Wales. When I saw an exhibition in Venice, I discovered they were a vast collection of tribes originating from Middle and Eastern Europe as far back as 500 BC, and that over the centuries they migrated and integrated with people all over the world. So I've used this cultural history as a creative muse. With THE BOOK OF SECRETS in particular, I was interested in beginning with their earlier and more Eastern history. I did a great deal of research in Italy, and in essence let the process of discovery evolve from that point.

M.S. Have you read any books on the history of the Celts? How do you research the motivations behind your music?

L.M. When I'm researching, the procedure takes many forms. I read a diversified collection of books – travel writing, fictional stories set in a period and locale of my interest – and I listen to a variety of music and study the instruments. I try to visit a place because I don't think there's any better way of absorbing and taking in all that essential information than breathing in the aroma of the streets and seeing the light in the sky. There is no book or radio documentary that can compare to that whole experience.

I discovered a wonderful book called *How The Irish Saved Civilization* written by Thomas Cahill. I knew there had been a lot of controversy about this book. But I think there is some aspect of its thesis that is sound historically. His thesis was that as the Roman Empire was disintegrating, numerous Irish monks were copying out ancient Greek and Latin classical and religious texts, and were re-introducing these texts to the continent. Were it not for their efforts, much of this material would have been lost to us forever. Another book I found to be of great value is William Dalrymple's *From the Holy Mountain*. He touched upon the connection between the Irish illuminated manuscripts and the sacred art coming from the East. This huge migration of people, who traveled across Europe and North Africa, had lost so many threads of those historical connections. He showed how the historical roots of these illuminated manuscripts, that we now so strongly associate with Ireland or Scotland, like The Book of Durrow and The Book of Kells, actually demonstrate a shared Indo-European origin.

M.S. I suppose you are often asked about your attraction for setting the classic writer's lyrics or poetry to music.

L.M. Yes, that's true. For example, in THE VISIT and THE MASK AND MIRROR, I incorporated some of Shakespeare's writings. I also added some phrases by W.B. Yeats and St John of the Cross. I suppose the reason I've done this is not only to give a different perspective to a recording, but also a certain kind of significance.

M.S. With the great variety of music that has inspired your creations, how would you define your musical 'stamp'?

L.M. Frequently, I call it eclectic Celtic, but in many respects it is more an expression of a hybrid form of world music. A lot of people associate world music with primarily African music, and, obviously, it's not African music. There were twenty-eight musicians involved in THE BOOK OF SECRETS. In some instances, there was a tin whistle playing along with a viola da gamba, or the St Petersburg Choir singing an orthodox Eastern hymn. The musicians and myself come from such a broad spectrum of musical styles there are bound to be these influences woven into the framework of my music. For example, I come from a classical and folk background. Brian Hughes, my guitarist, comes from a rock and jazz background, Rick Lazar, our percussionist, and Donald Quan come from a Latin and world music background, Hugh Marsh, my violinist, comes from a very experimental and imaginative musical background. At the essence of my music, there is a Celtic or an Irish resonance. But it is embroidered with Eastern and Middle Eastern influences. Since world music has impacted mainstream music so strongly, it is not unusual to find my albums nestled in the pop music section of record stores.

M.S. Tell us about your own philosophy and how that shapes your music and your lifestyle?

L.M. Creative people tend to have a great thirst for stimulation, and there are many ways to satisfy that need. A great deal of my inspiration comes from traveling, and it's fueled from my inquisitiveness. I consider myself extremely fortunate to be doing what I'm doing. I'm able to unite my passions and talents and interests, and make a living at the same time. I think there is a lot to be learned from the past and in finding out how, in these highly technological times, the history of our ancestors remains relevant.

One of the most wonderful and engaging things I've learned is that we are the culmination and extension of each other's histories and there is more that binds us together than separates us, and in discovering this, perhaps our needs are timeless and universal.

I have a very deep interest in religion and spirituality. I like the Sufi perspective, which suggests that it is better to participate in the world than to become detached from the world. Certainly, I think that isolated situations are good for different stages of one's own development. But the challenges that we encounter in life can offer opportunities that help us to grow. I find it difficult to comprehend what the mind was about five or six centuries ago, or any mind that is in the deepest of isolated circumstances. A lot of the ancient monks were usually physically alone with their books and prayers; they had very little companionship. They did write their own prose, which can offer us a deeper insight into their experience and intentions. In observing this segment of religious history, and the many questions that flow through the spiritually dedicated mind, one ponders what is the correlation between isolation and religious or spiritual experience. In a broader sense, we see our continuing lack of knowledge of the mechanics of the human soul.

(Answers to these questions were presented in written form by Loreena's staff at Quinlan Road.)

DISCOGRAPHY

LIVE IN PARIS AND TORONTO
Double album (1999)
(Quinlan Road/Warner Bros.)

THE BOOK OF SECRETS (1997)
(Quinlan Road/Warner Bros. Records)

A WINTER GARDEN:
FIVE SONGS FOR THE SEASON (1995)
(Quinlan Road/Warner Bros. Records)

THE MASK AND MIRROR (1994)
(Quinlan Road/Warner Bros.)

THE VISIT (1992)
(Quinlan Road/Warner Bros. Records)

PARALLEL DREAMS (1989)
(Quinlan Road)

TO DRIVE THE
COLD WINTER AWAY (1987)
(Quinlan Road)

ELEMENTAL (1985)
(Quinlan Road)

Compilations

The Chieftans' "Tears Of Stone" (1999)

Videos

NO JOURNEY'S END (1996)

SUSAN MCKEOWN

BIOGRAPHY

Susan McKeown was born in Rathfarnham, Dublin, Ireland, in 1967, the fifth of five children. Encouraged by her composer mother, she pursued music and theater interests from an early age. Religious and classical music was what she listened to as a child, but as a teenager she discovered singers like Mary Margaret O'Hara, Michelle Shocked, and June Tabor. At fifteen, she began intensive study with Ireland's leading opera trainer but left after a year. Busking on Dublin's streets followed, where Susan explored rock, folk, jazz, and blues.

Susan arrived in New York in 1990 to take up the scholarship she was awarded to attend the American Musical and Dramatic Academy. Quickly immersing herself in the East Village music scene, Susan was one of the original performers at the Sin-e Cafe, and is featured in a soon-to-be-released documentary on the legendary club. While she has headlined at The Bottom Line and The Bowery Ballroom, Susan's home gig is at Manhattan's Fez, where she has given a record of thirty plus consecutively sold-out performances. She has released four solo albums and appears on such compilations as WOMEN OF THE WORLD: CELTIC MUSIC II from Putamayo World Music.

Labeling Susan's music has proven quite a challenge. Her songs and music are original; the sound is acoustic-rock, blending progressive, jazz, and Celtic influences. Formerly mis-tagged as solely a Celtic artist, audiences now recognize Susan as a performer with the unique ability to cross genres and defy categorization.

INTERVIEW

MAIRÉID SULLIVAN   How do you describe your music?

SUSAN MCKEOWN   I reluctantly describe it as acoustic-rock with Celtic and jazz influences.

M.S.   Tell us about your philosophy and how that shapes your music and your personal lifestyle?

S.M.   I like to live simply. I learned from my father the value of being content with what you already have, and I often find that I am blessed with more than enough.

M.S.   Where do you like to live?

S.M.   I like to live either in the thick of things or in a remote place, nothing in between. Currently I live in Manhattan, but I have plans to live in a very rural area. I have been spending most of my time on the road recently, and while I enjoy that immensely, I have found it a bit distracting and not always conducive to creativity. I like to bring a candle on the road for the hotel rooms. I've been doing a little yoga recently, which brings great calm and a great space in my head, and that's a great thing to bring to a hotel room, or rather, to take you away from it.

M.S.   Can you tell us some of your favorite themes from the traditional songs and original songs you perform?

S.M.   The traditional song *Tam Lin*, made famous by the singing of Sandy Denny, has always held a fascination for me, and has influenced one of my own songs, entitled *Snakes*. In *Tam Lin*, when our heroine, Janet, discovers that Tam Lin is a captive of the Faerie Queen, he describes to her how she might save him and warns her:

> They will turn me in your arms to a newt or a snake
> Hold me tight and fear not and you will love your child
> They will turn me in your arms into a lion bold
> Hold me tight and fear not, I am your baby's father
> They will turn me in your arms into a naked knight
> Cloak me in your mantle and keep me out of sight.

In one quick verse, Janet accomplishes all Tam Lin has instructed and saves the day – and the man. I love dark, magical songs, songs where people are changed, and I have a special interest in songs concerning women. So this song does it for me on many levels.

In my own song *Snakes*, which appears on my first album BONES there are the lines:

> There's crosses and stars in the night overhead
> You can turn in my arms into a bird and fly there.

I am a great believer in people's capacity for change and good. The song is about how I felt concerning the Catholic Church in Ireland and its oppression of women, from its suppression of the ancient keening women, down to this century, where it had the power over the government to deprive women in Ireland of their reproductive rights. I've cast the Church as the snakes which I recall seeing under the foot of the Virgin Mary in Christian art since I was a child. It bothered me that it was all Eve's fault. It bothers me when people think feminism is damaging. At the end of *Snakes* I had the idea to segue into O'Riada and O'Doirnín's *Mná na hEireann* (Women of Ireland). That's how I usually end my gigs.

Another of my favorite traditional songs is *In London So Fair*, a song which I learned from the singing of Mary Ann Carolan and recorded for an album of traditional songs called BUSHES & BRIARS in 1998. It's one of those broken token songs, except the token is a phrase that the loyal woman repeats to her lover and in doing so reunites them. Her lover had gone off to sea and she gets her playful revenge by dressing up as a sailor. Seems like they're at sea for awhile when one day, while she's in his cabin, he's overwhelmed with emotion and tells her that he(she) reminds him of his girlfriend whom he left on the shore. All is revealed and they live happily ever after.

I've recorded an album, MOTHER, with Cathie Ryan and Robin Spielberg, which was a most rewarding experience for all of us. The song *Ancient Mother* is a traditional Native American poem for which I wrote music and translated the lyrics into Gaelic. It's very simple:

> Ancient mother I hear you calling
> Ancient mother I hear your song
> Ancient mother I hear your laughter
> Ancient mother I taste your tears.

Bones, from my first album of the same name, is an archaeological kind of song about the things left behind by a woman after her life. The emotions and lifeblood which made her so alive can't be used as evidence of her life, only the objects which are recovered and used to describe her life.

Dirt in my nails and I'm scavenging pieces
I'm searching for evidence,
Some part of life I can claim
Some people seduce you with stories and old myths to live by
Wrench through my hair with such anger
I break off a gold tooth of my haircomb ornament
Shining finding, wet with my tears
So don't throw the dirt away.

M.S. What are some of your other interests, besides music?

S.M. Genealogy, literature, especially poetry, good films, politics/current events. Genealogical research has taught me a lot about who I am, because of the stories I learned about my family and ancestors long gone. I encourage everyone to take it up now, rather than later in life, when it might be too late to find some of the answers.

M.S. Why do you think you chose a musical career?

S.M. Sometimes I feel this career chose me, and yet everything I have done in my life seems to have been leading me to this. My mother was a musician, and she is the person who has been the greatest influence in my life. She rose to some prominence in her chosen field of religious music: she was asked to select the music to be played when the Pope came to Ireland, she was awarded a medal by the Pope in recognition of her service to the Church, and she was also the Hammond Organ Company's demonstrator in Ireland. She made her own work, booking her own gigs, arranging rehearsals with other musicians and singers, and so I learned from her, and feel her influence, as I do the same thing in my own career. It has meant that I have always felt comfortable pursuing a musical career and working for myself.

I've been singing as long as I can remember, encouraged by my mother. And it feels like people have always been asking me to sing. It was after studying with one teacher in New York that I really found my voice and accepted it as my own instrument, reflective of who I am. This teacher took a very holistic approach, which I embraced. I made changes in my life which resulted in changes in my voice, and allowed it room to grow and develop in tone and expression the more I came to know myself. I believe it's a gift that I'm lucky to have been given so I try to respect that.

M.S. Can you trace your musical background influences for us? Who or what inspired you?

S.M. I think my style combines the old and the new; that is, I've always been conscious of a desire to adapt traditional music in a progressive way. As I grew up in Ireland, I have traditional influences, but my music is essentially original. I wasn't brought up on traditional music, but it is a part of me. What also interests me is the female, the spiritual. My own journey leads me to explore the chaos along with the order, the sorrow along with the joy, and how these can co-exist.

I'm interested in women's emotional states and how women are represented in folklore – things of that nature. In my teens I was listening to June Tabor, Clannad, and Geraldine McGowan, and then I remember hearing Michelle Shocked and Mary Margaret O'Hara on the radio and running to switch up the volume each time. The first single I bought was Kate Bush's *The Man With The Child In His Eyes*. Currently I have wide ranging musical taste, such as Mercedes Sosa, Massive Attack, Lúnasa, Sheryl Crow, Ani DiFranco, Carthy Waterson, Kíla, Natalie Merchant, Richard Thompson, Astor Piazzolla, Morcheeba, Portishead, Lauryn Hill …

M.S. Who were your mentors?

S.M. My mother was a mentor and an inspiration. She encouraged me to be creative and independent and was a feminist herself. She was fearless and strong and accepting when facing her own death in 1982. I remember her expressing gratitude, then, for the fulfilling life she had led, and the happiness she had known. That will be with me always. Since 1991, I have used her maiden name McKeown as my last name.

I have also been inspired by people who exhibit fearlessness, who challenge authority when they see wrong even when it is dangerous to do so, people such as Bernadette Devlin-McAliskey and Nelson Mandela.

M.S. Did you get a 'big break' as a professional musician?

S.M. I had been a long-time fan of Natalie Merchant's when she called me last year to invite me to sing with her on the PBS TV show *Sessions at West 54th*. Then she took me on tour with her for a couple of weeks, which was fun and exciting and a thoroughly great musical experience. That was a big break for me, for which I am most grateful.

M.S. Do you like touring and what kinds of venues do you prefer?

S.M. I still enjoy traveling, and my favorite venues are those where you can have intimate concerts. While on tour in Germany and Switzerland recently, I performed in some very old concert halls with capacity for over a thousand people, but the acoustics were so great that I performed a cappella songs completely away from the microphone.

M.S. What do you feel about live performance? Does it take a few songs to warm up and get to know the audience? How do you prepare for the stage?

S.M. To me it is all 'about' the live performance, the singing of it on the stage. If I need to warm up, I like to do it before I get there. When I first started out, I was shy when I wasn't singing and never knew what to say. Thankfully, I've gotten over that!

M.S. How do you feel about singing in the studio?

S.M.   It's such a different process: I definitely take a different approach. When I'm working with traditional material I often look for a simple approach which can be easily reproduced live. On the other hand, for my own compositions, I like to take advantage of new technologies and do things that I just couldn't do live. On *Bones*, the title track, the engineer Oliver Straus put my vocals through an amplifier he had in his studio from the 1940s, and the result is an eerie, distorted vocal, which was just what I was looking for.

M.S.   What do you think are the reasons for the overwhelming popularity of Celtic music now?

S.M.   We all get asked that question a lot, don't we? Enya and *Riverdance* have done their share, but it hasn't escaped my notice that there has been a surge of interest in things Celtic at the close of the last two centuries (for example, the Belfast Harp Festival and Hyde's "Love Songs of Connaught"), and now that we're at the millennium's end, we could be witnessing a larger version of that.

M.S.   What do you think is the essence of the genre?

S.M.   This is difficult: there are so many elements. It can be serene and meditative, while the traditional tunes bring an exuberance and joy. However, from what people have told me, there is something about this music which moves people in a way unto itself, something you can't quite put your finger on. A well known British folk musician recently talked to me about what it was in the Irish and their music that had such an effect on people the world over. He said, "Being Irish distinguishes you from other Europeans, and you're almost expected to have a song to sing or a story to tell." Similarly, with the other Celts.

DISCOGRAPHY

MIGHTY RAIN (1998)

BUSHES & BRIARS (1998)

THROUGH THE BITTER

FROST & SNOW (1997)

BONES (1996)

Soundtracks and Compilations

A WINTER'S TALE (1998)

THOMAS MOORE'S

SOUL OF CHRISTMAS (1997)

PETER & WENDY (1997)

WOMEN OF THE WORLD CELTIC II (1997)

STRAIGHT OUTTA IRELAND (1993)

Website: www.susanmckeown.com

MÁIRE NÍ CHATHASAIGH

BIOGRAPHY

Máire Ní Chathasaigh (pronounced Moira Nee Ha-ha-sig) is, according to Derek Bell of The Chieftans, "the most interesting and original player of our Irish Harp today." She grew up in a well-known West Cork musical family and began to play the piano at age six, the tin-whistle at age ten, and the harp at age eleven, subsequently developing a variety of new techniques, particularly in relation to ornamentation, with the aim of establishing an authentically traditional style of harping. She's been credited with "a single-handed reinvention of the harp" and won the All-Ireland and Pan-Celtic Harp Competitions on several occasions in the 1970s. In 1985 she recorded the first harp album ever to concentrate on traditional Irish dance music, THE NEW-STRUNG HARP. Her unique approach to her instrument has had a profound influence on a whole generation of Irish harpers. A book of her harp arrangements, *The Irish Harper*, was published by Old Bridge Music in 1991.

Máire's musical partnership with Chris Newman, one of the UK's more revered acoustic guitarists, made its début at the 1987 Cambridge Folk Festival. They've played in twenty-one countries on five continents. The most recent of their four critically acclaimed albums together is LIVE IN THE HIGHLANDS. Máire and Chris are also featured on CELTIC HARPESTRY, a major Celtic harp album and associated TV special recently released by

Polygram U.S.A. and currently listed on the *Billboard* charts.

The Goldcrest feature film *Driftwood* features Máire's singing over the closing credits, and her harping and compositions appear with other luminaries of the Celtic music world on the major Sony (France) album FINISTERRES by Dan ar Braz et l'Héritage des Celtes, which recently received a Gold Disc. MISSA CELTICA, a new work by English composer John Cameron, has just been released on Warner Classics, and features the New English Chamber Orchestra, the Choir of New College Oxford, and a number of soloists – including Máire, on harp and voice.

interview

máirétd sullivan How did you first discover the harp, Máire?

máire ní chathasaigh Well I'm not really sure how I did. I grew up in a very musical family. There has been a very long tradition in both my mother's and my father's families. My mother is from Allihies, in West Cork, right at the tip of the Beara Peninsula. That's not far from where you come from. Her mother was O'Dwyer and she is an O'Sullivan. There have been fiddle-players in the O'Dwyer family for the last two hundred years. My mother and grandmother were singers.

m.s. Someone told me that there aren't a lot of the old sean-nós songs specifically written for women singers left in Ireland because most of the collectors were men collecting from men. I wonder whether your mother and grandmother knew any of the old Gaelic sean-nós women's songs, too.

m.n.c. They really didn't seem to me to make a distinction on the basis of gender. If they liked a song, they sang it regardless of whether it was a written from the angle of a man or a woman. That's always been part of the tradition.

But to get back to your question about how I discovered the harp, my mother started me playing the piano when I was six. Then I started playing the fiddle for a while and then the tin whistle. When I was eleven, I started playing the harp. My mother has told me that I'd always wanted to play the harp from the time that I was very small, though I've got no memory of this myself – my memories of my childhood are quite patchy really. She says that they could never figure out why the harp, particularly, or where I'd even heard one! So when the opportunity came up, they bought one for me. I've discovered since that quite a few harp players I know had the same experience: they'd always wanted to play the harp from when they were really tiny. My sister, Nollaig Casey, and I started the harp at the same time. We both started the fiddle at the same time as well, but though I've always loved the fiddle, I was more drawn to the harp. I just seemed to have a very strong natural affinity for it – and I'm now a professional harper, while Nollaig was drawn to the fiddle and is now a professional fiddle-player!

On my father's side of the family, there has been an enormous tradition of Seanchas (shanahus) which means lore and learning of all kinds: historical information, genealogical information, heroic tales, poetry. My father can trace his maternal ancestry, purely in the maternal line, back to the 16th century. That is an oral tradition: it's never been written down. That is the sort of thing they preserved in my father's family. Many of them, throughout the 18th and 19th centuries, were poets in the Irish language. Some of the poems they composed were preserved in the form of songs, which were still sung in West Cork up until the 1930s. As a child I remember learning a few of what are often described as "occasional verses" from my father. I remember learning one in particular, a humorous extempore verse composed by a 19th-century ancestor of mine, Donncha Óg Ó hIarlaithe, where he pokes fun at his daughter who liked staying in bed late in the mornings. It was passed down orally in the family – it's never been written down. It's full of puns and word play, which don't work so well when translated. Apart from anything else, it sounds perfectly okay in Irish, but when translated seems very vulgar all of a sudden! Irish is a very earthy language.

My father's grandfather was apparently a very fine singer and the family tradition is that some songs were collected from him by George Petrie, the famous 19th century collector of traditional music. So, on both sides of my family, there's been a very long tradition of knowledge of all sorts of Irish artistic activities, like composing poetry, playing music, preserving historical and genealogical information and lore of all kinds.

I grew up steeped in this. It wasn't until I was an adult that I realized how very unusual it is to know so much about your own lineage: lots of people, even in Ireland, know very little about their background, their ancestors, where they came from. I think that this feeling of connection to the past is probably one of the reasons that I feel so passionate about the music that I play. I feel a very strong affinity and love for all aspects of the Irish tradition and Irish culture, not just music, inspired purely by the family I was born into and its long collective memory – a long artistic collective memory which reaches back over two hundred years. My father himself, although he's a highly literate and learned man, has an extraordinary memory. It's the sort of memory which was probably once common in pre-literate societies, but which is now incredibly rare, probably because it's no longer necessary. I remember him once declaiming a forty-verse poem which he'd learned from an old neighbor in the 1930s: he'd only heard the poem twice but was able to remember every word of it! I've always been completely in awe of this gift, but unfortunately I haven't inherited it. He's always been a voracious reader and his extraordinary memory also means that he's forgotten very little of what he's ever read – he told me once that he'd memorized three of Shakespeare's plays by the time he was fourteen years old. On the other hand, he's never been able to remember what he did yesterday, or where he put his car keys! He's now eighty-five and his memory is not what it used to be – it's been fading for the last few years – but it's still remarkable.

My father grew up in quite a remote part of the parish of Caheragh, between Skibbereen and Bantry. His family was the last family of native Irish speakers in the district, because his grandmother was still alive when he was a little boy: she'd lived through the Famine, and wouldn't allow any English to be spoken in the house because she blamed the English for the Famine. That's one of the reasons why so much lore was passed on.

M.S. Was the Catholic Church very strong in your family?

M.n.C. It's a completely natural part of everybody's life in Ireland.

M.S. Is it separate from the other beliefs they held on to?

M.n.C. No it isn't. It could perhaps be interpreted as an extension of the ancient belief in the otherworld and the associated belief in the centrality of a spiritual dimension to life that we were just talking about. Several members of my mother's extended family were nuns and priests, which is probably not accidental. I have an aunt who's a nun, a very serene and spiritual person, who's also quite psychic, I think.

Christianity in Ireland is shot through with all sorts of other beliefs that have nothing to do with Christianity. Most people in Ireland think they are Christian beliefs. At least the old people thought they were. In fact, they are pre-Christian beliefs that are completely wound up with Catholicism. If you actually examine them, you will find that they have nothing to do with the Church at all, but the people, themselves, are convinced that they are.

Celtic Christianity developed in its own way over many centuries in relative isolation, incorporating within it many aspects of a pre-Christian, pagan Celtic belief system, before it was made to conform to Roman practices in the 12th century – though even then it was never completely stamped out. Because Celtic Christianity was so inclusive of all sorts of ancient beliefs, these beliefs were remarkably tenacious and survived in Ireland until the 20th century.

The rigidity that is associated with the late 19th- and early 20th-century Irish Church is a post-Famine phenomenon, a reaction to the severe psychological trauma inflicted on the whole country by the Famine. People were terrified that it might happen again. Whereas before the Famine most people married young, after it, people were afraid that they mightn't be able to feed their children. So very often only one member of the family inherited the land and married and had children. The other siblings either remained unmarried on the family farm or emigrated in the hope of earning enough money to be able to marry. The Irish people were never puritanical; the Irish language is not a puritanical language, even today. The Puritanism that some people associate with the Irish Church is an extremely recent thing, which developed purely as a consequence of the Famine; it was aided and abetted of course by the huge decline in the Irish language after the Famine. When people became more exposed to English, they also became more exposed to the stifling influence of Victorian England. Puritanism wasn't a cultural feature of pre-Famine Ireland. It's interesting that if you speak to native Irish speakers, they'll express themselves in Irish with enormous freedom, in a way that they never would in English. The freedom of expression characteristic of the Irish language is not acceptable in English, even today. Irish is a very earthy language and the Irish people were very earthy, but spiritual too.

M.S. Do you think the traditional music is affected by that stoical restriction?

M.N.C. Oh no! Well, certainly not now. During the heyday of the puritanical phase of the Irish Church in the late 19th- and early 20th centuries, some puritanical priests put a stop to crossroads dancing and house dances. The great collector of Irish traditional dance-music, Francis O'Neill, who, like my father, was born in the parish of Caheragh, was full of resentment about this. He says in his book *Irish Minstrels and Musicians* that a piper he knew in the parish who made his living from playing for dances was thrown into poverty as a result of the ban and ended his days in the workhouse, and that a number of other musicians he knew emigrated out of despair. But Irish people have always had a great *joie de vivre*, a great delight in being alive, which can never be repressed for long. Neither the trauma of the Famine nor clerical misguidedness managed to crush their spirit completely: the minute it got a chance again it bubbled up. So, no. I don't think it has affected the music long-term. Obviously a lot of musicians must have died in the Famine and thousands more emigrated. The music could have died, but miraculously, it never did.

M.S. What do you think is the source of that natural spring of energy, that *joie de vivre*, as you say?

M.N.C. It was always there, but there have been an awful lot of traumas in the last few hundred years of Irish history which have repressed it for a while. The Cromwellian wars were very traumatic, the forced movements of population and the huge massacres. For example, in 1649 thirty thousand people, just in Drogheda, were put to the sword by Cromwell's soldiers. The Penal Laws were appalling. Things calmed down for a bit and then came the Famine, the most recent large-scale trauma. The Irish psyche has always recovered and bubbled to the surface again. The current generation is now 'back to normal', you could say. Irish culture, in itself, has always been very expressive, very free, and very unfettered, very unrepressed. Sometimes you meet people who, in themselves, are damaged by very rigid nuns or priests who taught them thirty or forty years ago. They have blamed the Church for ruining their lives. That doesn't mean anything to me, really, because I grew up after The Second Vatican Council. I think there is an enormous difference between people who grew up after and before The Second Vatican Council. That is because the whole way of approaching religion completely changed. Hell didn't mean anything to me when I was growing up. The way religion was taught before that was very authoritative, whereas after, it was much looser and freer. It was much more participative. There was much less fear. So, I don't associate the Church with being afraid. My view of it is as a benign force, not a malign force. People, who are twenty years older than me, in their sixties, who talk about how they were mistreated and damaged by the Christian Brothers, etc., might as well be talking about two hundred years ago, as far as I am concerned. That bore no relationship to the way I grew up. It doesn't mean, of course, that I want to belittle their pain in any way.

There has always been, in Irish culture, an enormous exuberance of spirit which external events have crushed from time to time, but we've always bounced back from that because our culture is so incredibly strong: the springs of creativity in us are so strong. A part of our whole identity as people is a creative identity. Creativeness is completely central to who we are.

I do an enormous amount of traveling and I have not seen any other country where the ability to do something artistic is so highly valued. I live in England now, and though we are very successful in what we do, this society's view of musicians is that they are not perceived to be appreciated as much as in Ireland, where an artist is revered. If you are a musician, you are down a bit in the social pecking order, rather than up at the top.

m.s. Wouldn't that be related to the royal hierarchy?

m.n.c. No, it's not that, actually. It's something extremely fundamental. You see, in early Irish society, as among other Celtic peoples, the *file* or poet had the same status as the king. The word *file* originally meant a seer or wise man, and the *file* retained some of the prestige of the Druid. In the very earliest times, the Druids were the highest class in society, just like the Brahmins were in India. Because the poets had a very high status in society, what they said was revered. In the earliest periods, they were considered to have the ability to bless or curse. In the medieval period, every chieftain had his own hereditary professional court poet, whose main function was to praise the deeds of his chieftain in panegyric or praise poems. The poet could, equally, if he didn't like what the chieftain was doing, write an 'aor' or satire to criticize the king or chieftain. In the earliest periods, this was considered to have the power of a curse. So, the power of the word and of the creative person producing new words was enormous. That is a very, very ancient tradition.

The harpers had a very high status in society as well, but not as high as the poets did. Whereas in the earliest times the poets had the same status as the kings, the harpers were freemen – the only class of musicians who were allowed to become freemen! The word was always the main thing in Ireland. All of the descriptions of Celtic society talk of their love of poetry and their love of music. It is intrinsic to our sense of ourselves.

There was a high-ranking Norman/Welsh monk called Giraldus Cambrensis, whose uncle Maurice Fitzgerald was one of the principal leaders of the Norman invasion of Ireland, who visited Ireland in 1185 in the retinue of Prince John, the youngest son of King Henry II of England. While he was there he wrote *Topographia Hiberniae* (The History and Topography of Ireland), which is very interesting. He didn't travel very widely in Ireland, so some of what he wrote is based on hearsay, and of course it's colored by the fact that he came to Ireland with a conqueror. He was very credulous and seems to have believed every tall tale he was told by the locals! Maybe he thought he was such a superior being that he couldn't believe that anyone would dare to pull his leg. It's always in the interest of conquerors to disparage those who are being conquered. Giraldus's natural tendency would be to disparage everything he saw. He thought we were a barbarous people, with far too great a love of leisure and liberty, who spent ridiculous amounts of time listening to music and poetry. He thought this was a waste of time. What he said was absolutely true of the native Irish aristocracy, who despised manual labor. They believed in using the lower orders and plenty of slaves to do all the donkey-work, leaving them free to devote their time to the finer things in life, like making and appreciating art of all kinds. Slavery was apparently so widespread that the Irish bishops at a 12th-century synod in Armagh came to the conclusion that the Norman invasion was the judgement of God on the Irish for their purchase and enslavement of English people! Kind of ironic really. Anyway, Giraldus disparaged plenty, but one of the few positive things he said is that he had never seen harpers to compare with the Irish harpers. He said he'd never heard such accomplished playing, anywhere. He described the music of the harp as being highly ornamented and as being of an extraordinarily high standard. Giraldus was actually a very sophisticated person, who had studied in Paris and was familiar with all of the most advanced European literary and artistic movements. The Cathedral of Notre Dame in Paris was the center of the avant-garde in music at the time, what is known as the Ars Antiqua, "old art." This makes his testimony absolutely fascinating and very valuable to us today. He wasn't an ignorant observer. And since his natural tendency would have been to disparage rather than praise, the harpers he heard must have been truly extraordinary.

This love of ornament and decoration, which is very characteristic of Irish music, still, to this day, has a very long history. It's part of how we want to express ourselves. It's completely part of us. I think creativity has never happened just by chance in Irish society. I think Ireland, by its very nature, has nurtured artists because it has always appreciated them. You'll find in even the smallest place, with people who have never been any-where, that they adore music. They have the greatest regard for creative artists of any kind.

M.S.   It is so satisfying to hear that you have found that evidence. Let me ask you about your harp. What kind of strings do you use on your harp?

M.N.C.   It's a nylon string harp. The harp that I play is, strictly speaking, a neo-Irish harp. It looks like the ancient Irish harp but it is strung with nylon strings. It can also be strung with gut strings.

M.S.   Have you tried both sounds?

M.N.C.   I specifically like the nylon. I'll tell you why. When I was in my early teens, I'd already been playing the whistle and the fiddle and lots of different things. I grew up playing both traditional and classical music, side by side. But what I wanted to do is play traditional music on the harp. I wanted to play dance music on the harp, which hadn't been done before. At that point in Ireland, the harp was used mainly as accompa-niment to songs. There were hardly any harp teachers outside of Dublin. There was nobody decent at all outside Dublin, actually. The harp had become very much an urban instrument. It had become completely dis-associated with the oral tradition, with people who played music in the countryside. The people who played dance music and slow airs, who were part of the oral tradition, learnt the music orally.

The old Irish harpers played for an aristocratic clientele. A lot of their music has survived in various collections, but it's very complex and sophis-ticated and technically extremely demanding and it's not very accessible really: it sounds a little strange to modern ears. It doesn't sound like what we now think of as Irish music. Another large chunk of the music they played has survived in the oral tradition; for example, the really famous Irish airs like *The Derry Air* were almost certainly composed by harpers. Most of these airs, like a lot of the current music associated with Ireland, go back only two or three centuries and not further. The harpers didn't play dance music at all; in fact, they would have looked down their noses at people who played dance music because that was the music of 'the people'.

But that is what I always wanted to do because that is the tradition I grew up in. I was playing the uilleann pipes, which is an instrument that I've always loved and which was my main inspiration. What I wanted to do was to develop a way of playing that music on the harp, so in my early teens I started developing the necessary new techniques of fingering and ornamentation. I've been teaching people how to play dance music on the harp since the mid-seventies. There are people who have learnt from people who've learnt from people who have learnt from me a long time ago. So now, there are hundreds of young harpers in Ireland and elsewhere who use the techniques that I developed and their own variants of them, which is great.

m.s. You were the forerunner of that approach.

m.n.c. Yes. But to get back to your question about the nylon strings, I started playing on gut strings. The second harp my parents bought for me, when I was thirteen, was a Japanese-made harp. A Japanese man called Kunzo Aoyama started to make nylon-strung Irish harps in the late sixties. They also had thirty-four strings and a new, improved, way of changing key, using up-and-down semi-tone levers. It was a much better system than the one that was there before, much more suitable for instrumental music. I thought it was absolutely fantastic. It was the sound of the nylon that made me think I could make dance music work on this instrument. I couldn't have made it work on the gut-strung harp I had before because gut has a very mellow sound, which, of course, is lovely if you want to accompany songs and play slow music. If you want to play very fast dance music, which has a lot of ornamentation, you need a much brighter sound, and the nylon provided a very bright sound. So, that was the sound I was looking for.

m.s. Did you find yourself playing the harp in sessions?

m.n.c. Yes, when I was a kid. I was a very shy teenager. I didn't like to play for people unless I was asked.

m.s. So your desire to play dance music wasn't actually related to your wish to play with everyone else.

m.n.c. No. It was nothing to do with that. It was more a personal, artistic aim, for its own sake. I had always played with other people but not on the harp. I always played the whistle in sessions and that. You don't attract so much attention, which suited me fine! I would venture to say that I find playing the harp with lots of other musicians to be very frustrating. I don't feel I am contributing anything because I don't make enough noise. I always enjoyed playing with, maybe, a couple of other people. Then it has an artistic purpose and you're interacting in a very creative way.

m.s. How did people react when they heard dance music on the harp for the first time?

m.n.c. I remember when I first entered the under fourteen All-Ireland Fleadh Cheoil. Comhaltas Ceoltóirí Éireann organizes the Fleadh Cheoils every year. I got an awful lot of encouragement from people I met at that time. People said they'd never thought they'd see the day that they'd hear dance music on the harp. A lot of older traditional musicians, at that time, thought the harp was a useless instrument, that you couldn't play anything decent on it. But once they heard what I was trying to do, they were immensely supportive and full of praise and encouragement. They gave me the confidence to develop what I was doing even further. There isn't, of course, anything at all wrong with the harp, in itself, as a means of playing traditional music in an authentic style. You just have to know the traditional music, you have to grow up with it and be immersed in that style. Otherwise you're not going to play the right thing. It doesn't matter how good you are if you don't know the style. I grew up with the style and then developed the techniques to transfer the sound I heard in my head onto the harp-strings.

m.s. You had the instrument that would allow you to play the music efficiently.

m.n.c. Yes. So, from then on I entered a lot of Fleadh Cheoils. I won a lot of the competitions and got a lot of attention because what I was doing was very new. I appreciated that because when I was growing up I was extremely shy. A lot of musicians, when interviewed, disparage the whole idea of competitions. I actually think that I would still be playing to myself in my own front room if I hadn't entered those competitions. At that time, it really wasn't the done thing for females to put themselves forward. Male musicians have always been able to go into a place and ask for gigs. At that time a female couldn't do that. It's still more difficult for young females, though it's delightful to see how much more confident the new young generation of female traditional musicians is by comparison with my own.

m.s. When were you a teenager?

m.n.c. In the early seventies. If you enter a competition, as a girl, and you win, basically it's an objective validation of what you've done. Somebody else has said you are good. You don't have to say it yourself. You don't have to push yourself, which a nicely brought up young girl is not supposed to do. Even still, if you grew up in that way, you can never really overcome that.

m.s. That is certainly true still.

m.n.c. There are some people who are born pushy, but most women are not, if they are brought up in a particular way. In England, I am often asked, "Why are there such enormous numbers of really wonderful Irish female musicians?" There have been for the last thirty or forty years. I think one of the reasons is that the whole competition system brought a lot of female musicians to prominence when they were in their teens. A purely objective assessment is made that you are the winner, the best, so the whole musical culture hears about you. It benefited us females enormously. It brought us to prominence without ourselves having to say that we were brilliant. It gave a great boost to our self-esteem in those shaky teenage years and the confidence to develop our talents even further.

Sometimes you'll hear people, almost always men, disparaging the whole competition system. This annoys me as I think it's been of enormous benefit to women in Ireland.

M.S. So, if you were good, people would come to find you.

M.N.C. Absolutely, I didn't enter to win, necessarily, those events also provided a very important social function. But, if you did win, people would seek you out.

M.S. Where are you today in terms of your vision of what the past has brought you to and where you want to go with that understanding?

M.N.C. I keep working, especially on the older music. I do a lot of composition these days. My first solo album was in 1985. I've done four recordings since, with Chris Newman. I am working on another solo album, at the moment, completely solo. And, of course, I love performing. I get great pleasure out of giving people pleasure. We do a lot of touring.

My original mission in life was, I suppose, to reintegrate the harp into the oral Irish tradition, from which it had become separated in the last few centuries. That is very much the case now, and that is an enormous change.

I have always felt a mission to explain Irish music, not just to non-Irish people, but also to other Irish people. Given half a chance, I will expound my theories to anybody. (Laughter). I try to explain why Irish musicians play the way they do and what the actual aesthetic of the music is. A lot of people involved in Irish music play, but they can't really explain why they do what they do, very well. So, I feel it is necessary to explain. If somebody asks me I simply launch into it.

M.S. Please, go ahead, the floor is yours.

M.N.C. My central belief about Irish music is connected to my belief about Irish society, which I was talking about earlier on. It is that Irish music has always been a miniature art. If you think of the music of Beethoven as a landscape painting – his music is painted in broad strokes so that you have long crescendos and diminuendos – in comparison, Irish music is like a miniature painting. There are huge changes of dynamics within one bar of music. Some people think there are no dynamics in Irish music. If you take a reel, for example, it seems the same from beginning to end. In fact, there are enormous changes, but they all happen on a tiny scale. The overall sound seems the same from start to finish, but it isn't. It changes all the time. A really, really good traditional musician will never play the same thing twice in the same way. There will always be a slight change. But it will be done in a very, very subtle way. Subtlety is completely central to the whole Irish aesthetic. For the Irish, artistry equals subtlety, basically. One of the descriptions, from the earliest times, of the art of the Irish poets states that, to them, art that conceals art is the greatest of all. It was true of the Irish poets in the 8th century; it was true of the harpers described by Giraldus Cambrensis, in the 12th century.

I've actually got the book, which quotes the 12th-century monk Giraldus Cambrensis right here. I'll read it to you. This is the translation from the Latin: "The movement is not, as in the British instrument to which we are accustomed, slow and easy, but rather quick and lively, while at the same time the melody is sweet and pleasant. It is remarkable how, in spite of the great speed of the fingers, the musical proportion is maintained. The melody is kept perfect and full with unimpaired art through everything… with a rapidity that charms, a rhythmic pattern that is varied, and a concord achieved through elements discordant. They harmonize at intervals of the octave and the fifth. . . . They glide so subtly from one mode to another, and the grace notes so freely sport with such abandon and bewitching charm around the steady tone of the heavier sound, that the perfection of their art seems to lie in their concealing it, as if 'it were the better for being hidden. An art revealed brings shame.'"

m.s.　Is it that the Irish have hidden their ancient aesthetics under the current of the mainstream, and that it still is perceivably active?

m.n.c.　The whole Irish cultural aesthetic is to venerate the subtle over the obvious. The Irish cultural consciousness has always revered subtlety. Before the Irish were ever under threat from an outside power, they revered the subtle. It's a very ancient thing; it has nothing to do with what has happened to us.

Giraldus goes on to say: "Hence it happens that the very things that afford unspeakable delight to the minds of those who have a fine perception and can penetrate carefully to the secrets of the art, bore, rather than delight, those who have no such perception – who look without seeing, and hear without being able to understand. When the audience is unsympathetic, they succeed only in causing boredom with what appears to be but confused and disordered noise."

What this is basically saying is that to be able to appreciate the music of the harpers, you need to be educated in that music: that it was a very subtle art which needs to be appreciated. People, who really, really know and can penetrate the art, experience an unspeakable delight on hearing it. The same is actually true of a traditional fiddle player, for example, in the 20th century, especially of the older traditional musicians. If you hear them describing music, what they really respect in other musicians is subtlety. Not obviousness, not variations that jump up and scream at you, as if to say, "I am a variation, look how brilliant I am." What they absolutely love, in the playing of other musicians, is subtlety. It's interesting that that should be as true of musicians of the 20th century as it was of the harpers in the 12th century. That whole view of the nature of art is very ancient and very Irish.

In the case of the visual arts, just look at the old and very, very beautiful jewelry that was made two to three thousand years ago. Likewise, objects like the Ardagh Chalice, the Tara Brooch, and the *Book of Kells*, which were produced in the 8th century, when Irish art reached a peak of virtuosity. All the illuminated manuscripts produced from the 6th century onwards were highly ornamented, but the *Book of Kells*, which was the most famous illuminated manuscript of all, was extraordinarily lavishly ornamented. But again, you look at a page and the whole looks beautiful, but it is so detailed that even if you look at one tiny bit by itself, it'll have something interesting to say. For example, a tiny little figure inside a capital letter might be doing something interesting. That's very much, again, a miniature art. And, again, subtlety is exalted over the obvious. Giraldus Cambrensis described the *Book of Kells* as being "the work, not of men, but of angels."

M.S.   Have you looked into the history of those manuscripts at all? Someone was saying that those books are a hybrid of eastern and western design.

M.D.C.   Well yes, though their motifs show striking parallels with Irish jewelry and metalwork. Irish monasteries seem to have kept in close contact with the very earliest monastic foundations, those of the Near East, particularly Egypt and Syria. One characteristic feature of the Irish manuscripts, which was also found in Egyptian Coptic manuscripts, is the surrounding of capital letters with decorative red dots. It's been a feature of Irish manuscripts since at least the 6th century and appears at about the same time in Byzantine manuscripts. The extraordinarily beautiful "carpet pages" also seem to have been inspired by Coptic models. What is interesting, of course, is that Celtic society, particularly Irish society, preserves a way of life which is very ancient. The Romans never conquered Ireland, so it was able to preserve its Celtic culture in a pure form. The Celtic languages are a part of the Indo-European family of languages. One of the interesting things to observe is that the structure of ancient Aryan society in India, which is described in the *Rig-Veda*, is the same as the structure of society described by the early Irish writers. So that, in a way, Ireland preserved a very ancient form of society, shared with the ancestors of both the Indian culture and the Celtic culture.

M.S.   The Vedas are said to have been taken to the East, to India, around 1500 BC.

M.N.C.   The Indo-European peoples are said to have originated in the steppes of southern Russia, between the Caucasus and the Carpathian Mountains and spread from there east to India and west to Europe. They're supposed to have reached Central Europe around 3000 BC and the Punjab in India between 3000 and 1500 BC. Presumably, they brought the Vedas with them to India. Ireland has always been consciously conservative; I mean that in the positive sense of preserving things from the past. Preserving a type of society. The society described in the old Irish law tracts is a very ancient type of society, which is also described in the early Indian tracts. It isn't because Irish society was based on Aryan society in India. It is that ancient Indian and Celtic societies were both the descendents of an original Indo-European society.

M.S.   Well said.

M.N.C.   Thank you. There are some parallels between the *Book of Kells* and the art of the Middle East, but that doesn't mean that one directly influenced the other. I don't think it's as simple as that. The exaltation of the subtle and the importance of ornament are two things that go back a long way in Irish society. The Continental Celts were very much admired by the Romans for their eloquence and their polished and artistic speech. If you look at Irish poetry, it's very clear that it's always been very highly ornamented, even when the structure changed drastically at various times. There was enormous change in Irish society after the defeat of the Irish at the Battle of Kinsale in 1601. Later in the 17th century came the Cromwellian wars, which caused one of the real seismic shifts in Ireland. In the hundred years after 1601 eighty-five percent of Irish land was forcibly transferred into the hands of the new English colonists and the old Irish aristocratic order collapsed. The chieftains were no longer in a position to support either harpers or poets in the style to which they had become accustomed.

The poets then had to change the style of poetry they composed, practically totally. The harpers changed what they played, also, because now, in very short order, they had to find new audiences. Because the music and the poetry were actually aimed, very much, at a cultured and learned audience, they now had to aim what they were doing at everybody, so they had to change what they did quite drastically. The court poets of the medieval period, and right down to the 17th century, composed mainly praise poetry, but it was extremely formal. They used a lot of very complex meters, for example. They used complex forms of word ornament. They also used a standardized language.

That's an interesting thing, which shows the continuity and conservatism of Irish society. From the 12th to the end of the 16th century, the

Irish language, the Gaelic language, was standardized in grammar and spelling. It was the first standardized vernacular (non-Latin) language in Europe. It was standardized in grammar and spelling long before English was, for example. This language was used by the learned classes and poets both in Ireland and in Gaelic speaking Scotland. A poet writing in Gaelic in 12th century Scotland would be completely understood by someone writing in Ireland in the 16th century because they used exactly the same language, the same grammar and spelling.

Old Irish and Modern Irish seem quite a long way apart, but you can see how the language developed quite clearly. The earliest surviving examples of written Old Irish are in the form of glosses, or explanations written by an Irish monk in the margins of a manuscript of the Gospels in Latin, which is preserved in the library of the cathedral of St. Gallen in Switzerland. The monks also wrote some lovely poems in the margins when they got bored with copying out Gospels. There's one particularly sweet one, which a monk wrote about the antics of his cat, Pangur Bán.

St. Gallen is an Irish medieval settlement, a monastic foundation of St. Gall, built during the Dark Ages. After the fall of the old Roman Empire, civilization collapsed in Europe, even royal families became illiterate, and knowledge of the ancient learning of Greece and Rome practically disappeared. Irish monks re-civilized Europe between the 6th and the 8th centuries by founding monasteries and teaching all over Europe. St. Columbanus founded a monastery in Bobbio, south of Milan, around 590; St. Gall was one of his disciples. St. Colmcille founded the monastery of Iona in Scotland in about 561. Irish missionary work in England began with the foundation of an abbey at Lindisfarne by St. Aidan who came from Iona in 635. Another Irishman, St. Killian, was a missionary at Würzburg in Germany, where he was martyred in 689. And so on, etc.

M.S. Tell us more about the poets.

M.N.C. As I said earlier on, after the collapse of the old Irish order in the 17th century, the poets abandoned writing in the standardized, classical language in order to compose poetry in the language of the people, the dialects of the regions they lived in. The structure of the poetry they started to compose changed completely as well. Instead of the very formal court poetry, which was based on the number of syllables in the line and complex schemes of rhyme and alliteration, they started to write poetry which had more of a song meter. They abandoned the syllabic poetry. Even though the whole form of the poetry changed, it retained the very beautiful, very musical, very highly ornate style. The importance of ornament was retained. The very same thing happened with the harp music. The famous harper, Turlough O'Carolan, exemplifies this transitional period in music. His music is a hybrid of the more ancient Irish court music and the music that was popular in contemporary Europe, the music of the baroque style. Again, the harpers wanted to make their music accessible to the new landowners who were of English origin and, of course, to the ordinary people as well. But they retained their love for ornamentation and variation, and for subtlety in expression. Even though the forms changed over the centuries, the bedrock of the tradition never changed. That's why I believe there is a specifically Irish aesthetic. It's an aesthetic which reveres the subtle over the obvious, and is expressed in every art form. The artistic impulse has remained the same down through the ages.

One of the things that worries me slightly is that this aesthetic may not survive modern methods of communication and the drive towards homogeneity in music. This applies even within traditional music, with everybody hearing the same thing, played over and over, the same way, on recordings. It runs against the individualism, which is very much part of the Irish tradition. The harp and the uilleann pipes are solo instruments in the tradition. They are about an individual making an artistic statement. The modern world obscures this slightly, but it is still very much there. There's still an enormous number of discriminating listeners to Irish music who will prefer hearing a solo player to hearing a bunch of people playing together, because then you can really hear the variations going on and that's what they look for in the individual interpretation.

I feel that this whole perception of the nature of the music, of why musicians do what they do, is seen in so many other Irish art forms and goes back so far that it is central to who we are. I say this over and over again because I really believe it. My primary aim is to draw people into the music in a more meaningful and deeper way, so that they can hear beyond the surface.

Discography

MÁIRE NÍ CHATHASAIGH (solo)

THE NEW STRUNG HARP (1985)
(Temple Records)

Máire Ní Chathasaigh & Chris Newman

LIVE IN THE HIGHLANDS (1995)
(Old Bridge Music)
OUT OF COURT (1991)
(Old Bridge Music)

THE CAROLAN ALBUMS (1994)
(Old Bridge Music)
THE LIVING WOOD (1988)
(Old Bridge Music)

Compilations

CELTIC HARPESTRY (1998)
(Imaginary Road Records – USA)
FINISTERRES: DAN AR BRAZ ET
  L'HÉRITAGE DES CELTES (1997)
(Sony – France)
L'IMAGINAIRE IRLANDAIS (1997)
(Keltia Musique – France)
A CELTIC TREASURE (1996)
(Narada Media – USA)
BRINGING IT ALL BACK HOME (1991)
(Hummingbird Records)

THE BEST OF THE
  IRISH FOLK FESTIVAL VOLUME 2 (1989)
(Wundertüte – Germany)
THE BEST OF THE IRISH
  FOLK FESTIVAL (1988)
(Wundertüte – Germany)
THE 5TH IRISH FOLK FESTIVAL (1978)
(Wundertüte – Germany)
MISSA CELTICA
(Warner Classics)

Website: www.oldbridgemusic.com

LOREENA MCKENNITT

MAURA O'CONNELL

TRÍONA NÍ DHOMHNAILL
(with nightnoise)

MÁIRE NÍ CHATHASAIGH

MADDY PRYOR

GAY WOODS
(WITH STEELEYE SPAN)

MAIGHREAD NÍ DHOMHNAILL

BIOGRAPHY

Maighread Ní Dhomhnaill (nee donnell) has strong roots in the musical world. She was encouraged and inspired by her father, who passed along a wealth of songs to his children, ensuring the preservation of what he considered a living tradition.

Maighread, her sister Tríona, and her brother Mícheál were members of the renowned Irish group, Skara Brae, in the early seventies. That group's first album was recorded in one afternoon and released when Maighread was only fifteen years old.

While Maighread stayed at home in the west of Ireland to raise a family, her brother and sister went on to fame in The Bothy Band, Relativity, and, more recently, Nightnoise. Recently, Maighread has returned to perform and tour with Donal Lunny's band, Coolfin.

She and her husband, Cathal Goan, have worked to acquire a large archive of songs, and their recordings and transcriptions of these tunes have been submitted to the Irish National Archive.

interview

mairéid sullivan How many children do you have, Maighread?

maighread ní dhomhnaill Two: my daughter Róise is 18, and my son Mánus is 14.

m.s. It must be wonderful for you, now that the children are grown up and you can go out traveling with your music again.

m.n.d. Yes. It is wonderful to be back in there. When they were small, it was much more difficult. I didn't do much at all outside, musically, when they were young.

m.s. Tell me what you were thinking at the time you were considering the possibility of going out to sing in concert again.

m.n.d. It sort of happened by chance. Over the years there has been some pressure on me to make another album, to get back out there, and I kept putting it off and putting it off. Eventually, about seven or eight years ago, I managed to produce another album. Then I was faced with the possibility of having to go on tour. At that stage I had a young teenager and an eight-year-old. So, we managed that and I went touring for about four weeks around Germany with the Irish Folk Festival. That was the first time I had ever toured for that length of time away from home and I found it very traumatic.

m.s. How were the children?

m.n.d. They got along fine – I had arranged everything for them – but they were very happy to see me coming home. They said they found it hard after the second week.

m.s. Did the fact that they got along fine while you were away take the pressure off you a little bit?

m.n.d. It did. I made the extra effort to ensure they were okay, and they knew that it was an important thing for me to do. After that, I knew I would never tour away from home that long, and I've never done it since. It was something I had to do, something I had to get out of my system.

But I've been doing a lot more touring recently. The whole world seems to be looking at Ireland these days. Everybody says that we have something special in the music. We have a music that seems to cross all the divides. People love it and find it very accessible. I don't know why that is, but it's fascinating. I played in Japan twice last year, and there were people crying in the audience, crying at the beauty of the songs. It actually is a bit overpowering at times. I think our songs are very beautiful, and I think the Irish language is very beautiful. We were in a concert last week in Belgium and nobody said anything about all the songs being in Irish. If you gave them an indication of what the song was about, they just closed their eyes and sat back and listened to it. I think that is something that has changed a lot in Ireland and I'm delighted about it.

M.S. They say that Gaelic is one of the most 'unchanged' languages in Europe because it was suppressed for so long – that it has a unique meaning in the sounding of the words and the structure of the phrases.

M.N.D. There are certain words in the Irish language that you just can't translate; you just know what they mean. There are dialects that are unique to each area, too. There is a great sense of belonging when you remember your childhood and you remember your roots. Just yesterday I was sitting here in the car, and I turned on the radio at half past three while I was waiting for my daughter to come. I was tuned in to Raidió na Gaeltachta, the Irish radio station, just as at the beginning of a half-hour program about the song tradition. The next thing I realized I was listening to the sound of my father's voice. They had used a recording of a radio program that he had done in August 1960. He sang four songs, and they did an interview with him. And my father's twenty-two years dead this week.

M.S. That must have been a profound moment for you.

M.N.D. It really was, I found myself in tears. It was unexpected. I didn't know about the program. I hadn't heard his voice in so long. I had listened to his recordings, but this was him talking, and I just sat in the car and listened to it. I was upset all day yesterday about it. I listened to his voice and realized that everything I have, the songs, the traditions, are because of him. He was so interested in it. Out of such a large family, he was the one who mostly kept the songs alive and was interested enough to pass them on to us. I have cousins who are interested, but none of them sing, none carry on the tradition in that way. I think it comes from your parent's generation. If he hadn't shown an interest, brought us around, we would have never been interested in it.

M.S. He wouldn't have thought of himself as strange or different for doing it. He would probably have known really interesting people who shared his interest in the culture.

M.N.D. In his generation, there weren't actually that many people interested in keeping it alive. At that stage it was a living tradition and nobody thought it was going to die. He probably had some foresight because he wanted to record it.

Now it has moved into a different plane; you don't have that kind of handed down tradition any more. You don't have house parties, you don't have people sitting in the house saying here's another song, here's another song. It's a terrible pity that it's gone. Now we sit down at a gathering on weekends, where people make a conscious effort to go to listen and exchange songs, but that old style of life is gone. Memories from childhood make up our heritage. The children of this generation have different memories and view of reality. We have no conception of what our parents went through.

M.S. I get the impression that you're pretty happy about what you're doing; you seem very cheerful about it all.

M.N.O. Absolutely! Basically, I have never sought a gig. Everything I've ever done so far has come into my lap. Probably because I haven't really been relying on it to earn my living. I gave up nursing years ago, and now I'm in the position where I have the time, and I'm able to do it. For me it's a matter of picking and choosing what I want to do.

M.S. How do you feel about being invited back into a circle of serious touring musicians, such as Donal Lunny's band, who are going to carry you off with them into the wide world?

M.N.O. I enjoy that and I feel very privileged by it, to be involved with people like Donal, my sister, Tríona, and my brother, Mícheál. Working with the band – Sharon Shannon, Nollaig Casey, and everybody else – has been really great. It has been great to tour with them. And I've worked once or twice with Steve Cooney, and it's fabulous. It's great to be away at festivals and meeting other musicians. Having been away touring for the last year and a half, it gets stale, though. I feel I have to get back home again to learn new songs and renew my energy so I can start enjoying touring again. That's what I'm doing at the moment.

M.S. I feel if I add a new song every week or two that keeps the juices flowing for all the rest of them.

M.N.O. Exactly, and even when you've played with a big band for a while, it's a bit daunting to go back and open your mouth on your own and sing unaccompanied. It's so nice to do it and enjoy it, and say, Oh God! I can do this again!

M.S. You would be just the person you always were, a singer of traditional songs, then you would be offered a chance to go away on a big concert tour, but when you come back home, everybody would be saying, "Oh God! She's going to be famous." Then you don't feel like the same 'you' back home anymore. How do you feel about that?

M.N.O. It's very difficult. For example, I'm forty-three years of age and I've been a mother, and I'm used to being the organizer, in a certain way. When I go away with a group of musicians, they are all doing their own thing, you know, getting up when they want to, etc. In that kind of situation, I have to very actively try to keep my mouth shut and mind my own business. I like to be out by nine or ten o'clock and make the best of the day. I don't like to lie around all day. It's just a very different life. But then, when you tour a lot, you find that you slip into that mode because the constant soundchecks, late nights, and traveling can be really exhausting. Then you come home and the day after you are literally sitting in the kitchen saying, "I have to cook a meal for the family." Everything is kept on hold, but once you're home, you're home. When we're away in a group like that, I think we tend to become children again. Everybody is taking care of you; you become silly, you become a child, and, also, the people you're with become your family while you're away. Then you come home and delight to see your family, but long for this other family. Lots of musicians feel this, and they find it hard to talk about it. You come back to this loneliness. It's another life, a double life really.

M.S. Even the traditional songs talk about the experience of leaving home and longing for home. Then, coming back home and longing for the people you left out in the world. It's a completely impossible dilemma.

M.N.D. It is, and I think it's one which so many musicians and people who live on the road experience. You have to be out there to know that, and then you're dying to meet up with them again, and go off on the road. The more you do it, the more difficult it is.

M.S. I interviewed Andy Irvine in the late eighties. He never tires of the road. He even wrote a song with that title – *Never Tire of the Road*. He has a great philosophy. He says that everywhere he goes it's like meeting his dearest friends. Most relationships are sublimely happy because there is no time for interpersonal conflicts, really.

M.N.D. I remember when we met up with him on a recent tour in Germany. He had friends in every town. He is an extraordinary individual. I came very late to that, I never toured extensively when I was younger, and now this is all new to me.

M.S. This is an interesting subject, too; so many women in their forties are suddenly finding themselves free to go back full time to their music and with a lot more strength than we would ever have had in our twenties. But the fact remains – we're not in our twenties anymore. We have a very different agenda now. How do you deal with that?

M.N.D. It's trying to get a balance. I usually pick one or two nights when we're away, and I'll say to my self, "I'll have a blast that night, I'll have a good time." The rest of the time it's a matter of unwinding slightly after the gig. You know, you need to come down a bit. Your constantly trying to get rest, trying to get to bed, trying to have some kind of pattern, even if you just get up every morning and go for a walk.

M.S. Have you tried yoga, by the way?

M.N.D. I've just started yoga. I came home really exhausted after the last tour and I knew I had to do something to get over the exhaustion and loosen up again. When you have younger people around, its go, go, go! But after the age of thirty-five or so it gets much more difficult or you just aren't interested in all that running around and partying anymore. Especially with the demands of touring, jet lag, that kind of thing.

M.S. The great thing about yoga is that you can do it while you're touring. The basic stretching will really help you keep limber. But back to the music. What are your future hopes and plans?

M.N.O. I'm looking forward to working with my sister, Tríona, trying to get an album going there, seeing how that goes, working with different musicians and possibly getting a small band together.

M.S. Will Donal Lunny be in it or just produce it?

M.N.O. I'd say Donal will just produce it. He's too involved in his own work in so many areas. He'll always be there for us in some capacity, but I think it would be nice for us to create our own sound, definitively. Triona and I have been known for so long with the tradition of the "O'Dhomhnaill sound" – Mícheál, Tríona, and myself – the sound from the first group we had together, Skara Brae. I was fifteen when we recorded our album for Gael Linn in 1971, and last year I worked very hard to finally have it re-issued on CD. It was recorded in one afternoon with a stereo pair of microphones hanging from the ceiling. We went in at two o'clock and it was done by six. It's really doing well. It's one of those archival collections. The sound we had was very distinctive, and now I want to bring it back in a modern sense.

M.S. I'm sure people will be very curious to see what you do. The 'purists' always talk about preserving the pure tradition, and not messing it up with anything contemporary. I think they'll certainly be interested to see how you handle the tradition in a modern time and setting.

M.N.O. My aim at the moment is to make it as accessible, as interesting as possible, to bring it to the widest possible audience. I've had extraordinary help through the years from my husband, Cathal Goan. He worked in the Folklore Department at UCD (University College Dublin) as a post graduate student and was very interested in song. I feel, in my own life, that he took over where my father left off. He's now in charge of the new television station here called Teilifís na Gaeilge. It's here in Baile na hAbhann, Connamara. He was very interested in songs and the tradition. He worked for years on the song tradition in Donegal. All along, he has helped me with transcribing songs. He'll also pick out songs for me to sing. He has been a wonderful support to me all through the years. When we first got married, we used to go up and visit my Aunt Neilí, who was ill. She was very interested in the music. It got to the point where she said, "Cathal, can you leave me a tape recorder? Sometimes I remember the words or the songs, but when you're here, I forget them." We were trying to get her a tape recorder with a raised button on it because she was blind. We actually did find something that had raised buttons on it. So, then when we would come up, she would have a tape ready to hand to us. She would say, "Take this song and make your own of it." It was extraordinary. Cathal actually submitted the whole archive that we gathered to the National Archive here in Ireland, and now they have all her recordings, all the songs that we collected.

Discography

SKARA BRAE
(Gael Linn)

MAIGHREAD NÍ DHOMHNAILL
(Gael Linn)

GAN DHÁ PHINGIN SPRÉ
(Gael Linn)

NO DOWRY
(JVC Victor)

TRÍONA
(Gael Linn)

CELTIC LEGACY –
NARADA COLLECTION SERIES
(Narada Records)

WOMEN OF THE WORLD
(Putamayo Records)

CELTIC CHRISTMAS VOL. I
(Windham Hill Records)

CELTIC CHRISTMAS VOL. II
(Windham Hill Records)

ÓIRCHISTE CEOIL – AMHRANÁIOCHT
   A TREASURY OF IRISH SONG
(Gael Linn)

CELTIC WOMEN
(Celtic Woman Records)

A WOMAN'S HEART 2
(Dara Records)

SAILING INTO WALPOLE'S MARSH
(Green Linnet)

SULT
(Windham Hill Records)

CELTIC CHRISTMAS VOL. III
(Hummingbird Records)

JOHN RENBOURNE
(Shanachie)

TRAVELLER'S PRAYER
CELTIC CHRISTMAS IV
(Windham Hill Records)

DONAL LUNNY – COOLFIN
LAMENT
(Real World)

BEGINISH
(Inis)

CRÍONA NÍ ÓHOMHNAILL
(NIGHTNOISE)

BÍOGRAPhY

Irish brother and sister Mícheál O'Dhomhnaill and Tríona Ní Dhomhnaill are veterans of the classic group The Bothy Band, as well as Skara Brae (with their sister Maighread) and Relativity. Both have had other collaborations: Tríona with Touchstone, Mícheál with Kevin Burke. They are now members of Nightnoise.

Nightnoise started as a partnership between Irish traditional musician Mícheál O'Dómhnaill and American violinist Billy Oskay in 1983 when Mícheál moved to Portland, Oregon. A demo tape recorded by Oskay was turned into the album NIGHTNOISE. The success of this album led to the formation of the band, with the addition of Tríona, who plays harpsichord, clavinet, and flutist Brian Dunning. Oskay left the group after their fourth album and was replaced by Johnny Cunningham, a founding member of Silly Wizard. The music of Nightnoise is a fusion of jazz, traditional Irish, and impressionistic chamber music, mostly written by the group's members. In most pieces, the Celtic influences are subtle, with some traditional tunes standing out. The overall impression is of graceful, polished playing and a mellow, but not stagnant atmosphere, occasionally almost Enya-esque. The group was based in Portland, Oregon until their recent return to Ireland. The band has recorded eight albums on the Windham Hill label.

INTERVIEW

MAIRÉID SULLIVAN What was it that attracted you to the harpsichord and the clavinet?

CRÍONA NÍ ÐHOMHNAILL What I thought was a harpsichord turned out to be an electric clavinet. I found it in a small shop in Dublin many moons ago, back in the early seventies, when I was playing in Skara Brae with my brother, Mícheál, and my sister, Maighread.

I was looking for some kind of keyboard to play, and it was down at the bottom of a shelf sitting on the floor on its side. I was intrigued with the fact that the colors of the keys were reversed. I tinkered around with it for a few minutes, and thought, "What a lovely sound!" I asked the owner of the shop what it was, and he said, "I'm not quite sure, I got it out of a recording studio." I just said, "I really love it, it sounds like a harpsichord." It wasn't until many years later that I found out it was a Hohner D6 clavinet. Stevie Wonder used one, and made it prominent in the rock world with his hit songs *Superstition* and *Higher Ground* from INNERVISIONS in 1973. I loved the sound of a real harpsichord, but only occasionally got the opportunity to play one. We did a few radio programs where one was available in the studios.

The harpsichord was Sean O'Riada's main instrument. I was greatly influenced by Sean O'Riada. I was particularly attracted to his treatment of traditional tunes and backing. Since I couldn't afford to always carry a harpsichord in my back pocket, the clavinet, which was basically an electric clavichord, was more practical. O'Riada's approach really caught my ear. It helped me a lot in figuring out what to do behind tunes. Before that I don't think anybody had really approached harmony lines for those old melodies.

M.S. Yes, he's famous for that.

C.N.Ð. A lot of what the Chieftains did was inspired by his arrangements. I remember seeing them on TV when I was in my early twenties, and they had a strong impact on my playing.

M.S. You spent a long time in America with the band Relativity first and then Nightnoise. How long did you live in America?

C.N.Ð. Seventeen years altogether.

M.S. When did you come back home?

C.N.Ð. We all moved back to Ireland about two and a half years ago.

M.S. How many of the members of Nightnoise are from Ireland?

C.N.Ð. There are three of us, myself, my brother Mícheál, and Brian Dunning.

M.S. So, what are you doing now?

t.n.o. We took a year off. We're talking about getting things together again, soon. We have a fiddle player, John Fitzpatrick, from Belfast who joined us when we moved back here.

m.s. How does it feel moving back to all the music? Is it better?

t.n.o. It's very alive here, musically. It's very vibrant with a lot of things going on. There couldn't be a better time for traditional music. We left all that behind twenty years ago.

m.s. I wonder how you feel, in yourself, about being back in Ireland where you're really quite free to explore. Did you feel free to explore with Nightnoise or was that considered radical in America?

t.n.o. No, because we played to a completely different audience. We were just Nightnoise. We never set out to be a traditional band or any particular style of band.

m.s. Did you win traditional audiences when you toured?

t.n.o. We played mainly the college circuit and concert halls, rather than the 'trad' circuit that traditional musicians would have been playing on. There were a few crossover concerts that we did here and there, a couple of festivals. Our main audience was a different one, a mixture. Being on Windham Hill, a New Age label, we were kind of unusual and the most hard to peg in that whole bunch during all those years. It opened up a whole other way of going into the music, writing our own material, and most of it instrumental. I didn't get to sing a lot during all the years I was away. So, it was nice to come back and to be singing with people again. It feels right being back home. It's only beginning to sink in. I think we were in shock for the first year. I just moved into a house here in Dublin where I'm close to my mother and two brothers.

m.s. I didn't ask Maighread about your mother. Is your mother in Dublin?

t.n.o. She is, indeed. She'll be eighty-three in May. She's doing great. She's a trooper. She doesn't miss a thing. When we're on the radio, she'll say, "You're on! You're on!"

m.s. My mother's exactly like that for me. Her energy is great. She's seventy-seven.

t.n.o. They put you to shame when you're only half their age.

m.s. It's important to see our parents doing well in a time when the general American attitude toward being old is like, you're out of it, you're gone.

t.n.o. There is not as much of that attitude here. But it seems to be creeping in. I was just talking to somebody the other day, a friend down in Cork, another musician. He was wondering about the kids now having the same level of respect for the older folks, their wisdom, and what they have to say. All those years we were away, we were very fortunate and worked hard and toured a lot. Outside of that whole scene, a few weeks each summer we would come home, and you didn't get a picture of what it was like living here with all these big changes. It's been interesting.

M.S. What's it like there now?

C.N.Ó. Everything is much more accessible.

M.S. So, musically do you plan to continue with the Nightnoise formula? Do you have any plans for changing that?

C.N.Ó. Well, we'll see what happens. We never have planned much. I'm sure we will be touring again. We had a lot of success in Spain during the past few years, and they want us back there. We'll probably tour the States again, too, once we get another album out there, which is a tentative plan. The first priority is the album with Maighread.

M.S. How's that going to be structured musically?

C.N.Ó. We don't know yet, though we've chosen the songs. We'll just see how it comes out. We did a couple last weekend, and it sounded good, so we're very gung-ho about it.

M.S. These are the old sean-nos songs?

C.N.Ó Yes.

M.S. It's great that you're doing it because there are not that many people singing those old songs, in the old way. At least, there aren't that many who are able to do it professionally. It's great that you've been given the opportunity to do it and that circumstances have allowed you to do it. Do you read a lot? Are you studying history at all?

C.N.Ó. No, I studied archeology and French way, way back. Since then I've been on the road. That's the only thing I really enjoyed. I'd like some day to come off the road and pursue other interests. I also enjoy working in the studio and collaborating with other people. I read whenever I can.

M.S. With a background in archeology, you're well qualified to look at the material that's out there now on Celtic culture. I'm sure you've seen the stacks of books that are piled up on the subject.

C.N.Ó. Well it's great. But along side that you get these people trying to put up awful monstrosities right next to ancient places, like in the Burren, a mountain there called Mullach Mor. There's been a big battle over many things like that here. There's so much going on that's both good and bad.

M.S. Since Ireland has only recently reached this new level of prosperity, and it has maintained an agricultural economy for so long, rather than industrial, and put so much into restoring the culture, you'd think there would be enough active people who will want to protect the environment and the heritage.

C.N.Ó. But then there are some powerful people that want to capitalize on it, and who are just greed driven and ignorant.

M.S. Through your study in archeology, did you learn to look at the old Celtic history or were you focusing on some other part of the world?

C.N.Ó. A big part of the course was the megalithic tombs of Ireland. Each professor had a different interest so we covered a good bit of ground.

m.s. Because you've lived in America so long, you might have an insight to offer on the tremendous fascination Americans have for the mystery and idealism surrounding ancient Celtic culture. The 'American Way' is about free speech, and civil rights, and the freedom of the individual, and these concepts have really moved ahead, for individual human freedom generally, in the American culture. These ideals were also a fundamental part of the very ancient Celtic philosophy. So, I'm wondering if you think it's a natural phenomenon for Americans, especially, and Australians, too, to be interested in the highest ideals of ancient Celtic culture, especially since they resonate with their own idealism?

c.n.o. Well, if you reckon that there are about forty million people of direct Celtic extraction, living there, that's a big percentage of people with stories going way back. The memory has traveled through many generations over there, during the past couple hundred years. That's an awful lot of history to not have an influence. All the knowledge and lore those people took with them was connected with the pre-Christian way of life back then. Of course, it's taken hold on another continent, not only in America, but also in other countries like Australia, where the Irish have gone in large numbers. There are more and more people from all over the world, particularly the Americans, coming here and seeing this ancient country with a heritage that goes back thousands of years. A lot of people get flippant about it here, because the tourists run around with their camera's saying "We gotta take a picture" and "The donkey's so cute."

People are getting hoofy and annoyed about that, but then it makes them think, "Hey, this is beautiful . . . this is worth preserving."

m.s. Yes, I know what you mean.

c.n.o But it is almost too romanticized. America, being such a melting pot of cultures, is hungry for a link with something ancient and wise and good. They go for that kind of thing to other corners of the world, too. Look at people going to the East on their spiritual quests, with a yearning to connect and belong to something. I think it's okay. I think it's good, if it focuses people on the beauty that surrounds us and on giving kids a better education. And musically, *Riverdance* and things like that are adding focus and awareness on what Ireland has to offer from its heritage.

m.s. Ireland is the Celtic Tiger, so the Americans who have their roots in Ireland have an new sense of self-esteem.

c.n.o. Celtic whiplash!

m.s. That's hilarious! What does that mean?

c.n.o. That it's just gotten out of hand. That it's been too much.

m.s. Still, the point I'm trying to make here is that Ireland's prosperity is affecting Irish Americans because they used to be the underdogs in

America, with popular racist slogans like "No dogs, and no Irish," "No Irish need apply," and all that kind of stuff.

τ.η.ο. No dogs, no Italians, no blacks, and no Jews, and all that.

η.s. Of course, but the Irish suddenly have a whole shift in their self-esteem because of what Ireland is achieving. If you were an American looking at Ireland ten or fifteen years ago when it was still the poorest country in Europe, there wouldn't be any kind of personal celebration going on for people. Now, it's "Yes! I'm Irish! (Laughter) There is a celebration in the Irish American culture.

τ.η.ο. (Continued laughter) Yes! But, prosperity does that for some people, and not for all, and not for a lot. A lot of young people that are under thirty in the work force are going abroad. A lot of this country's talent is still going abroad.

η.s. But it's always been like that. The intelligentsia left, in droves, in the 17th and 18th centuries.

τ.η.ο. The young people are tuned in, and looking to America. That's the irony. An awful lot are coming back this time.

η.s. Máire Brennan was saying it's just part of the Celtic tradition anyway to be nomadic, they've always been moving around. It's really interesting that we've woven this network of relationships all over the globe.

διSCOGRAPhy

TRÍONA (1972)
(Green Linnet)

With Nightnoise

THE WHITEHORSE SESSIONS
(LIVE) (1996, 1995)
(Windham Hill)
A DIFFERENT SHORE (1995)
(Windham Hill)
NIGHTNOISE:
   WINDHAM HILL RETROSPECTIVE (1992)
(Windham Hill)
SHADOW OF TIME (1993)
(Windham Hill)

THE PARTING TIDE (1990)
(Windham Hill)
AT THE END OF THE EVENING (1988)
(Windham Hill)
SOMETHING OF TIME (1987)
(Windham Hill)
NIGHTNOISE (1984)
(Windham Hill)

With The Bothy Band

THE BOTHY BAND –
LIVE IN CONCERT (1995)
(Green Linnet)
BEST OF THE BOTHY BAND (1983)
(Green Linnet)
AFTER HOURS (LIVE IN PARIS) (1979)
(Green Linnet)

OUT OF THE WIND (1977)
(Green Linnet)
OLD HAG YOU HAVE KILLED ME (1976)
(Green Linnet)
THE BOTHY BAND – 1975 (1975)
(Green Linnet)

With Relativity

GATHERING PLACE (1987)
(Green Linnet)

RELATIVITY (1985)
(Green Linnet)

With Skara Brae

SKARA BRAE (self-titled) (1971)
(Gael Linn)

With Touchstone

JEALOUSY (1983)
(Green Linnet)

TOUCHSTONE (self-titled) (1982)
(Green Linnet)

Nóirín Ní Riain

Biography

A teacher and scholar of Irish music, Nóirín Ní Riain has enchanted the world with her angelic voice. As a young girl growing up in County Cork, Noirin learned many traditional Gaelic songs directly from Pilib O'Laoghaire. She continues to perform these songs in the original sean-nos style as they have been sung for hundreds of years.

In 1979, Nóirín made the first of three important recordings with the choir of Benedictine monks at the Glenstal Abbey in Limerick, Ireland. For many years the monks at Glenstal personally filled orders for these precious works, restricting their distribution but adding to the legend of this voice of an angel.

For the last ten years Nóirín has performed worldwide often in association with international peace efforts. She has recorded seven albums, including CELTIC SOUL (1997) and RIVER OF STARS (1996). Her 1998 CD, GREGORIAN CHANT EXPERIENCES, is accompanied by a book of meditations. Nóirín has also published a collection of Celtic children's songs, *Im Bim Baboo*.

INTERVIEW

MAIRÉID SULLIVAN How are your views of the world at large shaped by your musical career?

NÓIRÍN NÍ RIAIN That question would bring up for me gender and the notion of the balance between the masculine and feminine in all of us. There are different songs for men and women. In our tradition they are very different.

M.S. Tell us about that. That's really interesting

N.N.R. Most of the religious songs, which are my area of research, come from the heart and the head, and come from a very feminine side, for instance, where Mary is looking upon a child that she carried nine months in her womb, her child on the cross, seeing him go to school for the first day . . . a very direct intimate metaphor in the relationship there which seems very soft. That's just in the words. Then if you look in the music, you find that mirrored in the music. So, you've got a lot of repetition, just a small range of the songs where it would seem that the music is very subservient to the words and emotions being expressed. You find if you look at men's songs, the big songs like *Bean duh á ghleanna* and *Sliabh Geal gCua* with the huge range, the music is as important as the song text.

I'm interested in that side of things because of my own identification. I remember the very first sean-nos song I learned was a song from a man called Pilib O'Laoghaire. He was a Cork singer who learned his songs in Waterford. He was a tremendous mentor. He more or less took over from my first teacher and was very much an influence on me. He died in 1976. When I first started learning songs from him, in the beginning it was very much classical music. I was in his choir; he was a famous choirmaster in Cork. He examined me for my leaving certificate (graduation diploma). At that point, when I was eighteen, I had never met him; he just came to examine me, as I was the only student doing music. I intended doing law at UCD at that time. He said, "Not at all. You're going to do music." He was a very powerful and persuasive man. He drove back to my parents, straight in the door and said, "Give her to me. I'll look after her." So he influenced greatly my song journey and he taught me all these wonderful sean-nos songs.

I didn't speak Irish at all. I was educated up in Dundalk and had the usual 'book' Irish – no fluency, and so on. And so he taught me, with no tape recorders at all, just person to person. He taught me 120 songs. He gave all the songs he could remember himself. But there was one I could particularly identify with just immediately. It was almost as if I knew it before; it was in my memory. That was *The Seven Sorrows of Mary*, a song he'd learnt in County Kerry. I kept on asking myself why, why, why do I find this song easier, and I think it was, perhaps, that a woman wrote it. And so it was meant to lie on a woman's body. It's something I haven't done much research on but I very strongly feel that.

I felt it all very strongly again when I came to the music of the 12th-century Abbess, Hildegard Von Bingen. There is something magical about that music. You have to learn it, but once you learn it, you are tapping into a memory there. It's tapping into that wisdom that is the butterfly. That is recovering the wisdom that we lost. That started me on the whole pursuit of women's songs.

I then got interested in the whole debate on women in the Church, the Catholic Church, and the very exciting things that are happening there. Also looking back at the founder of Christianity, I could see that he was surrounded by women. Somewhere along the line, around the second or third century, we lost our place and we shouldn't have. We lost it to the institution, as Church, once patriarchy took over. In the early Church, women were very important. You see that in the iconography that has come down to us. There are no less than six Marys mentioned in the New Testament, who were very dear friends of Christ.

I became interested in women in music and the move from rural culture to urban culture, and what that did to music. The move from rural religion during the penal times, when religion was house based. It then moved back to the Church as institution, during the establishment of the Church in Ireland in the 1870s. Then it lost the domestic intimacy that it had always had. The way we greet people, "Dia dhuit, God be with you." And "Dia's Muire dhuit." It moved back into patriarchy again, into sitting in cold churches, instead of celebrating Mass around the hearth. I am also very interested in the folklore collectors and how so few of the informants were women. The majority of collectors were men, male singers and male contributors. Maybe that's the reason why so few women's songs have been collected and preserved. There is the danger that the pendulum will swing to the other side now and that the whole feminist revival will become brash. Men are slightly wary of women, looking for a balance.

There are work songs, there are dandling songs for keeping the child going when its awake, suantraithe (soontrees) lullabies. The more magic songs (lullabies) are out of time, because you're inducing sleep, and you're affecting different parts of the psyche. Then there are songs for praying, songs for love where you're not just talking about love. You're talking about existence. They show the depth of emotion. Most Irish love songs are about unrequited love. Women turn to song as a healing, as coming to terms with grief. Messages are sent through subtle metaphors. Goltrai would be lamentations, slow songs, and crying. Geantrai would be the happy songs. Suantraithe would be the songs for soothing. These are styles from the harping tradition.

M.S. I understand that the singers stood alone in the old singing tradition.

N.N.R. Absolutely, we don't sing together. There are exceptions like the Keane sisters and the Kilmore Christmas Carol tradition of six men singing, and no women at all. Generally our tradition is solitary. And then there is the tradition that I find very powerful in that the singer would hold on to somebody while singing. It's called "turning a song." You would go in a circular motion, hold somebody else's hand, and while you were actually singing, you would do this circular business, which as we say in Irish to someone " Would you Cas-Ámhrán? " Which means would you "turn a song." It refers to the moves that the older singers did. Now the tradition is practically lost. You would hold on to someone near you and turn hands very slowly.

M.S. What do you think that was for?

N.N.R. I think it was the exchange of energy and that people were in solidarity with you. And so it forms compassion. It's very much what religion was too, a form of solidarity between people.

M.S. Why is it that we need to create solidarity in our intellectual practices? We explain the universe to ourselves and we are happiest when we create solidarity through our explanations. What do you think of that?

N.N.R. I agree, I think it's very powerful actually. There is an initial stage, where you first go through a certain process within yourself before you can identify with solidarity, with other people, otherwise you'll bring your own baggage to that solidarity, or *communitas*, as it's called in Latin. The first prophecy is really your own story. There's an old Gaelic proverb that translates, "my story, everybody's story." It's coming to terms with your own story first of all, and then you're in a position to share the cosmic story. Solidarity is the second stage, and the third is a transcendental one. That's the ultimate preparation that you're heading for, the kingdom. They are the three steps in the ladder of life, really.

M.S. So I guess you could say that first you stand alone, then you stand in community, then you can stand alone in a new way.

N.N.R. Yes, I agree with you. You know we're traveling from the womb to the tomb, acknowledging those three stages.

M.S. So, we have to resolve all our affairs before we can stand alone ultimately, on the most mundane and on the most sacred level.

N.N.R. Yes, that's true, they say the moment we're born is the ultimate time of love, the ultimate time of solitude. You're actually on your own then once the umbilical cord has been cut; there's a real moment of loss. Then in the interim you have all the social interaction with the cosmos.

M.S. How do you approach or utilize your dreams?

η.η.R. I dream very strongly, very vividly every night. I just started writing them down recently. I started listening to them because I see that from the Bible all the major moves were manifested or revealed through dreams. Often it just wasn't a dream for an individual, but a dream for the world. So I see importance in that, and I see in the Roman Catholic tradition, my tradition, that we've lost it. In that context, dreams were always suspect, you didn't listen to them, you didn't see them as signals from the divine.

m.S. I recently heard a well-known journalist say, "Let's not bother interpreting our dreams, but look at how we feel in the dreams." The symbolism is very hard to interpret.

η.η.R. I agree with you entirely, a very interesting point.

m.S. I'd like to bring up something from an earlier conversation, wondering about the history of women in the church, and how you see that as significant today.

η.η.R. This is an important time for women, not just in the Church, but in spirituality, being able to express that very intimate religion which is within us. I'm not saying that men don't have it – we all know the difference between the yin and yang, anima and animus, feminine and masculine. That balance of opposites must be achieved within ourselves. I think that we also have an outlet for expressing that balance through spirituality or when one comes to talking or trying to link the temporal and the divine. So, I think it's a very exciting time for women and what we can access together. I think it's important for female theologians, not feminists, because up until now there haven't been any women writing on theology.

If you look at an issue like communion, for me being able to receive the Eucharist is the pinnacle of companionship, of spirituality, of solidarity with people. It's like sitting down for a meal with people, sitting down with bread and wine, re-enacting the ultimate banquet, and you're also looking forward to that banquet psychologically that will be hopefully on the other side. We connect all that up with companionship; with wine, food, companionship, of which Jesus was the epitome of sharing, of being a charismatic figure. He drank wine with sinners and everybody. It's for everybody; it's the cosmological banquet.

m.S. You're in a sense, re-creating the perspective of the old Celtic Christianity. Are your saying there is a precedent for this celebration, saying we're not going to destroy what we've achieved so far?

η.η.R. Well, no, it's actually being reverent and respectful of what was there initially. All the great religions began with Goddesses, the Earth Mother, the Sky Mother, and all. Historically, it was a Goddess tradition, and then it's taken over in a very clever way by organized religion. As a matter of fact, I think the Roman Catholic Church did as good as anybody else in taking over the pagan gods and integrating them into their beliefs. We still have our four major feasts. I hold that we are all priests and priestesses. When I was seven, I wanted to be a priest, and I used to go in my parents' bedroom every day after school and I'd sing my chants, and I'd give out communion which was little sweets we had to give out to people. I remember coming down the stairs one day and saying to my brother that I wanted to be a priest, and he laughed. He said, "Listen, you can't even be an altar boy!" I was shocked. Then I looked up at the altar, and I saw that there are no women. I never realized that before. At the time, I was really hurt by all that, to find that exclusion.

M.S. Where were you born?

N.N.R. I was born in County Limerick, in a place called Cahcrconlish. Actually I was born near a big stone circle in Loch Gur. It's the oldest inhabited place in Ireland. You can feel it; it's a powerful spot. My parents were living there at the time, and I was conceived and born there, and then at the age of four we moved to Cahcrconlish. My father was a businessman, and my mother was a teacher.

M.S. What do you think about the stone circles and the revival of interest in this aspect of Celtic culture? And the fact that they say the Celts used those places, that they were there long before the Celts came to the islands, but they used them.

N.N.R. Just a few days ago there was a major archeological find on the Hill of Tara. This is the biggest; it's bigger than Stonehenge in England. It's an enormous pre-historic edifice. The problem with places like this is the access. They can't just become public, but you've got barriers all over the place. We should have access to them, and there's got to be reverence there for the soil. They were there so much earlier than we were, and you've got to show respect for that.

M.S. We can tune in to pick up the vibration if there is anything ... to make something of it?

N.N.R. Mairéid, I think touch is very important in our tradition. If you look at holy spaces, holy places, for example, when you go to a holy well, you touch the stone, you touch the tree, you touch the crucifix, and you kiss the cross. It's very much a tactile tradition. You can also go back to the Caf-Ámhrán, the turning song. It's all got to do with touch.

There's a tradition in the Church, where at a certain time you turn and wish the person next to you peace. Now I find that can be horrific because it's enforced. The moment you go into a church you think, "Who am I sitting next to, who?" I think touch can be a very sacred thing, connected with the divine.

M.S. You know it's the pews that do it, standing in straight lines in pews.

N.N.R. Absolutely. That whole thing lacks a sense of ritual, you know, going over the threshold. Going to Mass shouldn't be the same as going to the supermarket, but it is. You need to step over a threshold in order to create a ritual. In a way, going to Mass has become too mundane, too ordinary. We've lost the language, the ritual, and the incense. Even dressing up, I remember in the old days we would all dress up for Mass, and the minute you came home you had to take off your good clothes. We've lost all that ritual, and that's what we miss so much in life.

M.S. There's a new trend now to recreate that kind of thing in your own home. People create little altars, with sacred objects, reminders of things they want to think about, to create a sacred space. I think it's well informed.

N.N.R. I do, too. You know so much happens when you get together like that. There is a group of nine of us here that takes turns going to everybody else's house where we just pick books, theological books, where we pick something light, or something quite profound, and we will meet to discuss it. We find it incredible because we're all strangers.

M.S. That's great, no pre-conceived ideas.

N.N.R. Exactly, and also it helps form a community between us, just over that three hours we spend together. It's a sense of belonging to one another. I suppose going to a concert or theater is another form of ritual. You suddenly find a relationship with the person beside you. For the time that you're actually sitting there, you're laughing together, clapping together … you know … you're putting yourself apart from the rest of society.

M.S. I want to ask you how you prepare for the stage?

N.N.R. I prepare quite deeply, actually. The sound is in your head, but how do you know that sound will actually be there when you open your mouth? For me, in that moment, it's a numinous sound, it's a holy sound. It's a numinous time; it's a time of the spirits, numina meaning holy in the Latin. It's a time of the spirits, a time of the unknown, like Samhain, the time of the underworld. For me before I make a sound, it's a time of the underworld, a time of getting into that state and so I would be trying to call upon that sound, whatever that sound is going to be when you first open your mouth. It could be a totally unpredictable sound that comes out because it's not yours anymore. It's almost as if it's coming from somebody else, or somewhere else. It just doesn't belong to you anymore, you are just the medium; that's the word I'm looking for. You're very much the medium of the sound. I see the role of the artist as a medium. In fact, I think we are all media for other people at other times. That's our role, really, on this soil, on this planet. That would be the discipline I would be trying to call up before an actual performance.

M.S. Then what do you do?

N.N.R. I just let that go then. Jesus Christ said, "For those who want to save their life will lose it and those who lose their life for my sake will save it," from the Gospel of Mark. That means a lot to me. You must save your life; you must save your sound. But, if you keep that sound to yourself, it is lost. So, if you lose your sound, you actually save it. If you give it away, or let it go, more than give it away, you save it. Let it exist, let it be, let it go out, let it fly to wherever it is to go. Not become too overprotective.

M.S. That's a very good instruction. I imagine when you do that, you'd be feeling very tuned in, as in the beginning of a ritual.

N.N.R. And also very humble. Performing is about humility; it is about letting go. It is about being vulnerable to people when you sing, particularly.

M.S. Why do you say "particularly?"

N.N.R. If you play music or if you write a poem, you can distance yourself from it. Singing is a higher form of poetry because you are adding the layer of music onto it. But if you sit down and play the piano for people you can hide behind it, and the notes are going to be there. Whereas when you sing, in that moment of preparation before, the note might not be there. Playing an instrument, you can hide behind it, there is a kind of smoke-screen. I don't mean to take away from the creativity that is involved.

M.S. Let's talk about what the singer is doing. Because you are not hiding, you can't hide. Except that the form of the song gives security.

N.N.R. Yes, it does to a very limited extent, I think. First of all your are talking about choice there. You've got to choose, first of all, the song you are going to sing. For the moment let's say you're not talking about improvising, singing a song in a very unpremeditated way. You've got to choose, first of all, what song you want to sing.

M.S. Do you choose a song to sing before you go up on stage or do you allow the moment to reveal itself?

N.N.R. Always, always. That is the luxury of doing things on your own as an unaccompanied singer. Sometimes, if I am interacting with musicians, I find it very restrictive. That calls out another area of creativity all together. That area of *communitas*, that area or sharing with people; that needs a lot of preparation. I find when I work with a group of musicians, we have to do an awful lot of work together and being together before the sound is right, before something happens. Whereas when you're on your own, you have so much control. It comes back to your own wellbeing at the time that very much dictates what is going to happen at a performance.

Going back to improvising, you have got to decide and you have to be open to the decisions. It happens a lot when you're singing away on your own that something else flashes across your mind, some other song that you might not have sung for years and years and years but you have to sing it. It wants to be sung. I remember, now, that happening very powerfully in Bosnia and Croatia when I sang in the refugee camps there. They were always songs there that came out of my childhood. Songs I had never sung publicly before, songs that I never even knew I knew. Just by being in that situation of terrible despair, by being in a situation where people didn't know what I was saying or singing, but it was almost as if I had to sing particular songs to move people in a particular way. In that kind of circumstance, you can end up being quite a lateral singer, rather than a vertical singer. Do you know what I mean? Calling on an eclectic collection of songs.

To illustrate, I was doing a workshop in Limerick about two years ago, and it was one of those times that I was very heightened by a lot of things going on in my life. I was giving this workshop on spiritual music, and down the back there was a young girl who started to cry, you know, people were giving her tissues and it kept getting worse. I became very much aware that I had to address this woman. So I spoke with her. She said, "I just never thought there was someone else in the world like me. You are exactly like me. I thought I was mad until I met you – all over the shop."

M.S. What a way to meet somebody. "I thought I was mad until I met you." Are you saying that, "all over the shop" means letting yourself sing anything that comes out.

N.N.R. Yes, yes, you can have that luxury when you are singing on your own. It might not even be called singing; for me that is the greatest moment of healing; you can use your voice to heal the mind, the psyche, the soul, and the body.

M.S. Can I ask you how you feel when you are in the studio with headphones on and a microphone in front of you?

N.N.R. Awful! I rarely do it anymore.

M.S. How do you record then?

N.N.R. Acoustically. Most of my recordings have been recorded acoustically.

M.S. How did you do that when, for example, you were working with Paul Winter?

N.N.R. Now Paul was an exception, actually. Although not an exception entirely. What I did was I laid down about thirty tracks for him, for CELTIC SOUL. Which just meant going into his barn, with all these wonderful bats. I had a fear of bats until that particular time when I lived with them for three days. I just sang thirty songs for him, and he, in his own brilliant and inspired way, put the music on them.

M.S. That's a great solution.

N.N.R. Well I'm not able to work any other way. The other rule I have in recording is that I try to sing a song once. Naturally, in all my recordings there have been times when I break down that rule. I believe in that once-off rendition because I become quite empty when recording actually. I feel that I'm hiding behind something. It's like with any of us when we go to a live concert – you can say, I heard this person on tape but it is nothing like he or she is in person. I know the recordings allow things to be spread. But I just feel that the live performance is very powerful. And so, my only way of overcoming that in recording is through doing it acoustically, which means having one microphone and a small dat recorder and doing it once-off, and letting the spirit carry that. I approach the recording with twice, at least, the amount of songs I'll need so that I'm prepared to lose some songs and keep the ones that hit an inspired moment.

M.S. There is a huge circle, now, of very good singers and instrumentalists in the Celtic genre who each have a public profile for their music. What do you think of that? How do you feel about that growth?

D.D.R. I think it's wonderful, the more the merrier. May there be three times as many in six months' time. I think there will be if we encourage one another, if we share and are generous. This is a time for us to be generous and sharing in passing on both the memory that is inherent in each one of us, and also our own experience so that the culture doesn't die. We don't want to go to the grave without sharing. It's like having the opportunity to tell your mother you loved her. It's as important as that. We've got to stick together and we have got to share. I have found people to be very generous in sharing their songs and their stories. It would be much easier not to share, not to talk to people, not to sing. Much easier to hide behind a persona which as an artist you can do so easily. You go in to sing in front of three hundred people and you're out again and you really haven't given anything of yourself because it can be contrived. You can control and manipulate. It's the genuine sharing the truth, that will set us free. I think that is the reason there has been such an explosion. I think this is a time for sharing.

M.S. A circle of people who are going to choose not to compete, who are going to choose to support each other because they prefer that to the old paradigm, which is to compete.

D.D.R. And to be judgmental. The old way is to say, "She sings better than she does. I sing better than her or you. She has more songs. Ah! Sure she's not Irish at all." You know all the awful stuff that people say. Younger people have such energy. My generation was more stand-off-ish, in that we were taught that we should be seen rather than be heard. A group of young people I am working with now has so much energy. The ideas they come up with – for example, they would say, "There is no point in us performing and getting 250 pounds because we'd each end up with two-pence. So, we'll give it to a charity that we will choose. A charity that will be for young people." Ideas like coming up with a logo for the group. They are busy composing poems, songs, and instrumental pieces and sharing them with the group. Helping these young people is universal motherhood. For example, we sang for a Peace Conference here in Dublin on the first of February. The first of February is Brigid's day,

February second is Candlemas, and the third is the feast of St. Blaisé who is the patron saint of singers.

M.S. Tell us about St. Blaisé.

N.N.R. Blaisé was a 4th-century saint; all our throats are blessed here on his feast day, the third day of February. The story of how he got that role as patron saint of the throat has it that one day there was a chicken bone stuck in some young lad's throat and he removed it. And so every February third we all line up in church to get our throats blessed. I am always very careful about whom I will let bless my throat. It always has to be a very special priest. These are three days that are the highlight for me of the whole year. There is a lovely story about Candlemas and St. Brigid. You see Candlemas is the feast of the purification of Mary. There is a legend, then, an old Irish legend, that Mary and Jesus were on their way to Jerusalem and the soldiers stopped them. The myth says that Mary said, "Come on Brigid, help me out." So, Brigid appeared wearing a crown of lighted candles. The soldiers were mesmerized, and while they were looking at Brigid, Mary and Jesus slipped by. Then Mary looked back at Brigid and said to Brigid "Thanks Brigid, from now on your feast day will always be before mine."

DISCOGRAPHY

CELTIC SOUL (1997)

RIVER OF STARS (1996)

SOUNDINGS (1995)

STOR AMHRAN (1995)

THE DARKEST MIDNIGHT (1992)

VOX DE NUBE (1989)

THE VIRGIN'S LAMENT (1980)

Books

Im Bim Baboo (1976) – a collection of children's songs

Stor Amhran (1980) – companion to the CD of the same name

Gregorian Chant Experiences (1998) – a book and CD of meditations

MAURA O'CONNELL

BIOGRAPHY

Maura O'Connell embodies many paradoxes: lead singer for DeDannan, she is not a traditional Celtic singer; resident of Nashville, she is not American; collaborator with New Grass Revival, she is not a bluegrass performer. Nevertheless, O'Connell has made a name for herself on two continents as a superb singer.

Maura O'Connell was born and raised in County Clare, Ireland, where she began singing at an early age. Involvement in the folk club scene led to an invitation from Celtic traditionalists, DeDannan, to join their ranks. Her involvement with DeDannan resulted in the recording of STAR SPANGLED MOLLIE, a clear indication of interest in Trans-Atlantic culture. Maura then began to collaborate with members of New Grass Revival, and in particular with Bela Fleck, who produced several of her tracks. Together with Fleck and others, she recorded JUST IN TIME and made the decision to settle in Nashville, Tennessee. Since then, she has released HELPLESS HEART, BLUE IS THE COLOUR OF HOPE, and REAL LIFE STORY, each album registering a move toward a pop synthesis. STORIES followed in 1995, with WANDERING HOME appearing in 1997.

INTERVIEW

MAIRÉID SULLIVAN   How do you feel about the increasing demand on singers to write their own songs?

MAURA O'CONNELL   I believe there's too much pressure on singers to write their own material. I believe it completely dilutes the quality of the music. It's not just with traditional music. It's across the board. Not every singer needs to write, as not every writer needs to sing. There are very few really talented singer-songwriters out there. I believe the pressure on people to write has been detrimental to the art of writing. The only reason I've emphatically formed my opinion is that one of the questions I am most frequently asked is, "How come you don't write?" or "Do you write?" This assumes that if you're a singer, you automatically have the gift of writing. That's why there's so much poor material out there in the world these days. When I hear a good new song, I am shocked and excited to have found a person that can really write. It's come to the point now where I read the words first. If the words don't make any sense to me, I throw the whole thing out.

M.S.   How do you go about looking for a song?

M.O.   If I'm affected by a song, that's why I will sing it. The song is poetry and music put together. It depends on the style that you like. I like all forms of music if a song moves me, whether it's to joy or sadness.

Sometimes songs can be the most wonderful care-taking things. If I feel taken care of by a song, emotionally, then the listener will surely feel taken care of in the same way. If you're happy and you listen to a particular song, you feel happy. Someone else, who is depressed, may listen to the same song, and feel uplifted from the song. It will take care of their depression. I'm always taken care of, emotionally, by the poetry in the song.

I think, in most parts of the world, with Ireland as an exception, poetry doesn't have the same impact or clout that it used to have. So, as a result, popular music and folk music has taken over, in terms of where religion or poetry would have taken care of the emotional wellbeing.

M.S.   You have done wonderful things with your music over a long career. Have you noticed a change in attitude to singers over your career?

M.O.   In the past, the singers, male and female, never got as much respect as they're getting today. In Irish music, the traditional role for the singer in the session was that when the musicians got tired, the singer came in and sang a song, and, mostly, sang unaccompanied, unless she was very lucky to have someone beside her who played guitar. In ordinary, regular neighborhood entertainment, it's the singer who has the floor. If it's a dancehall or pub setting, it's the traditional musician who's going to be the one that's given the floor.

M.S. Tell us about the development of your identity as a singer.

M.O. My identity as a singer was formed very early on. You know, you just sing, it's not anything special. It's not that you have to feel wonderful about yourself. It was something that you shared with everybody. Like everybody else that grew up in a musical family, I was always amazed that there wasn't music in everybody else's family. As a teenager I was in a boarding school. I don't think a night went by before I became like the jukebox: the girls would say, "Sing this, sing that." It had nothing to do with me going on stage. There is something very different about folk music, and not necessarily Irish folk music. It is that you could have the identity as a singer without earning a penny for it. My mother did that. She was never a professional musician, but she sang in the opera and choirs. When I was growing up, everyone would say, "You're Mamby O'Connell's daughter, you must be a great singer."

My mother and I are from Ennis, in Clare, and my father was from North Cork, a little place called Medford. My dad was more of a traditional person than my mom was. He went to an Irish-language college, and was interested in the Irish language, and loved the ballads. He taught us all that stuff when we were kids.

The combination of both of those cultures is all around Ireland. I was born in 1958, and in the sixties the whole notion of the light opera was in every small town in Ireland. It was a part of our environment. It also includes the parlor song, which is very much a part of what I'm involved with, really, more than the strict traditional singer.

I have a theory: folk music is an ever-evolving form. That's the nature of the beast. It's a cultural mirror, a social mirror of the times. It includes the elements of times past. Classical music, through O'Carolan and others, has graced it as well. It's been influenced by opera, the great Irish tenors, from the late eighteen hundreds up through the nineteen-fifties. My father was a great fan of the opera, and these were all poor people. It's been taking in the forms of the sixties and seventies with the advent of the bouzouki and guitars and basses. If it's not doing that, it's not doing its job. It is now in finite form and it must take in everything around it. I spent a long time trying to disavow the notion of the folk singer. I felt it was too limiting. Then I found my own way to define it, and not to be defined by what the traditional folklorists would consider folk music. I do believe that there has to be some form of touchstone, where you can go and say, okay, this is it in a more pure form.

I think the distance between traditional folk music and contemporary folk music is strange, particularly in Ireland, I would say, although the gap has bridged a lot in the last few years. I wanted *not* to be defined as a folk singer. I wanted to be able to sing songs that appealed to me as a person, as a singer, rather than a particular kind of singer.

It was the right time for me, after the Irish music revolution in the seventies with the advent of Planxty and The Bothy Band. There was almost a paradigm shift during the seventies in the concept of traditional Irish music. Not everybody was raised on traditional music. There were very few traditional musicians in our town. How many times did you hear sean-nos when you were growing up? That's supposed to be the real deal, you know. Unless you went to the Common, or whatever you call it, you wouldn't hear that much ceilildh music, which is what traditional music was considered to be in the fifties. We all turned our backs on it then. When I began my professional career in the early eighties, there were very few Irish women involved in music. They were in the Irish show bands, which were considered a less than glorious deal to be involved in. In fact, it was almost akin to joining the circus.

When I was asked to join DeDannan in October of 1980, to tour with them in America for six weeks, I initially said no. I had no interest at all in traditional Irish music of any kind, in any shape or form. By then, it was ubiquitous. It was everywhere. You couldn't walk ten seconds down the streets of Ennis without hearing it. In every pub there'd be a whistle and ten bodhrans and some God-awful fellow with a guitar singing, "Come all ye." It was dreadful. It was like every half-reared child wanted to be a traditional musician because it was the hip thing at the time. As a singer, I found I didn't have as much interest in the traditional Irish music field because I didn't have a background. I didn't know the traditional singers and I genuinely wasn't interested.

M.S. Why do you think you felt that way?

M.O. As a singer, I've always been interested in the songs rather than the form.

M.S. Did the pub environment put you off?

M.O. I just never liked to be involved in something that everybody was doing. No, it's just that the songs weren't there for me as a singer. Also, I felt a lot of the songs I did hear were melodically limited. And, early on, I didn't know how to find the ones that, eventually, were attractive to me. I would hear songs that I thought were marvelous, that other singers sang, and I'd go, "How did they find that?" Then I'd realize they'd been into the traditional music for a long time and knew the people to talk to. I was a bit of a 'harum scarum', and still am. I'm actually coming back to it now. I made an album a couple of years ago called WANDERING HOME, you know . . . did a bit of making peace with my Celtic roots.

M.S. Having wandered home, what do you think now?

M.O. I never disliked it as itself, it's just that it wasn't something that interested me.

M.S.   I mean, do any of those songs interest you now, the ones that you rejected when you were younger?

M.O.   When I went home to make my record, I did the songs like *Teddy O'Neil*. That's a parlor song. But I did do *Astor Mo Chroî* because I heard the Kane sisters sing that one day, and it was like an old blues song. I finally understood the meaning. It's not everywhere. It's rare to find that beauty, to find that brilliance.

As teenagers, we're all affected by the society around us, and I was determined to be cosmopolitan. Coming from Ireland gave me a great love of poetry and a great love of great lyrics. That's different from the songs themselves. I think it's just an Irish trait. A beautifully turned phrase is just about as magic as having a big load of money. I had two wonderful English teachers in school who really showed me what poetry is. I would say that I was more influenced by my English teachers than I have been by any musical person.

The need to sing is an absolute disease! In the beginning I had no intention of becoming a professional singer. I had been singing with Mike Hanrahan, who later joined Stockton's Wing. I eventually told him I wasn't interested in traditional music and didn't want to be a professional traditional musician. So, after he left Ennis, I found that I didn't have anybody I could bounce ideas off. Mike played the guitar and I sang, and we would meet almost every evening and sit and talk, and play and sing and look at music. I did all of this just for fun, never intending to become a professional musician.

When Frankie Gavin called me and asked me to go to America for six weeks, my first reaction was just to say no, and second, I said, "I don't have any songs to sing for you, thank you very much." So he said, "Think about it, and you can sing whatever you want." Anyway, he called back the following week and I told him I'd go. I thought, hey, "I'll get a trip to America, I'll get to sing in big concert halls, and travel," and that was it. I've been on the road since.

M.S.   What happened when you got to the States? How did it feel to agree to go, and then actually find yourself on the stage?

M.O.   Oh, I was terrified, but the audience reaction was tremendous. My first gig was at the New York Town Hall. I can still see myself at the side of the stage just shaking. By the end of the evening I was fine. There was a lot of hostility back then to adding anything new to the old style. That was 1980, and I went out there singing *Love Has No Pride* and *Louise*. The only thing we put together that was vaguely Irish was a version of *I Walked Out*.

At that time, most of the audiences were Irish-American, and they had an idealized vision of Ireland. It had nothing to do with the reality. It's a lot better now. I got really great press, but I got a lot of bad reactions from the local Irish, which later helped form my notions about being in America. I refused for years and years to play Irish festivals, to go near any kind of Irish venue. It's not because I didn't like them. It was because I didn't want them to think I was something I wasn't.

M.S. How did you make that transition? You've grown up into it now.

M.O. You can rail against anything, but until you do something to change it, you might as well shut up. So, I moved to Dublin and then came to Nashville to make a recording with P. J. Curtis. I never intended to make the record in Nashville. All sorts of things happened to lead us to that. We were just coming over to look at some songs because he knew a lot of people in America, and I had a boyfriend here at the time, so I was anxious to come as well. The bulk of the record was made here, and it was very successful in Ireland.

So, then I got a lift and I went home and ignored that record because I didn't want anyone to think I was a country singer. People would see the word Nashville and say, "Maura O'Connell, country singer," and I'd say, "Oh God!" So, I turned around and ignored that and put together a big soul-revival thing, then I got over that. Soon after, I just stopped reacting to people.

Then I stripped the band down to just Charlie McGettigan and me. The live scene had become terrible in Ireland in the eighties. Musicians were just opening for discos, basically. Charlie and I would just go around and do songs that I liked. Then I built up from there. Arty McGlynn and Nollaig Casey played with me. I was still recording over here, and finally moved here to Nashville in 1986.

The reason I've had trouble with prefixes as a singer is that I'm not any one kind of singer. I am a singer. You can choose to be any kind of singer. If your nature is to sing and to emote those emotions, then they cannot be defined. There just aren't enough songs in each medium for me to be interested in one style. I signed with a major label, Warner Brothers, in 1990. I went through that whole thing and then realized that they, too, wanted me to have some sort of 'label'.

I always recorded songs from every genre in my albums, and I always got asked the questions, "What do you look for? Where do you find them?" Very few human beings, unless they are very closed minded, listen to just one kind of music. Whether they like it or not, they listen to all forms within that one format. If they have country radio on, there are many forms involved. I just wanted to find songs that interested me, not become parts of someone's genre. We are a product of our age, which is an information age. We have access to everything.

My point being, that when I grew up in Ireland, in the sixties and seventies, the radio had 90 percent popular music and 10 percent traditional.

That's the way we are. We are a product of that whether we realize it or not. I think that has broadened my interest in music, introducing me to the blues, and R&B, and folk music from all around the world. As I mentioned before, that is what folk music is. The more influences the society encounters, the more the country benefits. Music is a great leveler. It unites people.

M.S. What do you think is the basis of the artist's power of attraction?

M.O. Ego! Nobody gets up on stage and sings a song unless they think they can sing it better than the audience, or the people that sang the song before. That ego can be nurtured from your past. In my case, everybody encouraged me to sing and to become a singer when I was young.

M.S. You can look back to your earliest memories of singing as a little child, and you might find yourself asking, "Do I sing because people told me I could sing? Why do I love to sing?" Answering that can set you free.

M.O. Yes. I've always thought that I'm blessed to do what I love the best. Songs have become like prayers to people who have found themselves lost or in trouble emotionally. A good song can soothe the savage beast. It goes across the world. It doesn't matter where you're from. Having to do what I love most in the world for a living is the greatest achievement in my life, besides my personal relationships. The very fact that I can continue to do it at this age is the greatest gift there is.

M.S. In the last three years, you've developed a new perspective on your career. What has been the main outcome of that change?

M.O. I've stepped back from pursuing a career, or, I should say, being pursued by a career, and I've realized the joy that I have in performing and playing and coming to a part of my life where I don't have to go out and tour constantly. I'm taking the best step my career has to offer, and really enjoying it. Also, coming to the age of forty, I've found out that I don't have to prove myself to anybody anymore. I'm going to pursue what interests me. Hopefully, the audience will come along with me. They have so far.

M.S. You've established trust with your audience. Once you establish trust, you have to ask them to allow you to go further.

M.O. Exactly!

M.S. You have a child, don't you? You must love being a mother?

M.O. Yes, I do. I have one child, Jesse, who is three. It's amazing! Phenomenal! The best there is, no doubt about it!

DISCOGRAPHY

WANDERING HOME (1997)

STORIES (1995)

BLUE IS THE COLOUR OF HOPE (1992)

REAL LIFE STORY (1991)

HELPLESS HEART (1989)

JUST IN TIME (1988)

Compilations

THE FOLKSCENE COLLECTION (1998)

LIVE AT THE IRON HORSE (1997)

HOLDING UP HALF THE SKY, VOL. 1

    COLLECTION – WOMEN'S VOICE (1997)

TILL THEIR EYES SHINE – LULLABY (1992)

A WOMAN'S HEART –

    WOMAN'S HEART II (1994)

MOUNTAIN STAGE VOL. 2 –

    BEST OF MOUNTAIN STAGE (1991)

SÍOBHÁN PEOPLES

BíOGRAPHY

Born in 1972, Siobhán Peoples is an accomplished fiddle player who regularly performs with her father, the renowned fiddler, Tommy Peoples. Tommy got involved with the world of music in Dublin in the 1960s, where he was a founding member of the ceilidh band, The Green Linnet. In 1969, he married Marie Linnane, the daughter of Kitty Linnane who led the Kilfenora Ceili Band, from County Clare. In the 1970s, Tommy Peoples played with Tríona Ní Dhomhnaill and others in a group called 1691, and then moved on to join The Bothy Band for a short time.

Siobhán sang as a baby, played the piano by the time she was four years old, and has performed at ceilidhs since she was eleven.

Despite a mysterious ache in her hand, Siobhán has continued to play, adapting her technique to ease the pain. She now has two young daughters and spends most of her time teaching and playing locally.

Her music has been featured on five recordings, including CDs with her father, the band Grianán, the Mullagh More album, SOUND OF STONE, and two compilation albums.

INTERVIEW

MAIRÉID SULLIVAN Your father, Tommy Peoples, is one of the most famous fiddlers in Ireland. How old were you when you first played with him?

SIOBHÁN PEOPLES When we moved to Toonagh, between Ennis and Corofin, when I was seven.

M.S. Was he away playing on tour much when you were a little girl?

S.P. Yes, he was, when I was very young. I caught the tail-end of Dad's days with The Bothy Band and was very taken with the reaction they got – what their music did to people and that my dad was part of that. I was so very proud of him and his music – all I wanted to do was emulate all of that. It's funny, even today, I have a longing for the seventies and that music, even though it's a vague recollection.

Playing with my dad and hearing his ornamentation and sweetness and watching his fingers has often brought tears to my eyes. I remember nights at home, when he'd be home from one gig and I'd be home from another, we'd play a well-known tune together and time would stand still. I'd be trying to explain it to people but words were extremely ineffective, and I'd just end up saying, "Jesus, if only you could have been there." Powerful emotions!

M.S. What are your earliest musical memories?

S.P. My mother always said that as a baby I never slept. Some of my earliest memories are of rocking back and forward and singing tunes, not reels and jigs, but rambling airs that could last for hours until I was told, "For the last time, go to sleep." I remember living in my grandparent's house and my grandmother, Kitty, playing the piano. They had a ceilildh band and were always going off to play at gigs, and I suppose I thought that this was all very glamorous and exciting. Pop, my grandfather, would collect Paddy Mullins and they would come back to collect Kitty, my grandmother, and she'd be 'done up to the nines', smelling of powders and perfume, and all the men had suits and they were always laughing and joking. It was a mighty life, to my little eyes. So, I started to mess around on the piano. I would have been three or four, and it was the only instrument that was accessible to me at the time. I was always making up tunes and would play them non-stop, so often that I'd have to ask Kitty if they were real tunes, and she would always laugh and say, "No." I used to spend hours at it.

Later on, when my parents bought our house in Toonagh, my mother came home one day with a tune that Frank Custy, who later became my music mentor and teacher, had written out for me. I was thrilled! My first real tune. I remember someone bringing a whistle into the house, and I used to blow it and pretend I could play it, but I could hear real tunes even when others didn't. I was crazy for music.

We moved to Toonagh in August 1978, and I started school there in September. I had my first whistle lesson that month and I've never looked back. Within weeks Dad had noticed how keen I was. I remember Tola Custy, Frank Custy's son and a beautiful fiddle player, came to my house one day at lunchtime, and Dad taught me the scale on the fiddle. Tola and I were both seven at the time, and I can remember him telling me, "Don't worry about the screeches and stuff, that'll all get better if you practice!" I often laugh now at the little 'old man' that he was that day. So, the five or six tunes that I had on the whistle were quickly transferred onto the fiddle and I rarely played the whistle again. National School, years four through twelve, was, and still is, a beautiful place for me. We learned how to play hundreds of tunes, lots of songs, set dancing, step dancing – buckets of culture.

I got my first fiddle from Frank Custy and I used to carry it in a refuse sack until I got a case. I must have been some sight going up and down to school every day! As I got older I used to try to copy the 'big ones' at school who would be slurring and doing rolls and I felt frustrated that I couldn't do it all. I spent break times in the classroom playing concertina and accordion, banjo and even the snare drum. I have great memories of Fleadhs and concerts and ceilildhs. I loved every minute of it. I remember we got a concertina into the house, which belonged to Eddie Stack at one time, and I was hooked. I played it before school, during school, and after school for weeks. I have always loved the swell from the concertina. But the fiddle remains my 'big thing' and, luckily, I have a flare for it, I suppose. I felt important because I was good at something.

M.S. What kind of music do you like besides the traditional tunes?

S.P. I like old timey bluegrass and jazz, but I wouldn't have the confidence to play it on the fiddle. If it was a big mad session, I'd have a go at it, but I don't feel the music or know it enough. Eamonn Coyne, who plays banjo, used to play a lot of old timey music with me. I really enjoyed playing with him.

M.S. When did you first start playing out in sessions?

S.P. Well, Frank Custy, my teacher, used to bring us out to ceilildhs when we were very young. I used to play with my grandmother, Kitty, and Paddy Mullins on Sunday nights from the age of eleven. I started on two pounds and eventually graduated to being paid five pounds. Sure, I thought I had it made: gigs, money in my pocket, and, most important, I was doing adult things. I couldn't wait to be grown up.

M.S. So you were on the stage playing along with everybody else. That's a great way to learn.

S.P. They used to have events on Friday nights in Toonagh, at a community hall there. There would be set dances and singing and playing.

My secondary school years must have been torture for my mother. While she was trying to get me to study, I was either out playing or playing all evening at home. Around the age of sixteen, I met a crowd of musicians I still love today. We'd meet at Limerick Junction and be off on the train to Dublin. We all loved playing and we would have played anywhere for anyone. There were parties and sessions and trips abroad and weekends here and there. It was an addiction. Music and the craic – lots and lots of craic.

M.S. What kind of music do you play now?

S.P. It's all traditional. I play regularly with John Kelly, a flute player from Roscommon, Pat Marsh, who plays bouzouki, and guitar player Liam Murphy.

M.S. What do you call yourselves?

S.P. We don't have a name. We just get together at regular sessions.

M.S. Have you played on many albums?

S.P. I've been featured on a few Irish collections. I am on one of Dad's, called THE MUSIC OF TOMMY PEOPLES. There was another one with Mullagh More, called THE SOUND OF STONE. I recorded one called MAID OF EIREANN, with Grianán, a group here in Ennis. It's in some shops but was never released internationally.

M.S. Why do you think you were drawn to become a musician?

S.P. I've thought recently, in hindsight, that it was a great way to get attention. I must have liked, also, to gain my dad's approval. And there is no question of who you are when you play. It gives an identity. But I think it was mainly because Dad was away a lot when we were young that I wanted his attention. That also makes you want to work harder at it, I think.

M.S. How has becoming a mother changed your life?

S.P. Part of the beauty of having my two daughters, Eadaoin and Aoimhe, was the realization that I didn't have to be out seven nights a week to truly enjoy myself. I watch them for hours and I learn about the simple things in life from them all the time. They can be grumpy and content, happy and sad, and all these things delight me. Eadaoin's first steps blew me away – realizing that all this time I was spending with them and teaching them was just borrowed time. What'll I be like when they grow up and move out?

Being a mother changed me in a big way – all for the good, I must add. I'm always recommending it to friends of mine. Liam Murphy who has just had his sixth child, said to me, "You just can't describe it but you'll know what I'm talking about when you have yours." How right he was! Don and myself often talk about the two girls and we just end up shaking our heads in awe of it all. And we are two people who decided we were never going to have children!

I must admit I have pictured them with fiddle cases coming with me to a session, but I know I'm not the type to push them into music, still I'll encourage them, a lot!

M.S. Before you had children, you traveled as a headline performer in your own right. Where did your travels take you?

S.P. I did do a lot of traveling and performing when I was younger. But I have young children now, so I don't perform as much as I used to. I went to America and all over Europe, including the Nordic countries.

M.S. How old are you now?

S.P. I'm twenty-seven.

M.S. What was touring like for you?

S.P. Well, it was great. I learned a lot about the different people in each country. When I was in Finland, I had a strange experience. We were traveling around giving concerts and the audience always gave a very polite clap at the end of the concert. We weren't used to that at home. When we were leaving one place, I finally said to the person who was taking care of us that I thought it was a pity the audience didn't enjoy the music more. She said, "God no! They loved it! You got a great reception." That was their idea of 'losing their heads'. I suppose when you come from a mad nation, anything that is more reserved you tend to take personally.

M.S. Why did you decide to become a music teacher?

S.P. When I was about twenty-one, I started to get a pain in my hand that would go away pretty quickly when I played for a few minutes, but eventually it got really bad, and I started to lose the power in my little finger. I was terrified! In denial and with an awful lot of fear that I'd be told to stop playing, I kept at it, pulling all sorts of configurations to knock out tunes. My playing deteriorated badly, but even then I wouldn't, and indeed couldn't, stop playing. I was losing my very identity, everything I had ever dreamed of, and I had no control over it what so ever. A very scary and lonely time in my life! It really challenged my self-esteem and my self-belief. I suppose I thought my friends would have no more use for me if I couldn't play and I would just be 'a nobody'. I eventually hit on the idea of playing with two fingers. With self-acceptance there has been an improvement. It is frustrating though, but not half as much as before.

I went to several people and they could never tell me what it was; only what it wasn't. I focused so much on the problem, and with my friends asking me to get it sorted out, I nearly went mad. So, I decided this is how it is meant to be, and, for now, to hell with it. Because of this injury, I got into teaching full time. After a couple of difficult 'finding my feet' years I have grown to love it.

Nothing can beat the joy of teaching someone a tune and how to play an instrument. It's like I'm passing on everything that I felt, which was very intense, when I discovered the fiddle. I've taught a couple of people who have said that learning the fiddle has changed their lives, and it's a beautiful life. Sharing music and stories and a bit of slagging around the table is an amazing feeling. Having love for people, for no other reason but their music, is an amazing feeling. There's something about the emotion and heart in Irish music, and indeed most music, that fills the soul like nothing else. It never ceases to amaze me how music without words can do such things to me. Every care and worry disappears when I play beautiful tunes that have so much to tell us about ourselves.

Having lost a brother to suicide and Kitty and Pop, my grandparents, all of whom I was very close to, threw me off course a lot. I lost a lot of myself with them and it's only with the birth of my own two daughters, that I've started to recover that part of myself. They are eighteen months and five months and they sit in on classes all the time. Don, my partner, brought Aoimhe to our end of term concert, for about fifty fiddlers, tonight. I was so proud that she was there to hear it. I'm so very proud that I have so much culture to pass on to them. It's something real and priceless in a world that has become obsessed with money and power, so much that people seem to be thrown to the side and forgotten about. For me, I have it all when I have my music; I really don't need anything else when I'm playing. The music is a very big passion. Around here we are so spoilt for it. There is so much music that I don't need to go outside the area to feel fulfilled with the playing. There are so many musicians and so much music around here that you'd never be short of tunes to learn. There are loads of pubs with sessions every night.

M.S.   What kind of pubs? Are they very commercial style places, where the musicians play up on the stage with spotlights on the stage?

S.P.   Oh God! No! They just sit around the table and play, very social like. You can go to a session seven nights a week, anywhere. There are lots of fiddles, lots of accordions and lots of flutes, guitars, and bodhrans. You have the commercial pub culture as well, but not as much, where the line up is usually about three players.

M.S.   Ennis sounds like a lovely place to live.

S.P.   It's a lovely town now. They have done a lot of work on it in the last few years and music has become very popular here. It has its black spots, like every where else. It's expanding at a savage rate.

M.S.   What is the main industry there?

S.P.   Computer components. You see, we are very near to Shannon airport. There are a lot of immigrants here, too, because of the airport, who can't work because they are refugees waiting for political asylum.

M.S.   There must be a lot of new nationalities there now.

S.P.   Over the last couple of years there has been a big influx. We have our first Indian restaurant. A local fellow owns it but the chefs are Indian. I am partial to Indian food. We have a lot of good Chinese restaurants with Chinese chefs too.

I wouldn't be fully sure where a lot of the immigrants come from. We had a lot of Cubans at one stage. They all just hang around the town while they are waiting for their papers to be processed. I've seen all kinds of foreigners dancing sets and listening to the music. They try to integrate themselves. There is a population of about twenty thousand here, I'd say. You'd still know all the newcomers to see them.

M.S. What is the local attitude to the growing prosperity? How are the older locals feeling about the change of life there?

S.P. Well, Ennis is a boomtown at the moment and everyone is making the most of it. The people here are pretty easy going, you know. They wouldn't be put out about it. Ennis, seven or eight years ago, was pretty much a dead town. Now you could go out seven nights a week and hit the nightclubs for dancing. There are three or four nightclubs for dancing. There are plenty of places to go for the craic after a session, to continue it on.

M.S. It is amazing what has been happening in Ireland over the last decade. The music is so popular.

S.P. It's like anything else in Ireland: it has to become popular somewhere else before an interest is taken in it here at home. They say that about all our rock groups, too. I just think the Irish in general have a shortage of self-belief, but that is changing now.

M.S. Do you see yourself coming back to playing music professionally when your children have grown up?

S.P. I couldn't ever see myself giving it up. I don't think I will change my focus much even when they are older. It's hard to say now, but I don't think I'd get into traveling too much again, maybe the odd trips away.

M.S. Do you improvise at all? Have you played with musicians who are playing rock music or world music variations and different styles besides the traditional tunes?

S.P. Well, I would have tried, but it is something I wouldn't have the confidence to do. You get so used to hearing Irish music played by people who obviously don't listen to it. It's like jazz. You really need to understand it to be able to play it. The traditional music has really stood the test of time. As for the future of Irish music and where it stands right now, I don't think that the essence of it has changed a bit. The music has changed a lot over the years and it has become a world-wide music now. But its still all about caring and sharing, for me anyway. It's still about making friends and swapping tunes, having the odd argument and stirring and lifting emotions. I hope that never changes, and the way things are looking, Irish music will boom for a long time, and when I'm older, I'll probably be giving out about the younger musicians, but I'll still play with them. It's just a part of life.

Discography

With Grianán

MAID OF EIREANN (1992)

With Music of Mullagh More

SOUND OF STONE (1991)

With Tommy Peoples

THE MUSIC OF TOMMY PEOPLES (1989)

Compilations

THE IRISH FOLK FESTIVAL (1993)
(Harvest Storm)

THE SANCTUARY SESSIONS (1992)
(Cruises)

Website (her father's site): http://homepage.tinet.ie/~logo/tommy.htm

MADDY PRYOR

BIOGRAPHY

A dedicated and thoroughly professional performer who worked as a roadie for Rev. Gary Davis during the 1960s folk scene, Maddy Pryor went on to form a successful duo with the traditionalist Tim Hart before both were absorbed into Steeleye Span in 1969. When Steeleye Span disbanded in 1978, she signed to Chrysalis and launched her solo career with WOMAN IN THE WINGS and CHANGING WINDS. Both albums contained several 'historical ballads' written by Pryor herself. During the 1980s, she also sang with the re-formed Steeleye Span. Her songs became more intimate and rootsy, and, with her backing group, the Answers, she recorded the pop album GOING FOR GLORY, which included work with the Eurythmics and Rick Kemp's impressive *Deep In The Darkest Night*. In 1984, a broadcast with the early music specialists the Carnival Band led to three mutual albums of richly varied music and annual tours. With Rick Kemp (her husband), she recorded HAPPY FAMILIES, a loose, swinging album, featuring his guitar playing.

Maddy Pryor has become a folk singing legend with her own show on BBC Radio 2, *In Good Voice*. Pryor remains one of the most diverse characters on the folk scene both as a solo artist and with the excellent Carnival Band. FLESH AND BLOOD, released in 1997, was possibly her finest album. Not only has her voice gained an edge of grit but also the choice of material was exemplary. The high point is the final track, *Heart Of Stone*, a masterpiece of considerable lyrical depth.

INTERVIEW

MAIRÉID SULLIVAN Do you have any opinions you've developed while you've been watching this whole resurgence of women's freedom and Celtic music, Maddy?

MADDY PRYOR These things tend to come attached to specific issues. It's interesting that in England at the moment there's a big move away from 'British' and towards 'English' as there has also been a move to Celtic. Obviously, the breakup of the Empire, etc. is a big part of that.

I've always considered myself English rather than British, but it's almost like there isn't any 'British' anymore. It's interesting how we've got the revolutions in Scotland and Wales, and the problems in Northern Ireland. I don't think the English have quite focused themselves on where we sit in all this because we've been British for so long and have spent our energies on that. Therefore, it's quite interesting to see the great rise in Celtic. I've always known a lot of Irish people and always known a lot of Irish music. That's always been a part of what I've been interested in. Welsh less so because there is less Welsh music available.

M.S. I know, I've had trouble finding Welsh songs. It's hard to find a Welsh song in English. It's surprising, since they are such great singers.

M.P. There are some Welsh-English songs, whereas there are quite a lot of Irish-English songs.

M.S. There's a lot of talk about the Glastonbury Tor, the crop circles, and everything; they're all happening in England. They talk about England being one of the important global magnetic centers.

M.P. At lot of it has to do with the Pagans. The pagan idea is based a lot on the Celtic Pagans, and yet there seems to be more interest in England, as you say. I've been reading a lot about the Celts lately. It's interesting that there are no real separation lines in England. It's so mixed; you have to look at the names of the places. If you try to find clarity in it, it gets ridiculous, you can't. I think of myself as English, but there's no way I can really say. I've got relatives called Henderson, which is Scottish; my grandparents are Hendersons, so you see there is no purity here. (Laughs) It's quite interesting, this urge to find the purity, which certainly exists.

M.S. Maybe the end result will be, hey, forget it! That might be healthy. You have to laugh!

M.P. Exactly, there is an urge to find one's roots and a place of belonging. Somehow the world is not enough. We think we want something more local. I do like the idea of English. I don't know why that should be. We have these issues about becoming part of Europe. It's a very bizarre discussion. Some people are very adamant about it. It depends on which grouping you're talking about.

M.S. It's like discussing the various categories of jazz; it seems to go on forever.

M.P. Yes, and like Celtic music, too. As I say, I've done some Celtic songs, but we haven't differentiated them in that way before. It's quite a recent thing. I always thought of them as songs of the British Isles, but having worked with Irish people, they don't think of it that way at all. So that kind of threw me a bit with the songs. It gets more complicated. I have to think, "Now what do I sing, how am I defining this anyway? Why am I defining it? What's the urge to define it?"

M.S. Actually, that's an interesting question in itself, because when you say, "Oh, that's a traditional song," suddenly you realize that it's got more implications than you ever thought. It might help if we thought of an example. You're working on a new album right now. Are there any traditional songs on that?

M.P. Oh yes, *Twankydillo* is a good one. That's English. It's a song I've known forever. Well, ever since I've been involved with the revival. All the people I know are revivalists; we're non-traditional. I think there are very few traditional singers.

M.S. I want to talk about that, too, in a minute. Carry on about *Twankydillo*, first.

M.P. *Twankydillo* is a quintessential English song. It's got a lovely melody. It's more chorus than verse. I think it's from the Cooper family of Rottingdean. They are a traditional singing family with hand-written books of songs that go back several generations. Anyway, I thought, "I can't sing a song called *Twankydillo*. It sounds ridiculous." In England we have a theatrical tradition called pantomime. At Christmas we have these slapstick plays, mainly for children, such as Aladdin. One of the characters in that is called Widow Twanky, and she is a dame. A dame, in pantomime, is a man dressed as a woman, and a very unattractive person. The ugly sisters in Cinderella would be dames. It's a very particular tradition that began in France. Then I discovered that Twanky is an old English slang for gin. Now, that completely changed the meaning of the song for me. The English find their own tradition really hard to cope with. We laugh at it.

M.S. It is very funny; it is very much like a caricature, isn't it?

M.P. It is. We have a very strange slant on things. There's no doubt about it. We're not at all like the Scots.

M.S. No wonder Monty Python happened.

M.P. Absolutely, The Scots do not have that humor, they're much straighter. The English are more bizarre. So the song is great. It brings up all the old English inhibitions. The English people find the song very embarrassing now.

M.S. How?

M.P. They would think the song silly, and yet we have an incredibly silly sense of humor as well. There's another song we're doing called *Rigs of the Time*. It was a topical song of tradesmen diddling or cheating customers. So, I just updated it.

M.S. You've touched on something I haven't heard anybody discuss before, and that's the bizarre sense of humor that has come out of England. The English language is made up of so many different influences. In a sense, you've got a new culture that's made up of all those cultures.

M.P. Latin and French are very fundamental, and of course Scandinavian. So the language is based on all those combinations. All languages have a lot of slang, but there is a lot of slang in English. We have all sorts of backward slang, and I don't know if other languages do that, and rhyming slang and all these different kinds of things we do.

M.S. You just mentioned before that you were a revivalist, not a traditionalist. What does that mean to you?

M.P. Just that I was involved with the revival of the music. I didn't learn it on my mother's knee. My father did teach me some songs from the Northeast. I just thought of them as everyone does who has a tradition. I just thought of them as the songs my father sang, and dismissed them consequently. It was the Music Hall side of the tradition, the more popular side. I just never thought of it that way, I just thought of them as the songs my dad sang.

M.S. Back in the late eighties, a lot of women were coming out to perform professionally, as musicians. What a wonderful time it was.

M.P. It's funny how there was a big movement for women to play instruments. When I began, it was quite rare for a woman to play an instrument professionally. We all sang. That's what girls did. Like June Tabor, I am not an instrumentalist. For singers, our musical intelligence comes in a much more portable form. It's very interesting to see that more girls have chosen to play instruments. I always thought of it as more technical, and it suited me more to be a singer. I've always been very impressed by instrumentalists, and the girls, coming into that area, have had a very positive influence on band life. Not that I ever found any problem with being a girl in a band, to be honest. I always got the feeling that everybody had the same problems. The gender thing has never been a big issue for me. I've been too aware of the problems of the blokes to feel that I was having a hard time anymore than anybody else. (Laughs)

M.S.   There has been a clichéd attitude towards a woman having children and having to pull out of the music business. It's not a cliché; it's the fact. It's very hard to stay in there when you have children. Then, back in our parent's generation, by the time your children grew up, you wouldn't allow yourself on stage. However, today everything is different. Most women I know who have strong careers are in their forties now, and they don't even think twice about it. They certainly don't let that stop them from pursuing their musical interests.

M.P.   It's hard to do. You have to have support from the family to survive it. It's very difficult to sustain.

M.S.   Do you have children?

M.P.   Yes, I've got two children: Alex is eighteen, and Rose is fourteen. Alex would travel with us when the band was on tour. I don't know with kids what works and what doesn't. This image that one has about staying at home – would things be different? For me, it would have been the same.

M.S.   What are your most obsessive thoughts? What are you most interested in?

M.P.   I don't think I'm that obsessive, but there is always a new dimension to realize. It probably applies to everything that people are interested in. I remember hearing that Churchill said he loved to be writing a book because it was somewhere to go. It was something that you always had to be doing. It's like the thing that's going on in the back of your mind all the time. You think, "Oh! I can go and do that." You get a good idea and if fires you up with enthusiasm. I do it with traditional music, history, and I've been doing a project on ravens for the past six months or so. It's a long piece called *In the Company of Ravens* that's going to be on the new album. We're mixing it at the moment. It's a series of six segments. I like to do these long pieces. It was actually instigated because they wanted music for a television program. I did one earlier, with a director, about hares. When he came to the ravens, he thought it would be nice to do it again. I've ventured into movement and visuals, which, as you can imagine with ravens, is fairly weird. It's taking people by surprise. But all in all, I'm really enjoying myself.

I was on my way to a concert with Jackie McShee of Pentangle – we recently toured together – and I overheard someone say, "I wonder what Maddy Pryor's got in store for us tonight?" I wander off on these ideas and I always think everybody else is following me. It's kind of filtering through now that the work I do is a bit off the wall. The great thing about traditional music is that you have so much depth. You get the big ballads with all the archetypal stuff. We could go on about that for hours. I've been so lucky that I just fell into this.

M.S. What happened to pull you there?

M.P. Well, it was a couple of Americans. I was traveling around with them singing American songs. That was in the mid-sixties, just as I was leaving school. They said, "Sing British songs!" At the time, the only folk songs I knew were ones I'd learnt in school, and nobody sings songs they've learnt in school. They said they had loads of tapes. I thought, "Well it all sound a bit bloomin' dull to me," and I thought these people sounded incredibly old. Then I started listening. They sort of, more or less, forced me to listen. They would say, "Here's a great song, have a go at that." At school I'd been terribly anti-history, I thought it was really old and irrelevant. I soon found more and more relevance in it, and I eventually became hooked. It's given me so much. You couldn't go in a nicer direction. You can use as much intellect as you want and you can dump it when you want. It's not an academic discussion. It's been a lovely avenue to travel in life because all of life is in traditional music. The humor, the tragedy, all the different aspects. What's interesting now is that there are no limitations.

DISCOGRAPHY

MEMENTO:

   THE BEST OF MADDY PRYOR (1995)

GOING FOR GLORY (1983)

HOOKED ON WINNING (1981)

WOMAN IN THE WINGS (1978)

CHANGING WINDS (1978)

With Steeleye Span

STACK OF STEELEYE SPAN (1999)

TIME (1996)

TONIGHT'S THE NIGHT LIVE (1992)

HARK! THE VILLAGE WAIT (1991)

BACK IN LINE (1986)

STORM FORCE 10 (1977)

ORIGINAL MASTERS (1977)

ROCKET COTTAGE (1976)

COMMONERS CROWN (1975)

NOW WE ARE SIX (1974)

PARCEL OF ROGUES (1973)

LIVE AT LAST

PLEASE TO SEE THE KING

ALL AROUND MY HAT

TEN MAN MOP

BELOW THE SALT

TEMPTED & TRIED

SAILS OF SILVER

BEST OF

HARK THE VILLAGE WAIT

   with Gay Woods

HILLS OF GREENMORE (AN ANTHOLOGY)

celtic women

With June Tabor

NO MORE TO THE DANCE (1988)   SILLY SISTERS (1987)

With Rick Kemp

HAPPY FAMILIES (1991)

With Tim Hart

SUMMER SOLSTICE (1991)   FOLK SONGS OF OLDE ENGLAND V.2
FOLK SONGS OF OLDE ENGLAND V.1

With The Carnival Band

FLESH AND BLOOD (1997)   HAPPY FAMILIES (1990)
HANG UP SORROW AND CARE (1996)   SING LUSTILY &
YEAR (1993)   WITH GOOD COURAGE (1986)
CAROLS & CAPERS (1991)   TAPESTRY OF CAROLS (1986)

BONNIE RIDEOUT

BIOGRAPHY

Bonnie Rideout was born December 18, 1962. One of the finest and most fiery Scottish fiddlers of our time, Bonnie is a showstopper, scholar, and three-time U.S. National Scottish Fiddle Champion who is known as "the piping fiddler" for her evocative renditions of Highland bagpipe music. She performs throughout North America and Europe and is a sanctioned Scottish F.I.R.F. teacher and adjudicator for Scottish festivals throughout the U.S. She was invited to present 18th-century and Highland fiddle styles at the Edinburgh International Festival '96, the first American ever so honored.

While searching for hidden Christmas presents in her mother's closet, Bonnie came upon a dusty, black, oblong-shaped cardboard box. The old violin resting inside became her first love. She received her formal violin training in Michigan, playing in public school orchestras and youth symphonies with private violin instruction at the University of Michigan. She began college as a viola major but returned to the violin to finish her music and fine arts degrees. At the time she knew nothing of the folk world but had happy memories of music making at home. It was the playing of renowned Scottish fiddler Dr John Turner that opened a 'new world' to her.

During the past ten years Bonnie has immersed herself in the music of her ancestral Scotland. She has lived and worked in Scotland, fusing the traditions of her Scottish-American upbringing with those of the old country. She played with numerous strathspey and reel societies in Scotland and learned the different styles of fiddling from such greats as Ron Gonnella, Bill Hardie, and Angus Cameron.

She records for the Maggie's Music label. Bonnie is a mother of three, who currently lives with her husband in Alexandria, Virginia.

interview

mairéid sullivan   Do you have any advice you would like to share with upcoming musicians who might be interested in traditional music?
Bonnie Rideout   I guess this will sound like I'm an old curmudgeon, but this is what I try to mention to young people playing music. Although traditional music is an ever-evolving art form, one should remain conscious and respectful of the existing and timeless indigenous qualities of ethnic music. It is enjoyable to fuse traditions and create new music, but it is extremely important to honor and try to understand the origins of a musical genre. The stylistic influences on folk music in the past were usually dictated by family members or other admired performers, and not from the pressures of trendy record labels. It is easy to lose perspective. Traditional music is entering a vast market-place and undergoing influences dictated by larger economic and social fads from a predominantly shallow music industry. We are a society concerned with the extinction of our wildlife and indigenous people. I am also concerned for the extinction of Scottish fiddle music, as I know it.
m.s.   Tell us about your own philosophy in life?
B.R.   The most difficult part of my life, whether raising children or playing music, is to stay in touch with my principles, maintain a balance, and constantly strive for simplicity . . . and to achieve all of this with good humor.
m.s.   What are some of your favorite traditional tunes?
B.R.   I love the old Gaelic melodies from Scotland's Highlands and Western Isles. The mouth music for dancing and working and the songs which provide emotional comfort, whether in a lullaby or the caoine (lamentation) over a deceased loved one – all this is present in both my every-day life and in my fiddle playing. I think it is splendid that so many exquisitely beautiful melodies were formed around such simple tasks as milking, building fires, preparing wool, and howking tatties.
m.s.   Can you tell us what you have gained from some of your travel experiences?
B.R.   Well, just recently, I embarked on a trip into the remote areas of

the Copan region in Honduras, Central America. My husband, Jesus, has many family members still living in the forests not too distant from the famous Mayan Ruinas de Copan. The earthen floored single-room dwellings filled with the aroma of open fires and the sounds of women singing brought me back to my days living on the Isle of Skye. In Scotland, my home, Somerled flat, was situated above the Clan Donald Centre's museum at Armadale Castle, overlooking the Sound of Sleat to the east and the beautiful Highlands of the western coast of Scotland. All day I could hear the recorded voices of Skye folk singing from days past. One of my favorites, which I recorded on KINDRED SPIRITS, was a milking song. The tradition of singing to the cow, often with soothing incantations, kept the animal safe from evil and also presented a reassuring atmosphere for the production of pure and plentiful milk. Much to the delight and amusement of my Honduran aunt, I sang each morning whilst milking her cow. It worked miracles, supplying another half pail-full for our labors! Often when I arise in the morning, I smile at the thought of Tia Carmen, an elderly Mayan lassie, humming a wee Gaelic melody to her contented cow in the misty mountainside dawn.

M.S. Do you compose music?

B.R. Yes. I write a lot of fiddle music. What comes naturally to me are simple melodies in the old tradition. The music from the 18th-century Patrick MacDonald Collection seems to have influenced my subconscious for the past decade, especially in my slow airs. I often try my new tunes out on my mom and dad. I grew up with no television, and our family spent many nights playing music together. My mother has played piano with me on several of my recordings. My father can be brutally frank with his opinion as to which tunes have merit and what "sounds like rubbish." I embrace their feedback and the opinions of my bandmates, especially when it comes to tunes that I think I have written, but perhaps could have picked up at a session, forgotten about, and then resurfaced. I'll play my tune for different musicians and ask; "Do you know this one?" When enough people say no, then I am content that my brain hasn't played any tricks on me.

M.S. What are some of your other interests?

B.R. Gardening, sailing, painting, mountain climbing, comfortable and honest discourse, and music making with friends and family, this is what especially makes the world a happy place for me. Having grown up in a rural setting, living with nature is essential to my well being. My husband and three young children are my greatest blessings.

M.S. Why do you think you chose a musical career?

B.R. Other than a short love affair with the vision of becoming a country vet, I have always wanted to be a musician. In addition to music, I have a degree in fine art. I have published my illustrations in the past, and hope to continue. It is a quieter discipline with no group rehearsals, just solitary practice. I like that too.

M.S. Tell us how you came to your own musical style?

B.R. I like to leave it to others to analyze my fiddling 'style'. People often tell me that they want to pick up my style or that they recognize my playing on the radio or on a recording. I really don't know what makes me different. I just play. I can't describe my playing any more than I can describe the scent of my favorite old sweater.

M.S. Who are your mentors?

B.R. Dr John Purser is a well-known authority on Scotland's music. He is a great friend and inspiration to me. In my youth, I stayed a few weeks each summer with a well-known fiddler named Ron Gonnella in Creiff, Scotland. His playing of jigs was so light and beautiful. I also lived and worked on a farm outside of Forfar in the Northeast. The farmer was Jim Falconer, a jolly man who played the fiddle and had definite sensibilities about the Northeast style of fiddling. He and his wife entered me into several competitions and I went with Jim each Thursday night to play in the Angus Strathspey and Reel Society. I have enjoyed listening to and playing with the "granddads" of fiddling like Burt Murray, Angus Cameron, Arthur Scott Robertson, Charlie Gore, Bill and Alastair Hardie, John Turner, and, of course, my favorite Cape Breton fiddler, Buddy MacMaster. Playing fiddle in Scotland back then was different than today. For many miles, I think I was only one of two female fiddlers. Almost twenty years ago the average age of a fiddler must have been seventy years old. Session playing was rare. This has all changed now. There are so many young fiddlers playing on both sides of the Atlantic. I think there has been a real renaissance over the past decade, not just in Scottish fiddling, but in many forms of fiddling.

M.S. Did you get a special 'big break' as a professional musician?

B.R. I'm not sure if I have had a big break, except maybe when I stopped having babies. Performing in the Edinburgh International Festival was fun and exciting. I played two concerts representing the fiddle music of 18th-century Scotland and the fiddling from the Highlands and Western Isles. I met many fiddlers and was reunited with others whom I had not seen in years.

When it comes to 'success', I have a famous quote by Ralph Waldo Emerson pasted to the inside of my fiddle case which I read every day: "To laugh often and much; to win the respect of intelligent people and affection of children; to earn the appreciation of honest critics and endure the betrayal of false friends; to appreciate beauty, to find the best in others; to leave the world a bit better, whether by a healthy child, a garden patch, or a redeemed social condition, to know even one life has breathed easier because I have lived. This is to have succeeded."

M.S.   Do you like touring? What kinds of venues do you prefer?

B.R.   I love touring. My favorite venues are restored theaters. They are peppered all over the U.S. They are very beautiful, intimate, filled with enthusiastic audiences, and managed by some of the most interesting and fun people I have met on the circuit.

M.S.   What do you feel about live performance? How do you prepare?

B.R.   I always get very nervous. Besides breathing deeply, I manage to get through it by not thinking about it. I hate making mistakes in front of people. My attitude has been shifted a bit by my husband's healthy perspective: "You are just another part of someone's enjoyable evening. They will be much harder on a chef that messes up their dinner than when you play a few bum notes!"

M.S.   How do you feel about playing in the recording studio?

B.R.   I love it. What a breeze to be able to fix things. Sometimes when I create a 'successful' album, I worry that I won't be able to do it again . . . that it was somehow a fluke. Beginning a recording career is almost as bad as dating: what if I'm so egregiously flawed that I come off as a big disaster! Thankfully, I now feel my music-making is in a stable relationship where I can express my weaknesses and explore endless nuance and possibility.

M.S.   How does playing with contemporary artists from different musical genres influence your playing style?

B.R.   I don't think being exposed to other musical genres has affected my style of playing. It would take a lot to change the sound and style of my fiddling since it goes back so far and deep in my childhood. This is concerning the music that I record on my solo albums. Not so with all the other studio projects I do. I just finished playing on the documentary *Africans in America* where I played a sort of bluesy fiddle lament with Bernice Johnson Reagon. Last month I produced a show entitled *Celtino* at the National Geographic Society here in Washington, D.C. We raised enough money to build a dozen schools, which were destroyed by hurricane Mitch. It was great fun exploring the commonalities of Celtic and Latin music with a lot of great musicians. There is no music that I don't like, but my influences and inspirations come from within, so any changes in my personal playing will be very slow in developing.

discography

GI'ME ELBOW ROOM (1998)
(Maggie's Music)
KINDRED SPIRITS (1996)
(Maggie's Music)

CELTIC CIRCLES (1994)
(Maggie's Music)
SOFT MAY MORN (1994)
(Maggie's Music)

In Ensemble

CELTIC ROOTS, HESPERUS (1999)
(Maggie's Music)
A SCOTTISH CHRISTMAS (1996)
(Maggie's Music)

MUSIC IN THE GREAT HALL (1993)
(Maggie's Music)

Website: http://www.maggiesmusic.com/mmbr.html

jeaN RitchiE

BioGRAphy

Jean Ritchie was born and raised in Viper, Kentucky in the heart of the Southern Appalachian Mountains, the youngest of fourteen children. Walled in by the rugged Cumberland ridges, the Ritchies and their neighbors farmed and entertained themselves with play-party games and ballads handed down through the generations from their Scottish, English, and Irish ancestors.

Remarkably, Jean became the first person to enroll and obtain a degree in social work from the University of Kentucky, then moved in 1947 to New York to work in the famous Henry Street Settlement.

By 1950, Jean Ritchie was an important figure on the New York folk scene, and today she is credited with almost single-handedly reviving interest in the mountain dulcimer. As Jean's reputation grew, Oxford University Press encouraged her to begin working on a book about her family and its music. *Singing Family of the Cumberlands* was published in 1955, and nine more books have followed, including the prizewinning *Celebration of Life*.

She was the first artist to record on Elektra Records with the 10-inch LP JEAN RITCHIE, SINGING TRADITIONAL SONGS OF HER KENTUCKY MOUNTAIN FAMILY. Since then, she has recorded more than 30 albums for different labels, including her own Greenhays label, which she set up with her husband

George in 1979 to assure availability of her records.

While the folk movement peaked in the 1960s, she still finds herself often in demand to perform in folk festivals, to guest lecture at such places as the University of California, Santa Cruz, or to serve as artist-in-residence, as she did at California State University, Fresno. She led 180,000 people in singing *Amazing Grace* for Pope John Paul II in Washington, and the Kentucky Network honored her with a program about her life and music, *Mountain Born: The Jean Ritchie Story.*

As to why she sings traditional music, she says it best: "I believe that old songs have things to say to the modern generation, and that's why they've stayed around. That's also why I am still singing. I'm not afraid to be myself. Agents say you have to change and grow, but I believe you can sing the same songs and sing them better and grow new songs out of the old. I guess if I had to categorize myself or pin down a description of what I do, I'd have to say I'm a carrier of tradition."

INTERVIEW

MAIRÉID SULLIVAN When you went to England and Ireland in 1952-53 to trace the traditional songs, how did you find out which people to talk to when you got there? You found some very obscure people.

JEAN RITCHIE On this end, I knew Douglas and Helen Kennedy from the Cecil Sharp House, the folklore people. They came over to the summer camp at Pine Woods, in Massachusetts. I was there, and we met and became good friends. When we wanted to go over and do our Fullbright Scholarship tour, they gave us names. Their son, Peter Kennedy, and Seamus Ennis had been working together collecting throughout Ireland and England and Scotland for the BBC Archives. Went we went to London, we became good friends with Seamus and Peter, and they gave us names of all the people they visited. Some were very obscure, and they led us to other people that Ennis and Kennedy had not seen. We had a great time because they were all such great people.

M.S. I'm doing something similar right now, with this project. I'm meeting so many wonderful women, singers, and instrumentalists. I've been promised lots of cups of tea, and lots of people said they will pull the chair out for me when I get back there. It's thrilling.

J.R. We did that; we had all that happen. We were there before the folk revival. When we interviewed Jimmy MacBeth, and Jeanie Robertson, and all the other people, they were still singing the old slow style. And even the Clancys on this end; we met Tom and Paddy, and they were not singing at all, they were acting. When they did sing, they sang in the old slow way. It wasn't until they began their stage career that they became more aggressive in their singing. They didn't bother to sing exciting songs in the old days. The songs themselves, the words, were exciting.

M.S. That's an important thing to say. Most of the singers I've talked to say they prefer to sing the old slow airs. Because they have to go onstage, they feel they have to get some up-tempo songs.

J.R. That's right, you have to become 'stage Irish' or you don't survive.

M.S. There you go. You're putting your finger right on it.

J.R. That's really the reason I never got to be a household word in this country, which is something I never strove for anyway. I didn't want it. I want to be the way I am, and I want to sing the way I sing.

M.S. Now why do you want to do that? Tell me about that.

J.R. Because that's the way I feel. I don't crave that kind of thing. I guess one of the reasons is that I've never had to earn a living with music. I got married in my twenties to a photographer, George Pickow, and he's always been able to support me, so my music is more of a hobby. It's what I want to do. It's something that I love, and I don't want to go out and commercialize it.

M.S. I was really fascinated to see that you have established the Ritchie/Pickow archive in the city of Galway.

J.R. Yes. What a grand thing to happen in our 'senior years'. In that year, 1952-53, when I got the Fullbright Scholarship, George went along for the trip. He was a photographer. He set up several interviews before we went over. So we both had our projects, and being not long married, it was fun to be working together.

M.S. That was very good fortune that he is a photographer.

J.R. We went around and saw all the singers. In addition to recording them, he was able to photograph them in their homes, giving depth to the music.

Not long ago, we met Dáibhí O'Cronin, who is from Galway. He teaches there at the university. One of the people we collected from, all those years ago, was his grandmother, Elizabeth Cronin. She didn't use the "O," just Cronin. Since he's a professor and teaches and speaks Gaelic, he's taken up the old ways. Anyway, he started writing to me about his grandmother. He was writing a book about her and he heard that we had photographed her, and had tapes etc. etc. So he came over, and we showed him what we had, and he was thrilled with the quality of the pictures and the quality of the recordings. Back in 1952, we had one of the first portable recorders of good quality. It was very heavy. We recorded and photographed singers all over Ireland, and England, and Scotland. Dáibhí was able to interest the people at his university. They wanted to have all our material for their library. They bought all our Irish pictures and tapes and now they have a traveling archive of Ireland in the fifties.

M.S. You must be very excited about that!

J.R. Yes! We've had some wonderful trips to Ireland, and it is marvelous that our work is preserved in that way. We were hoping that the Scots would also be interested in our Scottish collections. There's a new project started up there, in Aberdeen, but it's not quite on its feet yet.

M.S. About ten years ago, the Glasgow government became very interested in cultural tourism. Glasgow is now one of the top six cultural centers in Europe because the government decided to focus their economic growth on their cultural assets. The Irish did the same thing at about the same time, during the late eighties when the big boom was going on. But, when the Wall Street crash came, Ireland didn't stop; they kept it going and now Ireland is known as "The Celtic Tiger." They have moved from being the poorest to being one of the richest countries in Europe.

J.R. You can see that in the country. When we went over there this last time, it wasn't the way it used to be when we were collecting. It was like daylight and dark. Everything is prospering and thriving. Another thing that's happening in Aberdeen, Scotland, is a new cultural center, a place called the Elphinstone Institute. The curator there, the man who is helping set it up, is Dr James Porter. He wanted to do the same thing in Scotland. They're interested, but things are moving slowly as yet.

M.S. How do you feel about the rapid changes in communications technology? You've got yourself a website; you've got email now.

J.R. Well, I just have people in the family who can do that kind of thing. I never would have gotten around to it myself, but I love it. It puts you in instant touch with the whole world.

M.S. Have you got any new projects coming up?

J.R. One thing that we're doing that might interest you is that Phillip King, of Hummingbird Productions, wants to do the same show that we did last November in Belfast. They want to do it at the Barbicon in London. The show in Belfast was for "The Belfast Festival at Queens," and I went over, and Tommy Makem went over, and David Hammond came. So the three of us, with Donal Lunny, did a folk music program. Donal didn't sing, but accompanied everybody. I asked him to sing with me and he blushed (laughs), but he played beautifully and we did a program as part of that festival. The whole program is Irish, but it's going to be in London. I guess the British government wants to do something nice, make good feeling. I don't travel a lot now, but when something like this comes up, it's really great.

M.S. I'm very interested in how you feel about what you discovered in comparison to the music tradition in America. You had already been involved in music collecting in America before you went to Europe.

J.R. I was born and raised in the mountains of Kentucky, where we're all of Scottish, Irish, and English decent . . . mixed, of course. The motivation for me getting the scholarship in the first place was that I wanted to trace the sources of our old family ballads and songs that were all of Celtic origin.

M.S. How do you feel about the word Celtic nowadays?

J.R. I think it's sort of an umbrella term that people use, not always knowing what it means. It's a very descriptive word. It unites people in that feeling. Where I came from, we had some Irish, and some English, and some Scottish, mainly Scottish. The Ritchies came from Inverness. But we began our collecting in Ireland. It was fascinating to visit there and hear the same tunes that we sing in Kentucky, but maybe with different words. Then I'd go to Scotland and hear the same words with maybe an Irish tune. Therefore, in the mountains of Kentucky, we seem to have taken what we thought was the best of everything. If we liked the words we would put a pretty Irish tune to them. Everything sort of got wedded together. Pity that human beings can't do the same. It's part of my heritage, and it's been thrilling my whole life to be able to discover, more and more, the roots of the music, what folk music really is. To meet the people who keep the songs alive because they mean so much to them – a part of their oral history and their way of life.

M.S. Well, they stir up wonderful feelings.

J.R. When we met Dáibhí and were going to go to Ireland, we were invited especially to come to Cork for a party, as guests of honor, because it had been almost forty years since we had been there. Everybody we had collected from, their descendants and children, all came. We met in a hotel and had a big party and we put our pictures on the wall so they could all see what they used to look like. Everybody sang and everybody performed. It was a marvelous little party. There was a big recording studio next door, and the Chieftains were recording, so some of them looked in and joined us. Imagine my surprise and delight when Sean Keane came in, nodded to me, and proceeded to fiddle a medley of lovely traditional 'airs' in my honor!

M.S. I think one of the big lessons we have to share, as people who get our thrills from music, is that just by associating yourself more deeply with the music tradition, you get this great lifestyle. When you're into music, you can meet the musicians. If you're reading a book, you rarely get a chance to hang out with the author. Whereas, with the musicians, you can go and hear them live and participate in the energy, even play with them.

J.R. Yes, that's the way it's been for me, and I've been very happy. It's made my life a very joyful experience.

Discography

CLEAR WATERS REMEMBERED (1971)
(Geordie Records)
A TIME FOR SINGING (1965)
(Warner Brothers)
SHIVER! (1963)*
(Esoteric)
JEAN RITCHIE AND DOC WATSON
 AT FOLK CITY (1963)
(Folkways)
THE APPALACHIAN DULCIMER
(INSTRUCTION) (1963)
(Folkways)
THE BEST OF JEAN RITCHIE*
(Prestige)
PRECIOUS MEMORIES (1962)
(Folkways)
BRITISH TRADITIONAL BALLADS
 IN THE SOUTHERN MOUNTAINS (1961)
(Folkways)
RIDDLE ME THIS (1959)*
(Riverside)
CAROLS OF ALL SEASONS (1959)
(Tradition Records)
JEAN RITCHIE AND OSCAR BRAND
 AT TOWN HALL (1959)
(Folkways)
THE RITCHIE FAMILY OF KENTUCKY (1957)
(Folkways)
SONGS FROM KENTUCKY*
(Westminster)
SINGING FAMILY
 OF THE CUMBERLANDS (1957)
(Riverside)

CHILDREN'S SONGS AND GAMES
 FROM THE SOUTHERN MOUNTAINS
(Folkways)
SATURDAY NIGHT AND SUNDAY TOO*
(Riverside)
AMERICAN FOLK TALES AND SONGS (1956)
(Tradition Records)
JEAN RITCHIE
 FIELD TRIP COLLECTOR (1956)
(Limited Editions)
COURTING SONGS*
(Elektra-Stratford)
KENTUCKY MOUNTAIN SONGS
(Elektra-Stratford)
SONGS FROM KENTUCKY (1953)*
(Argo Record Co., Ltd. – England)
APPALACHIAN MOUNTAIN SONGS
 2 10-inch 78 rpm discs (1953)*
(HMV – England)
JEAN RITCHIE SINGING TRADITIONAL
 SONGS OF HER KENTUCKY
 MOUNTAIN FAMILY
(Elektra-Stratford)
THE MOST DULCIMER
(Greenhays)
O LOVE IS TEASIN
(Reissue of EKL-22 & EKL-25, etc.)
(Elektra Asylum)
KENTUCKY CHRISTMAS, OLD & NEW
(Greenhays)

Cassettes

JEAN RITCHIE CONCERT
(Greenhays)

BEGINNING APPALACHIAN
DULCIMER (instruction)
(Homespun Tapes)

Books

The Dulcimer People (1974)
(Oak Publications)
Celebration of Life
(New & old songs, and poems) (1971)
(Geordie Music Pub. Co.)
From Fair to Fair (1966)
(Henry Walck, Inc.)
The Newport Folk Festival Song Book
(J. Ritchie, editor) (1965)
(Henry Walck, Inc.)
Apple Seeds and Soda Straws (1965)*
(Alfred Music, Inc.)
Folk Songs of the
   Southern Appalachians (1965)
(Oak Publications)

The Dulcimer Book (1963)
(Oak Publications)
Singing Family of the Cumberlands
(Paperback Edition) (1963)
(Oak Publications)
Singing Family of
   of the Cumberlands (1955)
(Broadcast Music, Inc.)
A Garland of Mountain Song (1953)
(Oxford University Press)
The Swapping Song Book
(1952, Rev. 1964)
(Henry Walck, Inc.)

* Discontinued – all others available from Folklife Productions, 7A Locust Ave., Port Washington, N.Y. 11050

Website: http://members.aol.com/greenhays/page6.htm

KATE RUSBY
(THE POOZIES)

BiOGRAPHY

T here are still a few world class singer/songwriters who revel in the sounds and traditions of the past, but none are quite as unique and stirring as England's Kate Rusby. At twenty-three years old, Kate is the most sought after traditional folk phenomenon in England. She has set the U.K. on fire with her penchant for lyrics and melodies that are reminiscent of yesteryear.

A native of Yorkshire, England, Kate grew up immersed in the sort of singing tradition generally related, rather romantically, to generations of old. She was playing the fiddle by age five and had taken her place in the family ceilidh band by the time she was ten.

She went to college in Barnsley to study the technical side of music in performing arts. With childhood friend and fellow performer Kathryn Roberts she recorded KATE RUSBY & KATHRYN ROBERTS, which was voted 1995 Album of the Year by *Folk Roots Magazine*. That collaboration turned into the band The Equation, a group which continued on after Kate decided to leave. She later became a member of the highly acclaimed all female folk group The Poozies and the owner of her own label, Pure Records.

HOURGLASS, Kate's new album on Compass, her first U.S. solo release, became a top selling traditional album in the U.K.

INTERVIEW

MAIRÉID SULLIVAN   Do you a have a place where you can go to get centered and refresh your energy?

KATE RUSBY   The only place where I find peace of mind is at home amongst friends and family. I also know that if I am not at ease and relaxed, then I cannot be creative. I now plan time at home to find new material and also write.

M.S.   Tell us your favorite selected passages from the traditional songs that you sing.

K.R.   Most of the traditional songs I know are one way or another connected with love and usually loss, so they are about basic human emotions. People often ask me why I sing songs that aren't relevant to this day and age; I don't see it that way at all. We still feel love as we did hundreds of years ago and we feel loss the same way, too. Just because the songs and therefore the characters are from years past does not mean the sentiment of the songs belong back then. For me they are timeless themes. I find so much sadness, tragedy, and passion in them. For instance, there is a song called *As I Roved Out*. I have listened to this song being sung for years, and still it has the same effect on me. Roughly from Napoleonic times, it tells of a governmental decree that basically said, young men would be rewarded with lots of money if they married the wives of landed lords while the lords were away at war just so the land would then still be worked. So many young men could not afford not to do this. Some of them were already betrothed to other women. The song opens up with a young man bumping into "his own true lover." Immediately you can tell how much they are in love . . .

> I took off my hat and I did salute her,
> I did salute her most courageously,
> as she turned around the tears fell from her,
> saying false young man you've deluded me.

It then becomes apparent that he is engaged to this woman, but has had to marry . . . "the lassie who has the land."

He says . . .

> If I wed the lassie who has the land my love,
> It's that I'll rue till the day I die,

Then comes the verse that always gets me …

> At night when I go to my bed of slumber
> The thoughts of my love are in my mind,
> As I turn around to embrace my darling,
> Instead of gold, sure 'tis brass I find.

Then comes his plea, and you really feel for the man …

> I wish the queen would bring home her armies,
> from the West Indies, America and Spain,
> and every man to his wedded woman,
> In hopes that I might be with thee again.

The words are just so beautiful and honest. I find it heart wrenching, and end up really feeling for the guy because there is not a thing he can do. The tune for this song is so gorgeous, one of my favorite songs. It's not very often that I find the same passion from modern songs. Maybe because a lot of songs are written for commercial use, and from the word 'go' they are conforming to a commercialized pattern rather than just being written out of sheer emotion. When I do find contemporary songs that have the same effect on me, it restores my faith in songwriting.

M.S.   What are some of your other interests, besides music?

K.R.   I love reading, and I read a lot on tour, mainly escapism material. There's a writer over here called Terry Pratchett – I really enjoy his books. They are very sarcastic and very funny. When I'm at home, I love being outside. I am from the country so I really miss fresh air when I can't have it. I have recently gotten into gardening, and yes, I even buy gardening magazines!

M.S.   Why do you think you chose a musical career?

K.R.   I developed an early passion for music, from my parents. They have been involved in traditional music ever since I can remember. There were always instruments lying around the house, and therefore live music in general was never alien to me. I do know how lucky I am to have been brought up with music, and it makes me sad to think most kids don't see any live music till their teens, when they go to their first pop concert.

My parents used to sing a lot in the car to my older sister, Emma, and my younger brother, Joe, and I. We used to argue a lot, like all kids, and my parents quickly discovered that if they sang to us we were really nice kids. It was just like them telling us stories, only better because they had tunes. I learned so many songs from them. They also had, and still do, a ceilidh band. I play with them whenever I can make it, and my sister still plays with them.

M.S. When did you start playing the fiddle?

K.R. I played fiddle from the age of seven, then my dad taught me some chords on the guitar when I was about fifteen. I then taught myself the piano. When it came time for me to go to university, I was stuck because I didn't have a clue what I wanted to study, so I had a year out. It was then that one of our family friends asked me to do a spot at the folk festival that she helped to organize. Then other people asked me to play at other festivals and such like. Suddenly, I was a professional musician. It sneaked up on me, and I'm very pleased it did.

M.S. How did you how you discover your own musical style?

K.R. My own musical style came out of the way I learned to play. I listened a lot to other performers at the festivals I went to, and from my parents' records. Two people that I took to at an early age were Nic Jones and Dave Burland. While other kids were walking around with the latest pop music in their walkmans, I was walking around with those guys in mine. So I suppose somewhere along the line, influences like my parents and then Nic and Dave would have had an effect on what my style was going to be, but I never thought consciously about it, it just happened that way.

M.S. Who were your mentors? How did they inspire you?

K.R. Nic Jones and Dave Burland were two very early influences. I still listen to them now. They were both so good at interpreting traditional songs. If people come and ask me about some CDs to buy so they can get more into traditional music, they are the first ones I recommend, and every time they come back saying, "Wow!" When you listen to their music, you can really tell that they love the songs and that they are telling you a story, and that in itself draws you in and makes you want to listen and hear how it all turns out. From the younger end of the scale, two people that interpret traditional songs brilliantly are Karen Casey (Solas) and Cathy Jordan (Dervish). I listen to them both a lot when I'm on tour. They both have such wonderful voices, and also you can hear the love for the music in their singing. I can listen to them for hours.

M.S. Do you like touring? What kinds of venues do you prefer?

K.R. I do like touring, but I find touring abroad quite hard. I like playing in most venues really. I started off playing in folk clubs and love playing in them still. They are such intimate places, and you know that the audiences at them are interested in the music. They have come to listen. I know a lot of performers who don't like playing at folk clubs because they are put off by the audiences being so close physically to them, and how closely they listen, but that's why I like them. I have been going to them and playing at them for such a long time that the intimacy is not foreign to me and neither am I put off by it. I play such a broad range of venues, from festivals with 20,000 people listening, to theaters and arts centers. I don't really have a preference, just so long as I feel comfortable.

M.S. What do you feel about live performance?

K.R. If I didn't perform live, I think that I would go nuts. When I have time off at home, however much I need it, when it gets to about eight o'clock in the evening, I start to get really itchy fingers and I can't settle. It always makes me feel so lucky that people want to come and see me play the music that I love. I don't really get nervous any more, not like when I first started playing.

M.S. Does it take a few songs or pieces to warm up and get to know the audience?

K.R. I do get a bit uneasy if I'm involved in a new project and it's the first concert. I hate that feeling of not really knowing what I'm doing. Very occasionally, for no apparent reason, I get stage fright like I used to. It's very odd, and I can never identify the cause of it, but if I do feel like that, I'm usually over it by the first couple of numbers. I don't always play solo, and it's sometimes a bit strange changing from one to the other. I like both forms for different reasons. It makes the touring side of it a lot easier when there are other musicians. It's like going on a scout trip or something, everybody piling in the car that's loaded down with bags and instruments. It's such good fun. The performing side of it, as I've said, is strange chang-ing from one to the other. I have to concentrate a lot more with other musicians because there are set arrangements, but when I am solo, I miss verses out and put them in, move instrumentals, and, of course, it doesn't matter. Going back to solo from the band situation, for the first gig on my own, I miss the others. I soon get on with it, though.

M.S. How do you feel about singing and playing in the recording studio?

K.R. I very much enjoy singing in the recording studio. It's the only time I get to sing and not worry about what I'm playing on guitar or piano. I put the instrument tracks down first, which leaves me feeling very free and able to just get on with singing, the part I enjoy the most. It's a time when I can experiment with phrasing and decoration, so, apart from the enjoyment, it's also a very valuable time for me. I think it's very impor-tant that you have the right person producing. I am very lucky in that respect. I have always worked with John McCusker (Battlefield Band). He is somebody that I trust a great deal, and I think that we are a good team. I think being in the studio has to be enjoyable. You are in there day-in, day-out, so it's important that you are surrounded by people you like and trust. I find the whole thing a very enjoyable, fulfilling time.

M.S. What do you think are the reasons for the overwhelming popular-ity of Celtic music now?

K.R. Every now and again the media picks up on the Celtic music thing. I have seen it at least three times in my lifetime. You start to hear 'folkie' instruments and influences in pop songs, then the film music industry picks up on it, and all of a sudden the unsuspecting public are listening to folk music. Maybe the thing that sparked off this latest media attention is *Riverdance*, I don't know, but something that is apparent is that when people actually get to hear this kind of music, they usually like it. It doesn't necessarily mean it is an overall good effect on this music, though. When it is all going well, the media are interested and giving lots of coverage. It's not very easy to take a step back and see where the media fad will end, because it will. Fashion and trends govern the media, and they always come to an end. These songs and tunes have survived for years on their own with no media at all, and there will always be some people there who will care for it and look after it.

Discography

HOURGLASS (1998)
(Compass Records)

With The Poozies

INFINITE BLUE (1998)
(Compass Records)
DANZOOZIES (1995)
(Compass Records)

CHANTOOZIES (1993)
(Compass Records)

Website: http://www.compassrecords.com/rusby.htm

CAThIE RYAN

BíOGRAPhy

$\mathbb{C}$athie Ryan is an Irish American singer-songwriter whose moving interpretations of Irish traditional and original songs have been winning her a loyal following throughout North America. Born in Detroit and raised by Irish parents, Cathie grew up steeped in the music of Ireland and the folk music that flourished in America in the 1960s. "When I was a kid it was very Irish inside the house and very American outside," she remarks. "That duality informs my songwriting and my singing style. I feel blessed to have been grounded in the singing traditions of both countries."

During the 1990s she has performed as a member of the American women's band, Cherish The Ladies. In the past three years Cathie has released two critically acclaimed CDs on Shanachie Records, the first of which, CATHIE RYAN, inspired the *Boston Herald* to call her "a major talent." *The New York Daily News* states that her second release, THE MUSIC OF WHAT HAPPENS, "places her firmly in the upper echelons of Irish music singers." It was selected Best Celtic CD for 1998 by numerous folk radio programs nationwide. In 1999, Cathie was again voted Irish Traditional Female Vocalist of the Year by the *Irish American News* in Chicago.

INTERVIEW

MAIRÉID SULLIVAN Tell us how your life story has led you to this moment where you are able to practice your art, and what this means to you. How does this influence your views on the world at large?

CATHIE RYAN Being on the road and traveling through different towns and countries has allowed me to meet and get to know people from all over. I find that people are much better than bad news suggests. I believe that we all carry tremendous love and spirit but our high speed world challenges our ability to share or express it. Music helps us to connect to each other and something greater than ourselves, it helps dissolve the barriers we erect. I love the positive energy and connection that I feel from an audience and when I meet people through my music.

M.S. Can you tell us about your own philosophy and how that shapes your music and your personal lifestyle?

C.R. I moved out of the city about seven years ago. I had lived in an apartment in the Bronx for fourteen years and began to feel very crowded-in-upon. So we moved about an hour north into a more rural area. It's not completely cut off, but we are surrounded by trees and grass and water. I look out the window and see nature and that gives me comfort. My favorite place is the garden. When we moved in, I tore everything up and planted perennial and shrub gardens all around the house.

Working in the yard is like Zen for me. I can spend a whole day moving from one area to another doing different tasks. It is meditative. It's also great to dig my hands in the dirt, to be out in the sun and air, to work hard, and to see the landscape growing and changing year after year. The flowering of it all is a great reward.

M.S. Tell us your favorite selected passages from the traditional songs and originals that you sing.

C.R. I love the traditional song, *Caone na Maighdine* (The Lament of the Blessed Virgin). Mary sees her son on his way to Calvary, burdened by his cross and in great pain. At first she can't even recognize him. She then wants to lessen his pain. Their exchange is profound:

> Mary: A Leinbh, is moor e t'ualach is leig cuid de ar do Mhathair.
> Jesus: Iompruiodh gach einne a chrosa, a Mhaithrin.
> Mary: Child, your load is heavy let your Mother help you carry it.
> Jesus: We each must carry our own cross, Mother.

As a mother I found these lines deeply moving. There is wisdom for every parent here.

And the chorus of one of my own songs, *I'm Going Back*:

Wake my heart, play the Bucks of Oranmore
Shake my mind, put the devil in the bow once more
Fray the hair, bend the note, and lift the dancer's feet
I'm going, I'm gone
I'm going back to Ireland.

I was trying to capture the feeling I get when I listen to great traditional music being played. The music has such power to transport the listener, to move the soul, the spirit, and the mind.

When I was a child, music saved my life, so that need to hold onto the music is in the lyric, too. Music can be a lifeline, as in my song, *Eveline*:

It's alright Eveline, let the ship sail away.
Hold onto the railing and cry.
It won't be the last one I promise you that
They're only telling you lies.

I wrote this song after reading James Joyce's short story "Eveline" in *The Dubliners*. Joyce leaves Eveline stuck in a diminished life at the end of the story. She is completely incapable of taking the one chance she has to make her life better. I believe we get loads of chances in life and many of us are late bloomers !

Roisin Dubh is my favorite Irish song. I think it is the best song ever written. The melody is sweeping, brilliant. The lyrics are profoundly moving.

I have loved you from my heart now for a twelvemonth
An anguished love, a hapless love, a love tormented
A love that has left me without health, without vigor, without activity,
And for evermore I cannot win my small black rose.

Another theme I love in Irish song is the positive and accepting attitudes about sex in ditties like *Sheain Bhain*: "You and I in the one bed lie, The Widow of Westmoreland's Daughter." Those songs are lusty and fun. Growing up Irish Catholic, that's not how it was presented to me. What a pleasure to hear and learn some of these great old songs.

M.S. Tell us about some of your other interests.

C.R. I love to read. I'm most interested in autobiographies, biographies, and Irish literature, especially Irish mythology. I relish those old tales. They bring the landscape and the archeology of Ireland to another level for me. They also show me stronger women than the deferential 'good girl' I was encouraged to emulate as a child.

I am also a wife and mother. My husband, Michael, is a very important part of my life. After all, we are in this thing together! Michael teaches Celtic Mythology, so we have shelves of great books. Raising my son, Patrick, has been the greatest responsibility of my life and continues to be my greatest learning experience, as well. He is now nineteen years old. His absolute determination to be his own person has changed my views on everything I previously thought about parenting. For example, that our kids are a reflection of us; that they turn out the way they do because of what we do; that we have real power over their lives; and that we know what's best for them. I now believe that is all wrong. I do believe we have a duty to guide our children. But I have learned to let my son have his own spirit and fate. That has been good for all of us. In all my life, I am most proud of him and I know his father feels the same.

M.S. Why do you choose a musical career?

C.R. I don't really think that I chose a musical career. Every day a musical career chooses me! Certainly another job would be easier. I have a degree in Education and Literature and I do have moments when I wish I wanted to teach and make a regular wage in regular hours. That would make parenting and being a spouse easier. It would also eliminate the craziness I sometimes go through regarding bookings, publicity, making arrangements for the band, the road, the shows, etc. But when I'm writing a song – right in the middle of that perfect concentration that takes hold – or up singing this music – I know I am right where I am meant to be.

M.S. How did you come to your musical style?

C.R. My songwriting and singing style come from being raised in Detroit, Michigan. I was born in 1959 to two Irish immigrants who were mad about Irish music. Inside my house it was very Irish. There was always traditional music playing, my father was singing, or we were going downtown to the Gaelic League for sessions, concerts, and dances. Music was great fun for my parents, but it was also a way of holding on to their Irishness and not assimilating. By extension, it became that for me as a child. So, I learned the rudiments of the sean-nos songs and absorbed Irish traditional music. But Detroit began to get in there, too – especially as I got older.

My closest friend's parents were from Kentucky and West Virginia. Through her family, I learned about American Mountain music. Eventually my parents began to listen to country greats like Hank Williams and Johnny Cash. I was also surrounded by Motown music and the singer-songwriters of the sixties. So, my musical style is born of being Irish American. That duality informs my songwriting and the way I sing songs.

M.S. Can you tell us about your musical influences, your mentors?

C.R. My greatest influences musically were family. My dad was a great singer in his day and a great man to pick a song. He got his singing from his mother, who I am named for. She was a lovely singer and fiddle player. Visiting her in Ireland is one of my fondest memories. I have never seen anyone else who loved to sing and play the way she did. Music was her joy – it transformed her. No matter how old she was, when she sang she became a girl again. She loved sessions in the kitchen. Everyone had to sing or play or dance. Her joy in the sharing of music was contagious.

My mother's father was a storyteller. He used to just mesmerize us kids. I think that my attraction to a song with a strong story comes from him. I think my songwriting as well. He made some great stories for us and for anyone else who rambled in. He also loved the mythology and the folktales. He believed in the Bardic tradition that you are the carrier of the history and the emotion of the country and that's what you put forth in song and story. His spirit was palpable, you could feel the peace and wisdom in him. I realize now that he was a true Celt because he believed that we were very close to the otherworld always. He was deeply connected to the land and the seasons, and I'm sure he was a pagan because my grandmother was always praying for him.

Joe Heaney was a mentor to me. I appreciated every minute I spent with him singing and talking about songs. He gave me songs and inspired within me the confidence to sing them. He also put the whole world of traditional music into perspective for me. He had no time for the purist traditional view that Americans had no right to sing traditional music. That kind of exclusionary stuff used to infuriate him. What he gave me brought me further into the art of the sean-nos; but mostly he gave me great encouragement to sing.

At that point I began to incorporate all the other musical influences within me into my own singing style. It was unconscious, but I think that seeing and hearing how he sang what was in him made me want to do that too. Also, his disregard for the powers-that-be in traditional music freed me from wanting to be accepted by them. At that point it was just me and the music that was inside of me. Joe was also a great storyteller. He was very like my grandfather Rice in many ways – the closeness to the otherworld and the closeness to the land and the sea – but Joe had an edge to him. That's one of the things I liked about him.

M.S. Was there a special event or a 'big break' that helped you become a professional musician?

C.R. Yes, there was. In 1985, Mick Moloney, the folklorist, realized that there were many women playing and singing Irish traditional music in America who were not getting the recognition they deserved. At his suggestion, Ethel Raime, Martin Koenig, and Rick Luftglas of the Ethnic Folk Arts Center in NYC applied for and got grant money to fund nationwide touring and publicity for an all women's Irish traditional ensemble, Cherish the Ladies.

I was invited to join about one and a half years later. It was great. The project was all about the music and introducing it to a larger audience – Irish music wasn't even on the map yet in some of the areas we played. We were nine women on the road playing all the music that was in us. That was important to me since I had grown up listening to mostly men playing the music professionally. But mostly, those early days were fun, pure fun.

This was the beginning of my career as it is today. I still perform for those audiences. I'm grateful to EFAC and to the members of CTL (Cherish The Ladies) who came and went through the years, especially Bridget Fitzgerald, from Inverin, Co. Galway, who taught me how to sing in Irish. Bridget Fitzgerald was also a very important mentor for me. Without those years spent on the road with her I might not be singing in Irish today.

M.S. Do you like touring and what kinds of venues do you prefer?

C.R. I love touring. It puts me in a completely different consciousness. I go into 'the road zone'. I measure everything differently. The most important thing becomes the gig and getting to it. The band becomes family. In many ways, it is a much simpler life, yet it can be grueling. I appreciate all types of venues – each has its own reward. Festivals are great fun because you get to play to large crowds and also see other bands in performance and socially. It's great to get the chance to catch up with other musicians, chat and hang out. I love the intimacy of small venues, like coffeehouses that seat maybe 120 people or less, because it is like being in someone's living room. The connection seems more intense. I usually wind up talking more at those shows. Concert halls are great because you get a buzz being on a large stage with lighting and good sound. There is something grand and formal about the surroundings and something warm and cozy about the show. I like that dichotomy.

M.S. Do you feel nervous or confident on stage? How do you prepare?

C.R. I love singing on stage. It takes me one or two songs to get settled into the music and that place of centeredness and comfort where I begin to connect to the audience. It takes some time to get the feel of the audience, who they are and what kind of energy they are sending out. Sometimes, it takes me a song or two for the band to get in synch. We may have just gotten off a plane or out of a car after a long drive. We need to connect and get into performance mode. Before I go on stage I like to warm up my voice by doing scales and singing bits of songs. I also need to get focused, think about the set list and how I am going to present the show. After that the absolute dream would be to have about a half hour quiet time alone before I go on stage, but that doesn't always happen because there are business things to take care of and also dressing rooms are a big consideration. Is there the space to go off into for a while?

I feel a very easy mix of vulnerability and confidence on stage. I am vulnerable in being open to the song and the audience, but at the same time I am confident because I love what I'm doing and I'm completely in the moment on stage. There is no other place in my life where I am so in the minute I am standing and thinking in. That's probably why I love it so much. It's a great thing to have a single mind! Singing the songs I do also gives me confidence as a singer. I know that on a subconscious level the beauty and spirituality of them must ground me.

M.S. What do you think are reasons for overwhelming popularity of Celtic music now?

C.R. I think the Irish music scene and the audience for it has been growing for many, many years. From a practical point of view, the business built around Irish music is improving and the quality of the music is at a very high standard. Right now there are more bands, more venues, more people recording their interpretations of the music, easier access to top of the line recording studios that produce polished recordings, more record companies marketing the music, and artists putting out their own CDs. Also, the world is getting smaller, radio and the Internet broadcast Irish music everywhere. So more people are tuning in to hear this music and learning that it is music of the people – the songs speak of the human condition.

There is also an historical dimension. During the mass immigrations of the 1840s, and the steady immigration that followed, Irish music was spread across the world and it has been nurtured in those communities where the Irish settled. It became a lifeline for the Irish immigrant in a foreign land – a way of expressing his/her Irishness, a way of not completely assimilating, a way of retaining a strong community. I witnessed and was part of this in my own growing up. I think music was also a lifeline for the Irish in Ireland through the centuries. The songs and the music carried the history, the pain, and the healing of the country. Music fueled by this kind of passion and life cannot but be strong and attract attention. I think also that the Irish and Irish Americans have more confidence at this point in our history so we are out there expressing our vision and ourselves. It is a life force.

M.S. Why do you think there is growing interest in ancient Celtic culture?

C.R. I think the interest in Celtic culture has been growing since Yeats, Lady Gregory, and Hyde began to use the Irish myths as way of establishing an Irish identity, of looking to their own cultural experience. I don't think the interest has stopped since then. Now it appeals to a world market because the essence of the myths is the human condition and our need to reach beyond to something greater than ourselves. We are a generation of people searching for healing for our personal and societal ills – notice the size of the self-help and spirituality sections in bookstores. Something is missing in our lives and some of the Celtic traditions offer a way to fill that emptiness. They can bring us back to a greater wholeness and wisdom.

M.S. What do you consider relevant today from Celtic history?

C.R. I think the most relevant message for today from Celtic history is to be more conscious of our own souls, to honor our own divinity and the divinity of the earth, the sacredness of place, of land – the connection. The Celts had rituals and celebrations, which opened them up to themselves and the land they lived in communion with. That is missing for us today and it manifests itself in an unconsciousness that results in conflict and pain.

Also, the myths are not neat and tidy. There are no pat answers in them. That corresponds much more to what human life is like – something I need to constantly remind myself of! The myths are living. I think we as a people have carried them because they are meant to be a part of our lives today. They can help to heal and reconnect us to a more spiritual way of living.

DISCOGRAPHY

MOTHER (1999)
    with Robin Spielberg
    and Susan McKeown
(Northstar)
THE MUSIC OF WHAT HAPPENS (1998)
(Shanachie)
THE SOUL OF CHRISTMAS (1997)
    (compilation)
(Tommy Boy/Warner)

CATHIE RYAN (1997)
(Shanachie)
OUT AND ABOUT (1993)
    with Cherish the Ladies
(Green Linnet)
THE BACK DOOR (1991)
    with Cherish the Ladies
(Green Linnet)

Celtic Collections featuring Cathie Ryan:

HER INFINITE VARIETY:
    SONGS OF CELTIC WOMEN (1998)
(Green Linnet)
ONE AND ALL (1998)
    Cherish the Ladies Greatest Hits
(Green Linnet)
HOLDING UP HALF THE SKY (1997)
(Shanachie)

CELTIC LOVE SONGS (1997)
(Shanachie & Green Linnet)
THERE WAS A LADY:
    THE VOICE OF CELTIC WOMEN (1997)
(Shanachie)
GREEN LINNET 20TH
    ANNIVERSARY COLLECTION (1996)
(Green Linnet)

JUNE TABOR

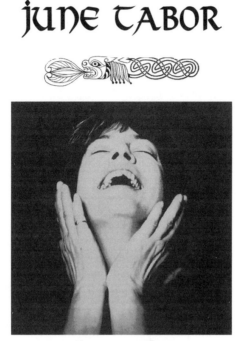

BIOGRAPHY

Anyone who has heard June Tabor sing is not likely to forget the experience. She has a voice that is startlingly different: smoky, velvet, brushing huskily into lower octaves. An interpreter of the first order, Tabor sings with a haunting power and with deep feeling for the song.

June Tabor began singing traditional music in her teens as a floor singer when the only folksongs she knew were *Kumbaya* and *Michael Row The Boat Ashore* which she had learned from television. It wasn't long, however, before she became captivated by the highly ornamented style of Anne Briggs, shutting herself up for days to emulate her recordings. As a student in Oxford, June encountered a large folk community, and a simpler vocal style began to appeal to her as she moved in the direction of the exquisite, controlled singing that today is her trademark.

June's acclaim and acceptance widened when she collaborated with Steeleye Span member Maddy Pryor in the duo called Silly Sisters. Tabor also teamed up with guitarist Martin Simpson for a series of albums; his interest in contemporary and American music broadened June's repertoire. A jazz album, SOME OTHER TIME, and the very well received recording with The Oyster Band followed. Her now classic "chamber folk" setting began to emerge with ANGEL TIGER (named *Pulse* magazine's Album of the Year in the British Isle/Celtic category). Tabor has been chosen Vocalist of the

Year so frequently by *Folk Roots Magazine* that they finally retired the category altogether, creating a Hall of Fame honor for her. June's fans include such artists as Richard Thompson. She frequently covers material by Richard Thompson, and contributed two tracks to Capitol's BEAT THE RETREAT: SONGS BY RICHARD THOMPSON. Elvis Costello, who considered it a goal to write a song for June to record, wrote two, *All This Useless Beauty* and *I Want To Vanish*. "If you don't like June Tabor," Costello proclaimed, "you should just stop listening to music."

interview

MAIRÉID SULLIVAN What does music mean to you?

JUNE TABOR I can, if you stick a pin in me, intellectualize about music and what it means to me. I like to sing. I let people draw whatever intellectual conclusions they want to, and I just get on with the music, telling stories in songs. That's what I'm most interested in.

Very often the stories I'm telling in song are ones that actually tear your heart in half. I'm responding to the feeling of the song, of the feeling that it engenders in me. I'm trying to communicate that to other people. What I'm trying to do is to make people think, make them laugh, make them cry, make them understand each other better, make them understand themselves. For me, it's part of the function of communication through song. It's quite a serious function. I am a great believer in the serious function of music. That doesn't mean that you can't enjoy it at the same time, but at its best music is on an equal footing with literature in whatever form it might take. If you can evoke the same reaction in someone while listening to a song as you can from confronting him or her with a very strong piece of theater, *King Lear*, for example, then it is just as valid an art form. Having said that, I think that song is probably one of the least regarded means of artistic communication, unless you happen to be singing in a foreign language. Take Grand Opera, for an example, which is given a much greater degree of serious interest and credence, and funding. Then compare it with the music that so many singers are making and it really has little comparison. If it has no commercial value, then the song doesn't really seem to be very important. It's a great shame and waste.

M.S. That's really interesting. One of the things that mystifies me about a lot of popular Celtic music at the moment is that the songs are in the Irish. Most people can't understand the words. So there is something else that draws people to it besides the meaning of the songs.

J.T. I think that one of the great appeals of a song sung in a foreign language is that it's completely unchallenging; you're not called upon to do anything but react to a nice sound. Possibly some emotional content within the performance, that's fine, but you actually don't have to understand anything. If you were similarly confronted with a short story in a foreign language, it would just be printed words on a page. You wouldn't even bother to look at it or attempt to read through it. However, if it's put into a musical context you can say, "Isn't that wonderful, isn't that imaginative!" You don't actually know what they're singing about. It could be "My tractor's broken down, and the man from the collective farm isn't going to come and mend it until Tuesday." But, if it's done by a Bulgarian choir, it makes you cry. The power of the word, the understood word, is something extremely important. You don't normally get it in the vast majority of popular music because the word is something that just goes along with everything else, including the arrangement and overall sound. What I like to look at, in terms of the importance of song, are the words – the meaning – something being understood. It's something in which every syllable counts. If it's somebody singing to you in a language you can't understand, you lose an awful lot. Of course, that doesn't mean you're gaining nothing at all.

m.s. Why do you think that has become the trend of the moment?

j.t. Because it is non-confrontational. There's no thinking required.

m.s. So the poet's in trouble?

j.t. Yes, that's true.

m.s. Through your long musical career you have had the opportunity to see these trends move back and forth, haven't you?

j.t. I suppose so. In some ways, you sit underneath it and it all goes on over your head because you have to consider what you're going to make of your own music, and what music is going to make of you. If you want to have any kind of professional relationship to it, then you may have to say, "I'm going to do what makes me money." And if you're lucky, you could have a degree of personal input, you might be given some degree of control. But it might be completely in the hands of somebody else, and that is the world of commercialism. Occasionally, what you really want to do and what people want to buy coincide. If it doesn't, then you probably won't make any money. But then you can do exactly what you want in many ways and let happen, what the music wants to happen to you. That's been my case.

For a long time I didn't have music as a solo career, it was a dual career along with something else. Then, when I turned forty, my life changed quite radically in a number of ways, and I felt I was ready to attempt a full-time career in music. I've done a lot of different things since, exploring different avenues in performance and selection of material, and I'm still learning about it. But it's all on my terms. The general terms of what music should be have changed, and very little of that has to do with what I do.

I'm so damned awkward. I just carry on doing what I feel is right for me. If you work on a small enough scale, which I do, you can do that. As long as enough people still want to listen to your personal view as an interpreter, then its working. It's very hard to be objective about your own work. It's very hard to say this is good or bad. Because when you've toiled and struggled with something, it is very hard to exert any kind of quality control over your output. So, I look for songs that other people have written, and decide if they move me sufficiently for me to want to perform them. It's a long search that's frequently unrewarded. When I do come up with something good that otherwise would have not reached a particularly wide audience, I feel I'm really doing the right thing. It's a wonderful feeling.

m.s. That just sends me to heaven. Tell me about that feeling from your point of view.

j.τ. When you come across a song, and you think, I want to be inside that song, and I want to share being inside that song, there is no better magic than doing it and sharing it with an audience who respond in the way that you hoped they would. When they get as many things from the song as you did on the first hearing, then that is nothing short of magnificent. In the end, the song is the most important thing. Everything else becomes subordinate to the song.

m.s. The industry seems to be dominated by very powerful men. How do you advise dealing with that?

j.τ. You could do it by not taking on the big boys. I suppose if you limit yourself to the less financially motivated end of the market, then people do tend to be, by and large, nicer and more accommodating to the way you want to do things. I think the more money that is involved, the harder it gets for anything to be regarded other than from a business point of view.

For a while, in the beginning of my singing career, I was working in a library at Oxford at the same time. It was the Taylorian Institute of Modern Languages. I once got caught singing in the back stairs at the modern language library: the room had great acoustics. I didn't realize that singing in the bowels of the building could actually be heard in the main room. When I came back down the ladder with some obscure linguistics textbook, a guy standing by the foot of the steps said, "That was a very interesting version of *Barbara Allen*. I've never heard that before. Where the heck did you get it?" Everybody in the main reading room had heard me singing thirteen verses of *Barbara Allen* while I was looking for a book. So there I was doing something I really enjoyed, and at the same time singing, though the Chief Librarian wasn't quite so pleased!

By the time I did come to choose music as a full-time career I was older. I think age and experience, whatever kind, does have a lot to do with it. It tends to make you more worldly and wary . . . not wise, but wary about what the pitfalls might be. I think confidence in the songs gives you sufficient belief to go out there and try it, and to say this is what's important. It's the songs that matter. I am just a vehicle for the songs. A Breton musician friend once said to me, "You slide into the song, like a serpent, and you become the song." I loved that! If often takes someone else to express or encapsulate what you do.

M.S. What about your mentors?

J.C. When I was a small child, my mother and father used to sing snippets of popular songs as they went about the house, so singing to me was a natural part of expression. I picked up things from listening to the radio and at children's parties where I would stand up and sing. And then, just flirting with learning popular songs. When I was fourteen, I wanted to be the remarkable early sixties French pop singer Françoise Hardy. She sang soulful French pop songs. She wore black. She was very melancholy. She did several huge-selling albums in France and then decided to become obscure. She just released a new album not long ago, and she is still incredibly beautiful.

At that time, around 1964, by a strange quirk of fate, a friend took me to a folk club, and it was just pure chance that I wandered into an acquaintance with folk music. I started to go regularly, and I became very good friends with the people who were resident musicians at the club. They taught me their songs. And then I discovered Anne Briggs and Belle Stewart.

M.S. The trend in the folk scene, until recently anyway, is that you just don't even think about recording. Live performance was the focus of the interest in the music. How did you first become interested in recording?

J.C. I got pushed and prodded into it. I just acquired a reputation through singing at the clubs and festivals in different parts of the country at open mic sessions. I got quite a reputation singing a cappella. At some stage in the early seventies, Topic Records asked me to do an album with them. They wanted me to submit a list of the songs I wanted to record, and I couldn't make my mind up as to what to put on it. So, I didn't do anything. Then I started singing with Maddy Pryor quite by accident. We discovered that our voices sounded rather unusual and striking together. We starting singing together for fun . . . worked out a small repertoire doing open mic spots in clubs just for the hell of it. And then Steeleye Span had two top twenty hits and Maddy was given the chance to do a solo album by Chrysalis Records, Steeleye's label, and she told them she wanted to do the project with me. That's how Silly Sisters came about. It was the first proper recording I had ever done. And then, having done that, I was finally induced to do an album of mainly traditional songs by the great Scottish singer, Isabelle Sutherland.

M.S. What are your favorite themes from the traditional songs?

J.T. 'Love gone wrong' definitely! I usually say that as one word 'love-gonewrong' or 'LGW' for short. Frequently, in traditional songs you come back to such a timeless expression of the pains and the joys of love, which could not be bettered. It's the freshness of words, which could be at least two hundred years old, that makes you feel you know exactly what that person means. How many times have these events happened to people over thousands of years? Such an economy of words in just four short verses, and yet they express many lifetimes of heartache. There's nothing quite like that.

Discography

ALEYN (1997)

AGAINST THE STREAMS (1994)

ANGEL TIGER (1992)

FREEDOM AND RAIN, JUNE TABOR &
   THE OYSTER BAND (1990)

SOME OTHER TIME (1989)

AQUABA (1988)

ABYSSINIANS (1983)

A CUT ABOVE, MARTIN SIMPSON (1980)

SILLY SISTERS, MADDY PRYOR
   & JUNE TABOR (1978)

ASHES AND DIAMONDS (1977)

AIRS & GRACES (1976)

KATHRYN TICKELL

BIOGRAPHY

K athryn Tickell was born on June 8, 1967, in Wark, North Tyne Valley, Northumberland, England, where many of her relatives still play traditional music. Her father, Mike Tickell, is an acclaimed performer of the songs of this area. Kathryn took up the Northumbrian smallpipes at the age of nine and by the age of thirteen had won all the traditional open smallpipes competitions and was also rapidly making a name for herself as a fiddle player. At the age of sixteen Kathryn released her first album, ON KIELDERSIDE, and two years later, in 1986, she recorded her second album, BORDERLANDS.

In 1987 a 60-minute TV documentary, *The Long Tradition*, broadcast on BBC Channel 4, chronicled her musical development and background. Kathryn's third album COMMON GROUND was chosen as one of 'Q' *Magazine*'s Records of the Year. Kathryn was also named as Top Instrumentalist in the Folk Roots Poll of 1988.

In 1990 The Kathryn Tickell Band was formed. The next few years saw Kathryn putting all her energy into the band, recording the albums THE KATHRYN TICKELL BAND and SIGNS and touring extensively throughout the world. She still found time to provide music for two of Newcastle's Live Theatre Company productions, to present a series of programs for Radio 2, record with the Penguin Café Orchestra and with The Chieftains. Kathryn has also contributed to three Sting albums. In 1997, Sting, Jimmy Nall, and

Kathryn hit the stage of Carnegie Hall, New York, performing *The Waters of Tyne* at a benefit concert in aid of The Rainforest Foundation. Kathryn has also founded the Young Musicians Fund to help young people in the Northeast region to realize their musical potential. In 1998 Kathryn released THE NORTHUMBERLAND COLLECTION, an album featuring various musicians and singers from Northumberland.

Interview

MAIRÉID SULLIVAN   You have recorded a great many albums, Kathryn. You must have been playing for quite a while.

KATHRYN TICKELL   I've been playing the pipes and the fiddle since I was about nine. Before that, I started on the piano and tin whistle when I was six. I made my first album when I was sixteen. It was a bit of a shock. I didn't really intend to do that recording.

M.S.   Really? How did that happen?

K.T.   I had made a cassette before that. I went into the local radio station to play a couple of tunes that were being recorded for an upcoming program. So, I recorded a couple of tunes, and they said, "You might as well record a few more while you're here." Eventually they said, "Do you realize you've just recorded over thirty-five minutes worth of tunes. Can you think of anymore? We can produce a cassette." So we did it, and they ran off a few copies. I was about fifteen at the time. One of the people there was the same person that organized the first official album. I didn't know anything about record companies, or the music business, or any of that.

M.S.   Do you sing also?

K.T.   No, my dad sings. That was always his thing, and he's also got a very loud voice. He's quite impressive. Having said that, I have been trying a bit recently around the house. There's a lot of musicians who have been going on at me for a while to give it a try.

M.S.   What do the Northumbrian pipes sound like? Do they sound anything like uilleann pipes?

K.T.   It's not tiny; it has a very pure sound, something between an oboe and a clarinet. It's a much purer sound than the uilleann pipes. On the positive side, its notes are very true. On the negative side, you don't always get the 'wildness' that you get in other pipes like bagpipes. It's an indoor instrument. Most people think of pipes as being very loud and blaring, but these are very sweet.

M.S.   Is it hard to keep it in tune on stage when you go from one climate environment to another?

K.T. Sometimes, yes, they have their moments.

M.S. Is it hard to get reeds?

K.T. No, but they rarely need replacing. I haven't changed mine in years. They are very different from Scottish and Irish pipes in that respect. The Scottish pipes are mouth blown. The Irish pipes are dryer, so they don't go out of tune as often. They're referred to as a "cauld wind pipe" because you don't blow into them, air is provided by bellows. The Northumbrian pipes are "cauld wind pipes."

M.S. Did many people play the Northumbrian pipes?

K.T. Yes, there's quite a lot. I just moved house to a different village in Northumberland, and my next door neighbor, who is eleven years old, is learning the pipes. The daughter of the village grocer is learning the pipes. She's eleven. There's a very famous Northumbrian piper, Joe Hutton, who lived in this valley and died several years ago. I was actually related to him, distantly. He did a lot to get the pipes going in this area. He gave classes and workshops. People would come from a great distance to get lessons. He was the shepherd from Northumberland, a very traditional player. He wasn't someone with a university education, who learned to play from books. He was someone who grew up with it, like I did.

M.S. You mean he was actually out there in the hills as a shepherd playing the pipes?

K.T. Yes, that's what he did. My grandfather was into forestry, and he was a shepherd and a mole catcher. He was one of the last mole catchers in Northumberland, actually.

M.S. It seems that Northumbrian pipers mainly comes from the Northeast corner of England. Why is that? What's the origin?

K.T. There used to be bagpipes all over the world. They were all over the country. Every county had its own bagpipes if you went back a few hundred years. For some reason, the Irish pipes survived, the Scottish pipes survived, the Northumbrian pipes survived, and also the Scottish small pipes, which are very similar to the Northumbrian pipes, and the Border pipes survived.

M.S. So, there are all these different kinds of pipes?

K.T. I think there are about five indigenous types of pipes in Britain that are still being played.

M.S. What attracted you to this particular instrument? You play the violin and penny whistle as well, right?

K.T. I used to play the whistle. It's mainly the pipes and the fiddle now.

M.S. Do you play the fiddle when you tour and record also?

K.T. Yes, I do.

M.S. It's unusual to find someone who actually has two lead instruments, like you, that you play on a professional level.

K.T. I desperately wanted to play the fiddle; it's the instrument that I would most like to play. I like to play the fiddle with other people. I love to play the pipes with other people also, but there's something about the pipes. You can play by yourself, and you sense something so old. The pipes are the instrument that is right for me. They are the instrument I feel more of a connection with when I play. Everybody's got an instrument which is right for them, and some people may never find it because it might be something rare and obscure, like Northumbrian pipes. I was lucky enough to be in Northumberland, so it was easy for me to find them. I would love to play the piano as well, but I would never be a piano player. With the pipes, it was a total accident that I took them up. They were just lying around. I don't really remember fully, but I think my dad had them. There were other instruments around, but I just had a go on them and made awful noises. I thought it was very funny. Then my dad came in and shouted at me and said, "Put those things down, and stick to the piano!" which was like showing red to a bull. It was at this point I decided I was going to play them properly. So, it's strange that although the fiddle was the one that I yearned for, the pipes just came naturally.

M.S. How do you feel about playing in front of an audience?

K.T. I've been doing it for a long time I suppose, so it's hard to put into words. Sometimes when I'm at home, I'm thinking, I'm pleased to be home. I don't want to go out and go away then. Then as soon as I get away, and I'm on stage, particularly with the band, when it's going well, I get the thought in my head, this is what I should be doing! I talk a lot on stage. For the first six years I did a lot of solo gigs, so I had to talk quite a bit. I'm quiet on stage, but not shy.

M.S. Do you tell stories about the tunes?

K.T. Yes. They're usually about my granddad, and uncles and people from the village, and where the tunes came from and where I came from. It's not like a historical debate. It's anecdotes. My interest is in how the tune has come down to me. I think it's important where you get the tunes from and how well you know the person you learnt it from. It's the value in the tune.

There's a fiddle player that I learnt a lot from, called Willie Taylor, who's another shepherd. He's still alive. He's eighty-two, and I spent New Year's Eve with him and his cousin, Will, who's ninety. He plays the mouth organ. With Willie, when I play a tune on stage, the audience is hearing me, but, although I don't feel that I'm playing exactly like him, they're also hearing him in my playing. They don't realize that they are, but they are.

M.S. So, then you tell something about him, to give the feeling of him? What would you tell about him?

K.T. He's only got three fingers on his left hand, and this is a source of great amusement to him. Everybody's always amazed when they suddenly notice. One of the stories I like is about the time he and his cousin came to play a concert, and my dad brought them up. They don't get out very often, you see. Anyway, they got lost and they drove onto the platform at the railway station instead of down the street. All this is going on with two eighty-year-olds and my dad, stranded, in the middle of the platform with the trains, in the car. Dad was in an absolute panic. And all that Willie and Will, the two retired shepherds, could say as they looked out at the station, undaunted by the situation, was, "Wow! what a great lambing shed this would make!" My dad's on the brink of destruction, and they're talking about sheep.

M.S. Those stories 'warm people up' for the music. They get more feeling and appreciate it more?

K.T. It's the feeling these people are real that comes across. They're not idealized shepherds out in the misty blue yonder. They're real people and they are funny. They might like a drop of whiskey on occasion, or indigestion tablets, and then they can play beautiful music. It's important to put it in context. It's really not one person standing up on stage with people that paid money sitting quietly as they listen. That's not what it's about. It's important to play the tunes, and talk about the context. I like it because it's so linked to this area. My family has been in this area for six hundred years. The tunes are written about people I know, plus tunes written hundreds of years ago. And the people around me are the descendents of those people from long ago. It all ties in with who I am and where I come from.

M.S. What's the mix in that part of the country in terms of ethnic background? Are there a lot of Danes there?

K.T. It's difficult to say because the history of Northumberland is a bit confused. This was one of the main centers of Celtic Christianity, the Holy Island, Lindisfarne, established by Ireland's St. Aiden long ago. Northumbria was a big country in the time we call the Dark Ages, when our history got lost. It was also the time of the Viking influence. Descendents of Vikings have been farmers in this valley for hundreds of years. They have that same tall blond look.

M.S. Do many people care about the history?

K.T. People in Northumberland are very concerned with identity. Unfortunately for us, we're still a part of England, while Scotland now has its devolution. We're far closer to Edinburgh than we are to London. So we always feel like we're left on the sidelines. The people in the north of England are very concerned that their identity doesn't get subsumed by London. We are quite isolated, and it is the border area where I live where it's actually been part of Scotland quite a few times. Scotland extends quite a bit further south than where I live, but I'm actually in England.

M.S. What do you think will happen?

K.T.   Well, there is talk of having a regional council and it's difficult to see what the best thing to do is. We're very strong with the culture. Especially the history and the poetry and the music as well.

M.S.   That will really be the way to preserve it, to preserve the identity.

K.T.   I think that's why people feel that they have a strong identity up here. There are so many songs that are indigenous to this area.

M.S.   Are they in the English language?

K.T.   Not as you would know it, no. There's a lot of words you wouldn't understand. The official language is English. It's just that a lot of old songs are written in dialect and the dialect is very strong. Some of these songs are over six hundred years old, so they're written in rather archaic language. My dad sings a few of them, and they go on for a long time.

M.S.   Does your father know a lot of them?

K.T.   They're difficult to know a lot of because they are very, very long. He vaguely knows a lot of them, and may need an evening to refresh his memory before deciding to sing one. He always has a couple that he can do all the way through.

M.S.   Does he ever record? Has he been collected?

K.T.   Yes, kind of. He's done a few songs. I've recorded an album of him. Not the border ballads because they are too long and it's difficult to work out what the context could be now, for border ballads. He did a ballad at a local charity concert, and it wasn't a folk music audience at all, just a local audience, and it was really powerful. It was amazing how it worked.

M.S.   Has the BBC done anything about it? They seem really interested in that sort of research.

K.T.   They have programs, every now and then, that investigate the history, to try to find out if these songs are really old, or if they are made up to sound old. They want to know if the ballads are actually true, etc. My dad really doesn't get involved with them. He just likes to sing the songs. He was brought up learning the songs outside of pubs when he was too young to go in. At that time people weren't really taking any notice. It's only more recently that people have been taking an interest. Dad's got a voice that can cut across a bar room.

Discography

THE NORTHUMBERLAND
   COLLECTION (1998)
GATHERING (1997)
SIGNS (1993)

THE KATHRYN TICKELL BAND (1991)
COMMON GROUND (1988)
BORDERLANDS (1987)
ON KIELDERSIDE (1984)

Compilations

FROM SEWINGSHIELDS TO GLENDALE (1985)

GAY WOODS
(STEELEYE SPAN)

BIOGRAPHY

Born in Dublin in 1948, Gay Woods started playing at fifteen with her brothers, and then with The Prentice Folk, whose members included her then husband Terry Woods. In 1969 she joined the newly formed Steeleye Span, founded by Terry Woods and Ashley Hutchings, and performed on their first album, HARK THE VILLAGE WAIT, in 1970. Soon after Maddy Pryor and Tim Hart were added to the band, she left to play in folk clubs in Ireland, England, and throughout Europe with Terry Woods and The Woods Band, until 1980. In 1980 Gay formed her own band in Holland, Auto Da Fe. In 1985 she spent just under a year with Operacket, a punk band, following which she gave up playing until 1994.

During these non-performing years, she diversified somewhat by studying the work of Carl Jung, finding in his theory of archetypes new meaning for the lyrics of tradtitional folk songs. In 1994 she was invited back into the fold of Steeleye Span, where she remains to this day, performing on their two most recent albums, HORSTOW GRANGE and TIME.

interview

mairéid sullivan   Where do you currently call home?

gay woods   I live in County Meath, which is only an hour's drive from Dublin. It's very lush meadowland. I'm a Dublin girl, originally.

m.s.   How did you get started with your musical interests?

g.w.   My father and mother used to sing around the house. My brother got me into playing in the folk scene because it was very popular in Dublin at the time. Both my brothers were really interested in the folk-revival that happened in Dublin in the sixties.

I had a strong attraction to play in E minor, so I learned that chord on the guitar and started singing. I didn't know then, when I was very young, why I was drawn to the minor keys, but I do now.

m.s.   Tell me what drew you to that?

g.w.   A depressed situation opens up so many doors, where as, if you're always in a major key, life just seems established the way it is – so called, happy. I think a depressive situation opens more doors, as long as one doesn't slip into clinical depression. Depression in song transforms us from being mommy's daughter or daddy's daughter. It transforms us, and it makes men and women of us. When I hear the minor key it touches something in me that I can start relating through. It was an unconscious thing I suppose; it just touched something in the unconscious. The pain and torture of just being alive got me into all sorts of messes and fixes. I think I'm at the other side now. I gave up music completely for about five years in 1986 because it was really draining me. I had my daughter, Lillian, who is now thirteen years old. I had to focus on being a mother. It was then that I started to study Carl Jung's work. That's why I can speak the way I speak now on subjects like depression. It took about four years before I got into the singing again.

m.s.   How different did the singing feel when you returned to it?

g.w.   Very different. The music Steeleye Span plays now is very different from the very beginning when I was first with the group. However, I'm enjoying singing the old traditional songs again because I have a new understanding of the mythological archetypes that I'm singing about in them.

m.s.   How do you see the archetypes in traditional songs now?

g.w.   Well, when I re-joined the band I had to do the songs the way they had been done, and that irks me a bit. I wish I had been there all the way through, from the beginning, because they've left out a lot of the symbols of transformation. For instance, *Thomas the Rhymer*: legend has it that he was Thomas of Ercledoune, who lived in the thirteenth century. In the original poem he comes back with the gift of the anima, shall we say, because he goes off with the Queen of Elf Land. She finds him sitting under an Elder tree, the Eildon Tree (some say it was a Hawthorn tree but I think the symbolism of the Elder is more potent). The Eildon Tree is the magic tree where the poets and seers go for inspiration. The poets used to sit under this tree because it was supposed to be an enchanted tree. It could have been a tree that grew something that would fall on them, or maybe, something grew near it, that would give them some kind of an altered state of consciousness, and this might be why they thought they saw the Queen of Elf Land. Thomas the Rhymer sees her, or thinks he sees her, and she takes him to Elf Land. "And till seven years were gone and past, True Thomas on earth was never seen." Seven is a magic number of transformation: seven planets, seven metals, etc.

According to Jungian thinking, she is actually taking him on a journey to the unconscious, and he becomes transformed by the events. She is his muse. The images give the impression that he's gone mad. This is an example of how I see these songs. I'm beginning to see something better, brighter, and deeper in them, and I do enjoy them more, for that reason.

M.S. How does he come back in the original poem?

G.W. The lyrics are, "He has gotten a new coat of the even cloth and a pair of shoes of the velvet green." He comes back more learned and wiser, but there is something wrong with one of his eyes. In these stories, they always come back with some kind of affliction. It may be just proof that they are transformed.

M.S. I love that concept. We can see it in ourselves. You're talking about coming back, and I could use that metaphor for myself too, coming back from a treacherous journey through life's adventures. We change and we do know our afflictions, our imperfections. But we also have a better understanding of our strengths.

G.W. Because the story is told as a poem, it seems metaphysical, but it's really about the invisible pain. The effect is a psychological change; we can't see it, but we do look different, as if we were traumatized and have come out of it. It's the story of life.

M.S. I have seen exhibitions of Buddhist statuary from the first century BC up to the eleventh century. What always stirs me is the expression on the faces – the sublime bliss, the joy, on the faces. Perfect bliss is plainly seen in those expressions. I think those ancient images are meant to show us how the face is transformed by heightened consciousness and that it is achievable; the expression on the face is there as an example.

G.W. I think we realize that we can evolve in a more pleasant way, now that we are more conscious of deeper meaning in all that is happening within and around us.

M.S. The Irish have some very old bog statues, and the meditation expression on the faces is exactly like the ones from as far away as Indonesia.

Human beings, when they get into that state, look pretty much the same anywhere, you know ... that state of inner peace.

G.W. I know what you're talking about. My brother does some paintings of these bog people, and I've got some on the wall here. The expressions are beautiful, very peaceful, but very dark. It's very 'this side' of the world; the furthest point west rather than the furthest point east. It's very dark. Have you read *Iron John*?

M.S. No, but I have heard of the story.

G.W. It's about a man who was found in the bog. It's based on a legend. I love it. It's quite Jungian as well.

M.S. It's really stimulating to see some of these creative perspectives take shape. It's part of the contemporary conversation all around the world; it's really interesting that the Celtic aspect is coming into it. What do you think of that?

G.W. I'm involved with a few projects at the Irish Association of Jungian Therapists. It's a very small membership. (Laughs) Yes, the ancient Celts have something to offer today, as long as people get it right. I like the whole Celtic thing, but we should make sure we take in the most ancient gods and goddesses. You know the dark underworld ones, the earliest, most ancient ones. The significant history doesn't start with Cuchullain (koo hoo lin) or the Celtic Twilight of W. B. Yeats.

As long as we go back far enough and go to, for example, Cernunnos (Ker noon os), lord of the animals, and Ogmios/Oghma (Og ma). Ogmios is like Hercules. Instead of brute strength, he is more a god of the strength of Eloquence, the binding power of poetry: he is the inventor of Ogham, the ancient Celtic alphabet. We find eloquence in a lot of the poets who come from a very deep Celtic, bog driven, merit system (laughs) – or whatever we want to call it. Cernunnos is the 'Horned One', the Stag God with antlers on his head. The God of Fertility. He's popular also in Nordic mythology. Dana would be at the top of the list for female goddesses. The supreme Goddess of the Tuatha de Danaan (Too a-haw day Dah nan). She was like Diana in Greek mythology; she had all the great traits.

M.S. Tell me about those archetypal traits?

G.W. Dana, or Danu, is the primal mother. Dana was also like Gaia, in Greek mythology, Mother Earth. I like her very much because she has great strength. She had three sons and one daughter, and then they started the whole thing rolling. She wasn't a wife; she was a companion to a male god, Bilé, (Bee-leh), Lord of Life and Death. The Tuatha de Danaan were her people, the tribe that descended from her. The Dagda is the male supreme god and father of the People, the tribe or children of Dana, The Tuatha de Danaan. He was famous for his great wisdom, as the 'Mighty One of Knowledge', which was the highest aspiration of The Tuatha de Danaan.

M.S.   How do you conjure up these archetypes?

G.W.   They are inherited parts of the psyche, patterns of psychological performance. Instinctive, primordial images. They are elements of the holy and demonic.

M.S.   I saw Seamus Heaney a couple of nights ago, and I gleaned what he said about going into the inner 'perfect' reality, within our inner experience. But he said we must also find that reflected in the external world. We look at our history, we sharpen our hindsight, to find that perfected reality, through our ancestry; so that we can prove the truth of our inner experience; so we can make it real in our lives by seeing that ancient precedent for perfection unfold in our own personal lives.

G.W.   Yes! I know! We are trying to make sense out of nothingness. I sometimes wonder why people get caught up in archetypes because they can lose their own sense of individuality through it. I think it's a crutch, and sometimes we do need crutches. You cannot mess with those archetypal images. They are very powerful. It can become schizophrenia for some people, and then you can start blaming them when you eat the dog or something. (Laughs)

Back to the music . . . I'm just singing traditional stuff now.

M.S.   But I thought you were writing a lot before.

G.W.   I was, and I hope to do it again. I'm finding something new in this old stuff, as I said earlier. With Steeleye Span, I'm doing some of their back catalog, and I'm also bringing some very Irish songs into the band. I'm also doing almost pantomime type songs because I'm attracted to them more. One of the modern ones I do is *I Wish That I Never Was Wed*, which is a Delia Murphy song from the 1940s. I heard her a lot when I was young. She was played a lot on the wireless. I loved the sound of her voice. The song is about domestic violence, but it was thought humorless at the time.

I do the *Old Turf Fire*, which was written in the late 1890s. More bog stuff. The bog is very big at the moment. Britain is very frightened that they're going to lose them because they are so beautiful. They are so important; there is nothing on them. It is sunken space, empty space with no trees. It's a completely different landscape. I love the bog. It's such a great place, a break from the bloody green. There is another song I found that I took to, it's called the *Bonnie Irish Boy*. It's from our most recent album, HORKESTOW GRANGE. It's a beautiful song that talks about how beautiful he is. I just stumbled across it. I love songs where the women praise the men.

You do realize that for a good five years I was singing in a punk band and writing my own songs. I didn't see it as a punk band, but it was judged like that. I thought I was just writing in the modern style.

M.S.   Oh! I shouldn't even be talking to you then! (Laughs)

G.W. Oh yes! You've probably got the wrong Celtic woman. (Laughs) I did all that experimenting by instinct. I needed a major breakaway from the 'folky' stuff, and I wanted, desperately, to stand up and sing – put more energy into it! I used to think folk music was just for sitting down. Everyone sat down when they sang in those days. That's how I felt at the time: I just had to stand up! I used to play the dulcimer and the autoharp, on my lap, in my folk days, but I said, "My God! I have to stand up and hold a microphone stand!" Thank God I did!

M.S. I have found a few people who have an 'attitude' about any experimentation with the various aspects of the music tradition. How did that affect you?

G.W. It annoys me because I think they're getting caught up in something that is very tight and 'twee'. In 1980, I realized I just couldn't stand it anymore. I'd just finished a tour of folk clubs in England, and I said, "I'm going to go mad if I don't get away from this stuff, and start writing and get some electricity behind me, as opposed to acoustic sound." That was great for me, because what I wrote about after that change was very important for me. It's what a lot of women were feeling at the time. I was with a group called Auto Da Fe, named after the Portuguese-Spanish Inquisition, where they used to burn women, mostly.

M.S. How do you feel about being back with Steeleye Span?

G.W. I suppose going back into Steeleye Span, since I was there in the beginning, is good. I left after the first record, and the band later became very English sounding. Before I left, there was a mixture. My former husband, Terry Woods, and Ashley Hutchings formed the group and then I joined the band. A little later, Tim Hart and Maddy Pryor joined the group, and the rest is history. So, there was the Irish influence at the very beginning, and we can call it the Celtic influence, the bog influence. The first album, HARK, THE VILLAGE WAIT, is great to listen to still. The voices were so young and pleasant, very innocent, and there were some good songs on it. Then, to go back to the band after such a long time was very interesting because the band had become so tightly English, Anglicized. I did it because it was a job in 1994. But I felt as if I was intruding most of the time. I was drawn to it, this time round, when they asked me to join them as a guest for one tour. But by the time the tour was finished, they wanted me to stay on.

Maddy Pryor had been in the band for twenty-six years and needed a break. So she left and I went on the road again last year. It was so weird for me to be there. I had to put up with a lot of projections from audiences who did not know the band in the very beginning.

DISCOGRAPHY

With Steeleye Span

HORKSTOW GRANGE (1998)
(Park Records)

TIME (1996)
(Park Records)

HARK THE VILLAGE WAIT (1970)
(RCA)

With Auto Da Fe

FIVE SINGLES AND
ONE SMOKED COD (1980)
(Spartan Records)

TATITUM
(Stoic UK)

With Gay and Terry Woods

TENDER HOOKS (1978)
(Mulligan Records)

BACKWOODS (1972/3)
(Polydor)

THE TIME IS RIGHT
(Polydor)

RENOWNED
(Polydor)

With The Woods Band

THE WOODS BAND (1971)
(Greenwich/Gramophone)

GRÁINNE YEATS

BIOGRAPHY

Gráinne Yeats was born in Dublin, Ireland, and was raised bilingual, in Irish and English. She has always combined a deep interest in traditional music and songs with a corresponding involvement in classical music.

At the same time she was studying piano, voice, and harp at the royal Irish Academy of Music in Dublin, she was also learning traditional songs from Gaeltacht singers. She has a particular interest in the Irish wire-strung harp, and was the first musician to revive and record the instrument on her double CD THE BELFAST HARP FESTIVAL 1792, released to celebrate the bicentennial of that event. Her companion book, *The Harp of Ireland*, relates the history of the instrument and explores the role of Edward Bunting in recording traditional Irish harp music in print. Gráinne plays both the wire-strung and gut/nylon-strung harps. She teaches in workshops, master classes, courses, and festivals. She is married to Michael Yeats, son of famous Irish poet and traditionalist W.B. Yeats, and they live mainly in Dublin.

INTERVIEW

MAIRÉID SULLIVAN How many children do you have, Gráinne?

GRÁINNE YEATS Four – they're all well grown up now.

M.S. Do any of them play music?

G.Y. My daughter Caítriona is a concert harpist with the Danish National Radio Symphony Orchestra. My daughter Siobhán is a genetic scientist in Munich. My third daughter, Síle, is a producer of a radio current affairs show here in Dublin. My son, Padraig, lives in Ohio, and he is an engineer.

M.S. You must be very proud! They're are all so creative.

G.Y. They are all doing great stuff, I think.

M.S. My mother says that each one of her seven children is like an only child to her. You have had an enormous career in music while bringing up your children. I know that you hold a very high place in Ireland as a singer and for your support of harp music. I want to find out why you were drawn to the harp?

G.Y. I can never remember a time when I didn't sing. I can't imagine not being able to sing. As a family, we used to spend two months in the Gaeltacht every year, and I learned a great many songs there. And, of course, we sang lots of lovely songs at school, which I still sing. And then I began studying piano, studying classical music. I have very wide interests in all kinds of music. I love all kinds of ethnic music, folk music, classical music, the whole gamut. So, my whole life has been filled with music.

I studied the piano and I studied singing, but I started my career as a singer. I was singing oratorio and giving recitals and that kind of thing. I used to sing unaccompanied songs in Irish. Whenever I gave a concert, I would always sing a few unaccompanied songs in Irish. But that is difficult for people to listen to if they don't know the language, since sean-nos is the old style of Gaelic singing.

I was invited to sing at a special function, and there I heard a harp player who impressed me. Before that the harp never affected me very much. I had heard it played at Gaelic League functions here in Dublin and it was used only as an accompaniment instrument.

I heard Joan O'Hara, who is an actress here in the Abbey Theatre, playing the harp, and I immediately thought I wanted to learn to play it. The next thing I had to do was find an instrument because harps were rarely played in Ireland at that time, around 1950. It was shortly after I was married that I became interested in it. I found a second-hand Scottish harp, a Briggs, in one of our music shops. It had gut strings because the traditional wire-strung harp, which had been played for hundreds of years, had given way to the much lighter gut-strung instrument in the nineteenth century. This harp was painted bright green. I got the shop to strip all the green off. I played that for quite a bit and, gradually, became increasingly interested in it.

I learnt basic harp technique from Sheila Larchet Cuthbert and Mercedes Bolger. Mercedes and I formed a duo and played all over the country for years and later on we taught together and we still do.

I majored in history in Trinity College, Dublin, so I have a strong interest in history. I discovered when I started playing the gut-strung harp that it has a very interesting history. So I read up on all that and I have all those precious books that nobody can get anymore in my library.

But I couldn't get anybody to make me a wire-strung harp. I went around to the harp maker, and said, "Can you make me a wire-strung harp?" And he looked at me and said "Mrs. Yeats, what would you want with that?" I just said, "I want to hear what it sounds like."

I continued with my search. I found a man who designed airplanes who was very interested, but he never did anything. I had an engineer who was interested in it and he never did anything. I had a man who made lovely furniture and the only thing that came of that were harp back chairs. He didn't even offer me one!

Finally a Welsh friend of mine said, "I have a friend who is a carpenter, and I'll get him to do something." So the carpenter in Wales made me a very small, rather inefficient wire-strung harp. At least, it was a wire-strung harp. This was about 1970.

M.S. Even then it was still hard to find one?

G.Y. Oh yes. You couldn't get them, they weren't made. Nobody was playing wire-strung harps then. I went to America on one of my regular tours there, and I landed in a place called Alamoso, a small college town in Colorado. After that concert I was talking to a man from the college, and he said, "By the way, we have an Irish harp." I expected it to be one of those Clark harps. They're gut-strung and very like a small Irish harp, but an American style Irish harp. He brought it out, and it was a Jay Witcher.

Well, Jay Witcher is the best harp maker of that kind in the world. At that time he lived in California but now he lives in Maine. He began to make replicas of well-known harps, so when I saw this I was enthralled. I wrote to him and asked him to make me a harp, which he did. He asked me which one I wanted. I asked for the 17th-century style SIRR harp, and he made it for me. He's been making harps for me ever since, and we became close friends. He revived the making of wire-strung harps. In addition, I revived the playing of them. So, between the two of us, we were proud of having re-started that.

M.S. That's why you are known as the grand matriarch of the Irish wire-strung harp.

G.Y. I've been described as a grand dame, which is not a name I like very much, but I will admit to being opinionated. (Laughter) Anyway that's how that started, so I have a number of Jay's harps now. I also have some of his nylon-strung harps. They are simply beautiful as well.

M.S. What is the difference between playing a wire-strung harp and a nylon-strung harp? Musically, how different are they?

G.Y. Totally different: they are simply two different harps. The big thing about the wire-strung harp is that it has a long decay of the notes. When you strike a wire-string, it goes on and on and on. When you strike nylon or gut, it will go on a little bit, but then it dies. It is such a different world. You have to dampen the strings on the wire-strung, and no matter how much you damp, the overtones always sound on. You get a very resonant sound. If you have a resonant room, it's not easy. It's a completely different technique.

M.S. That's what Ann Heymann was talking about.

G.Y. The great thing about Ann is that she has never played any other kind of harp, so she didn't come to it with her hands fixed in any sort of position. Also, she has worked very hard and she is very dedicated.

M.S. She actually mentioned something exciting about having played one particular Burns march that taught her to use both hands.

G.Y. (More laughter) I've known Ann since she began, and we've had some great sessions together. She used to come to Ireland and we would play together. It's very good to use your left hand to help out your right. We've both come to the same conclusions about that.

M.S. I got the impression that she was talking about the old lessons used in becoming a harper. These particular pieces of music were part of the very old training techniques for the wire-strung harp. They taught the skills one needs to develop to the next level.

G.Y. Oh yes, these are the studies, according to Edward Bunting, for teaching students the basics of wire-strung technique. His manuscripts are unique in that he collected music 'live', so to speak, from the last of the traditional harpers in the late 18th century. In many cases, he gives the names of the musicians so we know what harpers were playing. There are a number of earlier collections of Irish music but no prominence is given to the tunes, except in the case of Carolan, though it is clear that much of his music was collected from harpers.

Burns's *March* was the fourth lesson. We have lesson number one, and lesson number two, but number three is missing, so you have to invent your own. Bunting also wrote down lists of ornamentation and the traditional stories and lore of the harpers. In fact, he grilled them to extract all of the information that he could. He did wonderful work, and but for him, most of our harp music would have disappeared or, at best, become anonymous. I've covered a good deal of this in my book about the harp of Ireland.

M.S.   What's the name of your book?

G.Y.   *The Harp of Ireland: The Belfast Harp Festival of 1792, and the Saving of Ireland's Harp Music by Edward Bunting.* I have also recorded much of his music on a double CD, on which I play seven different harps.

As to how it should be played, with traditional music you have to make up your own mind. In classical music, once a composer has written it out, you're not supposed to change it, you're not allowed to. In traditional music it's up to you, although you shouldn't change the basic tune very much. It's more a change in rhythm here and there and the ornamentation.

M.S.   Maire Ni Chathasaigh has talked about the subtle miniature improvisation in the structure.

G.Y.   She's great! I never get tired of listening to her. She invented a new technique for playing dance music on the gut and nylon-strung harps. She invented that, and that has been great for the harp, because the harp has always been playing all kinds of things, but not dance music.

But back to the technique of the wire-strung instrument . . . if you don't do the damping properly, it just sounds horrible. The people who heard the Irish harp, of old, always talked about the booming of the bass and the tinkling of the treble notes. So, you can get all kinds of clues on how to play the music. The less bass you put in the better. I use selective dampening, so I get harmony from the tunes.

If I have a run of say five notes, C D E F G, and if I land on the G, I would dampen the D and the F and I would then be sounding a nice chord. You can only learn that by fiddling around with the instrument. I certainly don't dampen all the time. I dampen the dissonant notes. I do love to have this gorgeous noise going on, so long as it's not dissonant. I also use the harp as an accompaniment to an actor reciting poems. The old harpers used to do that. In that case, I've found that you can use it as a sound resource and can be as dissonant as you like. You don't have to play tunes all the time, you can use all kinds of peculiar things in it to illustrate the words. That is very exciting, too. It's a fascinating instrument.

M.S.   Do you get a thrill out of imagining how it might have been played in ancient times?

G.Y.   If anybody gave me a time machine, I would go back to Ireland in the 13th century.

M.S.   Why the 13th century?

G.Y.   The old style of playing began to decline when the Tudors came conquering. Before that the harp was at its height. I would have liked to have been present in the hall of one of the great Lords of Ireland, who would have had a wonderful harp player. I would just sit in the back with my video recorder and tape everything. Wouldn't that be wonderful? The only trouble with that is you might be terribly disappointed.

Most of my career has been with the gut-strung harp, and later the wire-strung harp. People have written all sorts of songs for me and music for me to perform. I used to perform music from many countries, but the second part of my program was always entirely Irish.

M.S. Do you have many recordings of your music?

G.Y. Yes, I have a double CD, which was recorded for the bicentennial celebration of the Belfast Harp Festival in 1992, and I have LPs which have been recorded on to cassette. I have been planning a new recording, but there have been so many interruptions that I have had to delay the process.

While things have improved tremendously for the music of the harp, not long ago, in Ireland, people were not very interested in it. The harp has been regarded for hundreds of years as the instrument of the great houses, not an instrument of the people. This is true to some extent.

In Norman times, the Normans were all Irish speaking and they adopted the Irish customs. Of course, harp players were professional musicians, paid by their patrons. From the 13th century up until the 16th and 17th, they played for the great houses. A lot of the harpers were resident in the homes of their patrons.

M.S. Your parents were involved with the establishment of the Irish Free State.

G.Y. Yes. My parents both worked for the 1916 Rising in their own ways. My father, P.S. O'Hegarty was on the IRB, which was the inner committee responsible for organizing things. My mother, Wilhelmina (Mina) Rebecca Smyth, was a member of Cumann na mBan, the equivalent woman's group. My mother was from Derry, and my father was from Cork.

When the civil war broke out, after the setting up of the Irish Free State, my parents supported the Free State but took no active part in that bitter struggle. My father became a civil servant, so politics was closed to him. It was not politics that brought them together but their desire to learn Irish.

Neither of my parents spoke Irish in their younger years, so they both had to learn it, which is how they met. They were both attending the Gaelic League in London. They were both learning Irish together.

We spoke both Irish and English at home. As time went on, we began to speak more English than Irish as there were always a lot of people coming to the house who didn't speak Irish. Irish was my first language, and I did go to an Irish-language school. Anyway, that was how I was brought up. Therefore, I have always had this great affection for anything to do with the language.

M.S. The thing that has enthralled me, in what Irish speakers say about their language, is its capacity for poetic expression. They say that the Irish language has a capacity to capture a much broader field of imagination than the English language.

G.Y. It is a very poetic language, and it is a very beautiful sounding language too. Our language has changed a great deal over hundreds of years. There's Old Irish, which I don't understand, which doesn't mean a thing to me. Middle Irish, I can make something out of, and modern Irish, from about 1600s, which I do understand. The language has changed quite a lot. Even in my lifetime, they've standardized it and changed the spelling.

M.S. The music has also changed. It must be a real pleasure, and a great source of inspiration, for you to see the revival of the harp by so many harpers who are really excellent musicians.

G.Y. It's a great pleasure. Mercedes Bolger, who's been my friend all these years, was the teacher at the Royal Irish Academy of Music. She and I, and few other teachers, were determined to try to raise the standards of playing.

M.S. So, you had a 'mission' back then?

G.Y. We had a mission; we were tired of people's attitudes to the harp. The attitude was that nobody could play and it was just being used for cabaret. We started on a little crusade. We were trying to teach some technique.

When Mercedes left the Academy to have a baby she 'dragooned' me into replacing her there, and I said, "Listen here, I can hardly play the harp myself, let alone teach anyone else." She said, "Oh yes, you can. Yes, you can! I'll show you." That shows how few people there were. Therefore, I went in to teach. I left because I was touring so much in America, and I couldn't keep up with it. But I then 'dragooned' a friend of mine, Elizabeth Hannon, and she said, "I can't possibly teach," and I said, " Oh yes, you can! I'll show you." She was there for about five years, and then there were one or two other people coming along. Now there are all kinds of teachers and pupils in many areas.

We also instituted harp schools around the country. We organized a team of teachers and laid out a course. We took turns going down to the country. For instance, we went to Derry, and we used to go to Wexford. We had everyone teaching the same thing, so that everyone had the same technique.

You might be interested in this little insight about the time before we really made our effort to improve the standards for teaching the harp. When the harp was beginning to come back, I went down to a conference at a local center to examine the students, on behalf of the Academy. I examined a few students who really weren't very good. Then their teacher, a nun, came to me, to do the exam, and she was just one step ahead of the pupils. That's the way it was before we launched our program.

The Wexford and the Derry Schools have gone, long since, but there are now schools in other parts of the country. There were practically no country harp teachers when I was learning. There were just a few around Dublin. I am delighted to have contributed to something like that.

M.S. Are you following the latest resurgence of interest in Celtic culture?

G.Y. I've always been conscious of the Celtic culture, if you want to call it that. The six Celtic countries – Brittany, Wales, Cornwall, Isle of Man, Ireland, and Scotland.

M.S. I know some academics that are frowning on the whole concept of Celtic being used to cover so many cultural ideas.

G.Y. We can't really call ourselves true Celts anymore, I think, because everybody is so mixed. I remember meeting an American man who had a real thing about the Celts. I said, "What do you mean by Celtic?" and he said, "Oh, you Irish are all Celtic," and I said, "We're not, you know," and I went through all the people that come into Ireland, and he was absolutely lost! I think you can say that there are the Celtic languages, there is the poetry that goes with these languages, and, in some cases, the music that goes with these languages, not always. I think in Cornwall, there's practically nothing left, and the Isle of Man is pretty weak. Brittany is very strong, but they never had a harp, up until Alan Stivell started to play the Irish harp. His father made him a replica of our old harp, the one you see on our coins. That was his first harp. He plays all kinds of harps now. I think it was he who coined the phrase "Celtic harp."

But anyway, I think the term Celtic is perfectly all right if you apply it properly. Now the term Celtic harp, I can't stand. It doesn't mean anything. We call it an Irish harp.

M.S. What about the ancient philosophy of the Druids? Do you know anything about that?

G.Y. I read books about the poets and Bards and Bardic poetry.

M.S. Any recommendations for books?

G.Y. I'd recommend Donal O'Sullivan's book on Carolan. It really is a must: *Turlough Carolan: Life, Times and Music of an Irish Harper*. I'd also recommend Edward Bunting's, *The Three Collections of Ancient Irish Music*, published in 1797, 1809, and 1840. They were republished about twenty years ago, all three together. They are very hard to get now, but well worth the effort for the serious scholar. These are books of music and about the music.

M.S. How did you manage a career and a household as well?

G.Y. When I was a young mother, you could still get house help very cheaply. I used to have a girl, who spoke beautiful Irish, living in with us.

When my children were born, I had that assistance, and I was able to go out and do things. I was always there when the children were small because I didn't want to hand my children over to anybody else. I wouldn't like to imagine what could happen if I did that. That is how I was able to cope with all that. I was about twenty-six, and it was then that I learned to play the harp. I was learning it between pregnancies. I remember there was always a period when I couldn't get close enough to the harp.

M.S. You're husband is Michael Yeats, son of W.B. Yeats. Did it make a major impact on your life to be married into such a great literary family?

G.Y. Well, we've been married nearly fifty years and I just married the man I fell in love with. People would always come up and say, "The son of W.B. Yeats!" and I said to him, not long ago, actually, "Probably, the first time I met you, I would have said, 'Oh! That's the son of W.B. Yeats, the man whose poetry I so love.'" I was nineteen when I met him, I don't really remember making much to do about that, but people make that comment all the time. My husband has always been a great help to me, with the rearing of the children, helping me to set up concerts, all that kind of thing, and he helps me with my typing. He is a marvelous man!

Discography

THE BELFAST HARP FESTIVAL 1792 (Double CD)

Book

The Harp of Ireland: The Belfast Harp Festival of 1792, and the Saving of Ireland's Harp Music by Edward Bunting

RECOMMENDED READING

Anam Cara: A Book of Celtic Wisdom,
by John O'Donohue

The Ancient Celts, by Barry Cunliffe

Ancient Irish Tales, edited by Tom P. Cross
and Clark Harris Slover

The Ancient Wisdom of the Celts,
by Murry Hope

The Arthurian Tradition,
by John Matthews

Atlantean Celts, by Simon James

Bagpipes and Tunings,
by Theodor H. Podnos

*Bardic Source Book: Inspirational Legacy
and Teachings of the Ancient Celts,*
by John Matthews

Bard, Odyssey of the Irish,
by Morgan Llywelyn

*The Bog Man and the Archaeology of
People,* by Don Brothwell

*Carolan: The Life, Times and Music of an
Irish Harper,* by Donal Joseph O'Sullivan

Celtic Bards, Celtic Druids,
by RJ Stewart & Robin Williamson

*The Celtic Book of Days: A Daily Guide to
Celtic Spirituality and Wisdom,*
by Caitlin Matthews

*Celtic Chiefdom, Celtic State: The
Evolution of Complex Social Systems in
Prehistoric Europe (New Directions in
Archaeology),* by Bettina Arnold

*Celtic Christianity: A Sacred Tradition, a
Vision of Hope,* by Timothy J. Joyce

*Celtic Harp Music of Carolan & Others for
Solo Guitar,* by Glenn Weiser

Celtic Heritage,
by Alwyn Rees and Brinley Rees

The Celtic Heroic Age,
edited by John T. Koch with John Carey

*Celtic Legends of the Beyond: A Celtic Book
of the Dead,* by Derek Bryce

*A Celtic Miscellany: Translations from the
Celtic Literatures,* by Kenneth Hurlstone

Celtic Mouth Music, by Matt Kopka

Celtic Music for Folk Harp,
by Laurie Riley and Leslie McMichael

Celtic Mythology, by John A. MacCulloch

*Celtic Pilgrimages: Sites, Seasons and Saints,
An Inspiration for Spiritual Journeys,*
by Elaine Gill

*The Celtic Quest in Art and Literature: An
Anthology from Merlin to Van Morrison,*
by Jane Lahr

*Celtic Tides: Traditional Music in a New
Age,* by Martin Melhuish

*Celtic Women: In Legend, Myth, and
History,* by Lyn Webster Wilde

*Celtic Women's Spirituality: Accessing the
Cauldron of Life,* by Edain McCoy

*Celtic Women, Women in Celtic Society and
Literature,* by Peter Berresford Ellis

The Celtic Year, by Toulson

The Celts, by Nora Chadwick

The Celts, by TG Powell

The Celts: Conquerors of Ancient Europe,
by Christiane Eluere and Daphne Briggs

The Celts: Life, Myth, and Art,
by Juliette Wood.

*The Celts: Uncovering the Mythic and
Historic Origins of Western Culture,*
by Jean Markale

The Chronicles of the Celts,
by Peter Berrisford Ellis

Complete Guide to Celtic Music: From the Highland Bagpipe to Riverdance and U2, by June Skinner Sawyers

The Confession of Saint Patrick,
translated by John Skinner

The Druids, by Peter Berrisford Ellis

The Druids, by Paul R. Lonigan

Early Medieval Ireland, by Daithi O'Cronin

The Elements of the Celtic Tradition,
by Caitlin Matthews

Fáeile na gCruitirái, Báeal Feirste, 1792: Gráinne Yeats assesses the music of Carolan and other harper composers which was collected by Edward Bunting at the Belfast Harpers' Festival, 1792, by Gráinne Yeats

Fiddle Music of Prince Edward Island: Celtic and Acadian Tunes in Living Tradition, by Ken Perlman

Fire in the Head: Shamanism and the Celtic Spirit, by Tom Cowan

The Flowering of Ireland,
by Kathleen Scherman

Gods and Fighting Men, Lady Gregory

The Great Cosmic Mother, Rediscovering the Religion of the Earth,
by Monica Sjöö and Barbara Mor

Hanes y delyn yng Nghymru, The story of the Harp in Wales, by Osian Ellis

The Harp of Brandiswhiere: A Suite for Celtic Harp, by Sylvia Woods

The Historical Method of the Celtic Harp: The Ancient British Small Harp, the Diatonic Welsh Bray Harp and the Irish Clairseach, by C. W. Bayer

A History of Ireland,
by Peter & Fiona Somerset Fry

How the Irish Became White,
by Noel Ignatiev

How the Irish Saved Civilization,
by Thomas Cahill

The Irish Harp Book,
by Shelia Larchet Cuthbert

Journey in Celtic Music, Cape Breton Style, by Sheldon MacInnes

King of the Celts, by Jean Markale

The Knight, The Lady, & The Priest,
by Georges Duby

Land of Women, Tales of Sex and Gender from Early Ireland, by Lisa M. Bitel

Last Night's Fun, by Kieran Carson

Lost Kingdoms, Celtic Scotland and the Middle Ages, by John L. Roberts

The Mabinogi,
translated and edited by Patrick K. Ford

The Middle Ages, a concise encyclopedia, edited by H.R. Loyn

Mythic Ireland, by Michael Dames

Myths and Legends of Ireland,
by Samuel Lover and Thomas Crocker

A Natural History of Love,
by Diane Ackerman

On the Edge of a Dream: Women in Celtic Myth & Legend, by Jennifer Heath

Over Nine Waves, A Book of Irish Legends, by Marie Heaney

Parzival, by Wolfram Von Eschenbach

The Penguin Atlas of Ancient history,
by Colin McEvedy

The Penguin Historical Atlas of the Vikings, by John Haywood

Pocket Guide to Celtic Spirituality,
by Sirona Knight

The Power of Myth,
by Joseph Campbell, with Bill Moyers

Power of Raven, Wisdom of Serpent: Celtic Women's Spirituality, by Noragh Jones

Prison Letters of Countess Markievicz,
by Consuitance Gore-Booth

Queen Maeve and Her Lovers: Reflections on a Celtic Archetype of Ecstasy, Addiction, and Healing, by Sylvia Brinton Perera

The Quest of Three Abbots,
by Brendan Lehane

Sacred Stones, Sacred Places,
by Marianna Lines

Secrets of the Gaelic Harp,
by Ann Heymann

The Serpent and the Goddess: Women, Religion, and Power in Celtic Ireland,
by Mary Condren

The Silver Wheel: Women's Myths and Mysteries in Celtic Tradition,
by Marguerite Elsbeth
and Kenneth Johnson

The Speech of the Grail, by Linda Sussman

The Story of the Irish Race,
by MacManus

The Tain,
translation by Thomas Kinsella.

Tree of Strings, by Alison Kinnaird

The Western Way,
by Caitlin and John Matthews

Women of the Celts, by Jean Markale

Women's Encyclopedia of Myths and Secrets,
by Barbara Walker

Women in Celtic Law & Culture,
by Jack Thompson

Women in Celtic Myth, by Moyra Caldecott

Women Troubadours, by Meg Bogin

The World of the Celts, by Simon James

Writing for the Pedal Harp,
by Ruth Inglefield and Lou Anne Neill

celtic music on the world wide web

For those of you interested in further exploration, here is a list of websites that are related to Celtic Music.

Altan's Home Page ...
http://www.altan.ie/index.html

Ancient Music of Ireland ...
http://services.worldnet.net/~pybertra/ceol/

Australian Folk Festivals ...
http://www.spirit.com.au/~grmac/festivals.html

Blix Street Records ...
http://www.blixstreet.com/home.html

Ceilildh Links ...
http://www.ceili.ie/Links_1.html

Celtic Guitar on the Web ...
http://www.celticguitarmusic.com/

Celtic Heartbeat Records ...
http://www.celticheartbeat.com/index2.html

Celtic Heritage Homepage ...
http://fox.nstn.ca/~celtic/

Celtic, Scottish, Irish & Welsh ...
http://www.lmce.com/~marko/celtic.html

Celtic/Irish/Scottish/Musicians ...
http://www.celticmusic.com/artists.html

CelticMusic.Com ...
http://www.celticmusic.com/home.shtml

Celtic Music on the Internet ...
http://celtic.stanford.edu//Internet_Sources.html#One

Ceolas ...
http://www.ceolas.org/

Claire Roche Homepage ...
http://indigo.ie/~croche/

Dirty Linen Magazine ...
http://www.dirtynelson.com/linen

Dunkeld Records/Dougie MacClean ...
http://dunkeld.co.uk/

Entertainment Ireland ...
http://entertainmentireland.ie/music/index.htm

Eileen McGann's Homepage ...

http://www.canuck.com/~jscown/mcgann/

Emma Christian's Homepage ...
http;//www.manxradio.com

Every Celtic Thing on the Web ...
http://www.celt.net/og/ething.htm

FestivalFinder: Music Festivals of Ireland ...
http://www.festivalfinder.com/

Fiona Joyce homepage ...
http://ireland.iol.ie/~planetx/fipage1.html

Folk Library.Com ...
http://www.execpc.com/~henkle/fbindex/home_pages.html

Folk Music.Org.Artists ...
http://www.folkmusic.org/artists/

Folk Roots Home Page ...
http://www.cityscape.co.uk/froots/

Galeforce Music Catalog ...
http://www.gaelforce.com/rec6.htm

Grace Griffith Homepage ...
http://www.loworbit.com/grace/

Green Linnet Artist links ...
http://www.greenlinnet.com/links/artlnx.htm

Harmony Music List ...
http://sdam.com/harmony/artists/indus/solo/

Home of Cherish The Ladies ...
http://www.cherishtheladies.com/

Hot Press Online ...
http://www.iol.ie/hotpress/

IMN – Irish Music Net ...
http://www.imn.ie/midi/title.html

Iona – Artists ...
http://www.lismor.co.uk/artists.html

Ireland's Internet Directory ...
http://www.niceone.com/

Irish Festivals ...
http://www.wco.com/~iaf/html/lineup.html

Irish folk song lyrics ...
http://www.cs.hut.fi/~zaphod/search/all_titles.html

Irish Music News ...
http://www.dararecords.com/imn/

IrishNet ...
http://celtic.stanford.edu/IrishNet/

Irish Traditional Music Archive ...
http://www.itma.ie/index.htm

Jacqui McShee's Pentangle ...
http://www.pavilion.co.uk/fdt/pent/

Jean Ritchie Home Page …
http://members.aol.com/greenhays/

Katell Keineg homepage …
http://www.users.interport.net/~slambert/katell.html

Kate Rusby Homepage …
http://www.compassrecords.com/rusby.htm

Keltria Home Page …
http://www.keltria.org/journal/

Kim Robertson Celtic Harp …
http://www.eldalamberon.com/friends/kimrobertson.html

Links to Celtic Music sites …
http://home.sprynet.com/~cottage/links.htm

Lismor Recordings …
http://www.lismor.co.uk/lismorhome.html

Liz Carroll …
http://www.musicblvd.com/cgibin/tw/0608798049921443314_104_11900

Llyfrgell Genedlaethol Cymru Na …
http://www.llgc.org.uk/index.htm

Loreena McKennitt Homepage …
http://www.quinlanroad.com/index2.html

Maggie's Music …
http://www.maggiesmusic.com/

Máire Brennan's Unofficial homepage …
http://www.jtwinc.com/clannad/clanhome.htm

Máire Ní Chathasaigh's website …
http://www.oldbridgemusic.com

Mairéid Sullivan's homepage …
http://www.maireid.com

Margaret Christl …
http://www.waterbug.com/christl.html

Mary Custy's Family Site …
http://www.custysmusic.com/

Natalie MacMaster Homepage …
http://www.nataliemacmaster.com/welcome.html

Nimbin Net – home page …
http://www.nimbin.net/index.htm#contents

Official Eileen Ivers Homepage …
http://historyoftheworld.com/music/blue/home/ivers.htm

Odilia Celtic Harp Archive …
http://www.odilia.ch/harp-agency.htm

Quarry Press …
http://www.quarrypress.com

The Pogues …
http://www.pogues.com/

Rita MacNeil Homepage …
http://www.ritamacneil.com/

Runrig Homepage ...
http://www.runrig.co.uk/

Sain Records, The Music of Wales ...
http://www.sain.wales.com/

Search Irish Net ...
http://www.ceolas.org/IrishNet/search.html

Shanachie Records ...
http://www.shanachie.com/Artists/

Sidestreet ...
http://www.elderly.com/sidestreet/M.htm

Susan McKeown's homepage ...
http://www.susanmckeown.com

Taylor's Traditional Tunebook ...
http://www3.islandnet.com/~btaylor/homepage.htm

Ted's Harp Links ...
http://www-personal.umich.edu/~tnichels/harplinks.html

Temple Records ...
http://www.rootsworld.com/temple/

The Harp Haven ...
http://www-personal.umich.edu/~tnichels/harpintro.html

The Irish Center of Southern California ...
http://gyw.com/irish_center/index.html

The Mudcat Cafe folk Search ...
http://www.mudcat.org/folksearch.html

The Talitha MacKenzie Homepage ...
http://members.aol.com/talithamac/html/

The Whirling Dervish ...
http://www.geocities.com/Paris/Metro/3858/dervish.html

Tommy & Siobhán Peoples Homepage ...
http://homepage.tinet.ie/~logo/bio.htm

Trad@Harp – Harp Links Page ...
http://www.harp.net/HarpLink.htm

Traditional Irish Tunes in MIDI format ...
http://www3.islandnet.com/~btaylor/irshmidi.htm

Tunes at Ceolas ...
http://www.ceolas.org/tunes/#midi

Welcome to Compass Records ...
http://www.compassrecords.com/

Welcome To The Doras Directory ...
http://doras.tinet.ie/Doras.nsf/Index

QUARRY MUSIC BOOKS

Wired For Sound: A Guitar Odyssey
Martin Melhuish and Mark Hall
$21.95 CDA/$16.95 USA

Willie Nelson: My Life
Doug Hall and Martin Melhuish
$21.95 CDA/$16.95 USA

The Real Patsy Cline
Doug Hall
$21.95 CDA/$15.95 USA

George Jones: Same Ole Me
Doug Hall
$21.95 CDA/$16.95 USA

Chicago: Feelin' Stronger Every Day
Ben Joseph
$21.95 CDA/$16.95 USA

The Mamas and the Papas: Straight Shooter
Doug Hall and Martin Melhuish
$21.95 CDA/$16.95 USA

The Other CD Guide: Extraordinary Music for Ordinary People
Raffaele Quirino
$34.95 CDA/$26.95 USA

Available at your favorite bookstore or directly from Quarry Music Books,
P.O. Box 1061, Kingston, Ontario, Canada, K7L 4Y5,
Tel (613) 548-8429, Fax (613) 548-1556,
E-mail: order@quarrypress.com